LARRY HOLMES: AGAINST THE ODDS

Larry Holmes

with

Phil Berger

THOMAS DUNNE BOOKS

ST. MARTIN'S PRESS
NEW YORK

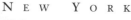

Photos courtesy of *The Express-Times*

THOMAS DUNNE BOOKS.
An imprint of St. Martin's Press.

Library of Congress Cataloging-in-Publication Data

Holmes, Larry.
    Against the odds / Larry Holmes with Phil Berger.—1st ed.
      p.   cm.
    "Thomas Dunne books."
    ISBN 0-312-18736-X
    1. Holmes, Larry. 2. Boxers (Sports)—United States—
Biography. I. Berger, Phil. II. Title.
GV1132.H65A3   1998
796.83'092—dc21   98-26973
    [B]   CIP

First edition: November 1998

Design: James Sinclair

10 9 8 7 6 5 4 3 2 1

To my wife, Diane, and my children, Larry Jr., Kandy, Misty, Lisa and Belinda, to my mother, Flossie, and to all my family and friends in the Lehigh Valley

—Larry Holmes

To my daughter, Julia, with love . . .
And to my friend, Michael Rakosi, with gratitude

—Phil Berger

We wish to thank Linda Ronan and Linda Wachtel at the Sports Illustrated Library and Sam Toperoff for access to and permission to use pertinent research materials.

Thanks to Ed Laubach, sports editor of *The Express-Times* in Easton, Pennsylvania, for access to and permission to use photos from the paper's files.

And finally, our gratitude to Tony Seidl, who was our agent on this book, and to Pete Wolverton of St. Martin's, who edited it.

Introduction

In my time, the great heavyweight champions were men whose path was made for them.

George Foreman, Muhammad Ali, and Smokin' Joe Frazier were fighters who won fame as Olympic gold medalists, attracted financial backers, and were accorded special treatment as young professionals.

It wasn't that way for me.

I was the equivalent of the youngster with his nose pressed up against the candy-store window. In other words, I was just another guy. Yet despite being a seventh-grade dropout and being regarded by the boxing establishment as nobody special, I went on to become heavyweight champion of the world, a title I held from 1978 to 1985.

I can tell you this: getting there was a helluva struggle. As a young professional, the money was chump change and my battle for recognition was hindered by the fact that I was a sparring partner for Muhammad Ali. For whatever reason, my being a sparring partner blinded boxing's movers and shakers to the talent I had. That included my so-called promoter, Don King, who treated me like dirt until his meal ticket, Ali, was winding down his career and King had to find his next heavyweight to exploit.

These days champions come and go, mostly go. With new governing bodies multiplying like rabbits—IBA, IBC, WBU, and WBF are just some of the late-blooming new organizations—a champion's title doesn't mean much anymore. Not so when I fought. Back then, there was no question who the heavyweight champion was. Oh sure, sometimes there would be more than one man claiming the title. But the public wasn't fooled. Frazier, Foreman, and Ali took turns being recognized as THE man. And when Ali said he was retired in 1979, then it was my turn.

During the years I held the title, I was a fighting champion, taking on all the bad boys in the division—Ken Norton, Mike Weaver, Earnie Shavers, Scott Le Doux, Ali (who did not stay retired), Trevor Berbick, Leon Spinks, Renaldo Snipes, Gerry Cooney, Tex Cobb, Tim Witherspoon, Marvis Frazier, Bone-crusher Smith, David Bey, and Carl "the Truth" Williams.

I fought the good fight in the ring, and out of it, battling dirty rotten Don King for my fair share and eventually reducing him to just another promoter, one among many, bidding for my services. I did what few fighters could: I became free to pick and choose for which promoter I'd fight, and even ended up as the promoter of a few title defenses of mine.

I also became that rarest of boxers, a man who still had his money after the fighting was done. That money enabled me to build a business empire here in Easton, Pennsylvania, my hometown. But believe me, none of it came easy. Then again, not much that's worthwhile does.

CHAPTER ONE

The sun was just coming up when the last of the Holmes family
of Cuthbert, Georgia, climbed into Uncle Willie's beat-up Chevy
and headed north.

All our belongings were loaded into the trunk of the car, or
strapped onto the roof. We were leaving the hard times of the
sharecropper's life for a better chance in a place called Easton,
Pennsylvania.

At least that's what my mother, Flossie, told me. And young
as I was, I knew that what we had in Cuthbert was no bargain.
So I wasn't shook about leaving. I was six years old that Georgia
morning in 1955 as the Chevy rolled past the fields where Mom
and her older children had once picked cotton to add a few dollars
to what my father, John Henry, made working the land. In that
time and in that place, farming was a hard way to go. And eventually my father decided the hell with it—there had to be a better
means of supporting a family. Up north in Easton were steel mills

1

and iron foundries and paper mills and sewing factories. John Henry figured chances were likelier he'd find regular work, and better pay, in that smokestack city.

John Henry had gone up north first, before any of us. Then, a few at a time, some of my older brothers and sisters followed. Mom and I and my brothers Lee, Bob, and Jake would be the last of the Holmeses to leave Cuthbert.

My memories of Cuthbert were not exactly warm and fuzzy. We had lived by the railroad tracks in a shack that sat on stilts and had few of the conveniences that most folks took for granted. It was stifling hot in summer, and chilled your bones when the temperature fell in winter. Our house in Cuthbert was too small for a family our size, had no plumbing, and, with the trains going by, made sleep sometimes difficult, more so when rain fell on the corrugated metal roof. Some nights I'd lie there in bed listening to raindrops pinging off that roof . . . until, utterly exhausted, I dropped off to sleep.

That the lives my folks led were exhausting—and unsatisfying—was plain enough even to a little boy like me. You only had to look at their faces as they returned home at the end of the working day to know all there was to know about life in the cotton fields . . . or out there in John Henry's hard damn acres.

I remember Mom and my brothers and sisters pulling prickles from cotton plants out of their clothes. If we had stayed in Cuthbert, I would have been expected to go into the cotton fields in a year or two.

I remember, too, the red clay roads of Georgia. That red clay got into everything—on the floor, in our clothes and towels, and even smudged the sheets we slept on. Now, as Uncle Willie drove north, I watched the red clay roads go by.

Because of the excitement of being on the longest trip of my life, I slept in little catnaps, waking up whenever we got to a big city. I'd never seen tall buildings before or so many people in one place. At night, I tipped my head back in the rear window of that Chevy and watched the moon and the stars. I thought the moon was following me.

Easton, population thirty thousand, is located at the fork of the Delaware and Lehigh Rivers, fifty miles north of Philadelphia. It had been founded in colonial times by sons of William Penn, who had named it after the English estate of some kin of theirs. With the building of canals, Easton came to be a water transportation hub in the 1800s for shipments to Philadelphia and eventually to New York.

Later came railroads and highways, and by the 1950s Easton was an established industrial city, doing business in textiles, finished products, paper, leather, paint, iron and steel foundries, and machinery.

That's what had drawn us and other poor blacks from the South to Easton. Jobs. There was said to be plenty of work there. But by the time Mom and I turned up, the Delaware Valley was recovering from a hurricane that had done millions of dollars of damage . . . and from a recession that put a crimp in the job market. Bad timing, folks said.

For Mom, what John Henry had to tell her must have seemed bad timing too. My father watched us settle in and then told Flossie that while up north he had fallen in love with another woman. So after a few weeks, he up and left for Connecticut, where this other woman lived. It near broke my mother's heart.

Every so often John Henry would come back and visit us in Easton, usually bringing the younger kids presents. I don't know if he gave my mom any money or not, but we sure as heck needed it. Yet as hurt as Mom felt, and as much as she missed him, she never bad-mouthed him to us.

From time to time I'd spend a week or two with him in Connecticut. John Henry was a no-nonsense, hardworking man. In the morning, he'd go to his construction job, then come home for dinner and be off to do yard work for the rich folks. I'd help him out. I'd cut grass, rake it up, and do whatever else needed doing. I loved my father even though I didn't really know him. I loved him because he was my father.

Our family ended up on the South Side of Easton, where

mostly poor black folks lived. The address was 208 East Lincoln Street—one of the identical government-subsidized Delaware Terrace row houses. Ours came with four bedrooms, a living room, a kitchen, and a bathroom for a family that eventually would include twelve children—nine boys and three girls.

In Easton, our part of town was known as "the projects"—just another way of saying the poor part of town. That meant we lived with no air-conditioning in the summer and inadequate heating in the winter. The only comfort we got was from a store-bought fan.

It also meant going hungry some nights. Mom would do what she could to stretch a bag of rice, and beans . . . and she made her own bread because it was cheaper. But every day was a struggle, and to keep our bellies full it took the welfare checks we got and the government-surplus Spam, powdered milk, blocks of cheese, lard, beans, and rice that we stood in line for once a month. At the welfare office you signed for a card you showed when it came your turn to stock up.

That's how it went. Folks from the South Side did what they had to in order to make it to the next day. For a family as large as ours, it meant watching what few pennies we had. Mom shopped for our clothes at the Salvation Army and at rummage sales, and was not too proud to accept help from Jack Paul, a local truant officer, a white man who made a habit of helping those who were poor. He was truly a decent man, who would take neighborhood kids into stores and get them clothes.

Jack Paul wasn't the only one who looked out for those less fortunate than they were. Around Christmas, on Northampton Street, where all the fancy stores were, they'd be selling poppies to benefit the YMCA, which would then turn around and use the proceeds to take the kids from the projects shopping for Christmas gifts, five dollars a kid. It wasn't much, but it was a gesture from the heart and we appreciated it.

Some of my brothers and sisters worked in the factories in and around Easton and would give a portion of their wages to Mom. But let's face it: it was never enough. In fact, some of my siblings, when they were financially pinched, would scoop up my loose

4

change—just out-and-out steal what was mine. That led me as a grade-schooler to start hiding what money I had under the bed, in pillowcases, and in flowerpots. But there were times when I'd see that my mother was in real need of money and I would raid the flowerpot to help her out.

As a grade-schooler I made money shining shoes. The routine went like this. When the school day ended, I'd grab my shoeshine kit and walk the Lehigh Valley railroad tracks from Easton, then cross the bridge over the Delaware River that took you into the next town, Phillipsburg, New Jersey. With my brother Lee, or sometimes with other kids from the neighborhood, I'd go bar to bar. You'd open the door of the joint, look in, and say: "Shine? Anyone need a shine?" If somebody looked up from his drink and said yes, you'd walk in and go to work. Slap the rag across the man's brogans, fifteen cents a shine . . . and hope for a tip. We might work as late as ten o'clock, and on a good day I'd come home with ten, fifteen bucks.

Although we were poor folk, I didn't get hung up on it. I knew we were doing the best we could . . . and nobody around us had a whole lot more. But I must admit that sometimes when I'd watch that TV show *The Millionaire*, I would think: When the heck is Michael Anthony gonna come knock on our door, give my mom a million dollars? Remember that show? Wednesday nights on CBS. This eccentric billionaire John Beresford Tipton (whose face you never saw) would instruct his personal secretary, Michael Anthony, to hand some average joe a cashier's check for a million bucks, tax free. The idea was to see how this new money would change that individual's life.

Our lives back then didn't change much. It was a struggle. But let me say it right here: Flossie Holmes is a truly great woman. She raised the twelve of us with very little help. She could have easily lost hope and maybe given some of us away—we knew some families that did that. I wouldn't have blamed her if she did. But I'm glad she didn't. She was very proud and very strong. I believe I got those same qualities from her.

She would never admit it, but I believe she treated me as her special child. Whenever I tease her about it now, she says, "*All of my children were special to me.*" Maybe, but I was a little more special to her because I was born with six fingers on each hand. The tiny "extra" fingers were right alongside my pinkies, and they were taken off by a doctor in Georgia when I was a baby. If you look close now, you can still see the scars and tiny stubs. My mother always told me those fingers were a sign from God that I must have been singled out for some special purpose.

I guess my youngest brother, Perry, wasn't put on earth for a special purpose. He died suddenly of a heart murmur when he was only five. Perry's death still haunts me. I never could figure out why, if there was a God, Perry had to die for no reason whatsoever. He never did anything cruel or evil to anyone. I was mad at God about that for a long time. I still am. But my mother is a very religious woman and she accepts everything as God's will. That's the source of her great strength. I never could be that accepting. Maybe someday I will be.

Although where we lived people were poor, there were neighbors of ours who would put on airs and ridicule us for being on welfare because they happened not to be. They were the same folks who, when later on I overcame those humble beginnings and rose up in the world as a fighter, would say: "Well, shoot, he'll end up broke 'cause he lacks the education to know what to do with his money."

It was true I didn't have much education. In Cuthbert I hadn't had any schooling whatsoever. So when I went into the first grade at Taylor Elementary School in Easton, I was behind the other kids. If only my teachers cared, school might have been a better experience. But the way it worked was that the slower students—and most of us were black—got branded as lacking the intelligence worth a teacher's time. So where you'd see the teacher urge the white kid to sound out a spelling word, that teacher wouldn't bother to try that with the so-called backward black boys and girls. The teachers viewed their job with us as simply to baby-sit us.

Without their help, I could never acquire reading skills, and without being able to read, I began to fall even further behind in every subject. The teachers treated me like I was stupid. I knew I wasn't, but it was hard to show it in school. Since I wasn't getting any attention from my teachers, I began to slide into the role of class wise guy to get respect from the other kids.

It was only in sports where I seemed to get a fair shake, and could shine. I was good at all the sports, but as a grade-schooler I excelled in wrestling. I wrestled for the St. Anthony's Youth Center, which was located in a predominantly Italian neighborhood, and won lots of trophies in competitions against other youth centers, first as an eighty-pounder and then, as I grew older, as a ninety-pound rassler. Through my grade-school years, I rarely lost.

Poor though we were, the kids in the neighborhood and I managed to find fun in lots of simple ways. With homemade fishing poles, we'd pass hours fishing the Delaware River. Or in cutoff trousers or even butt-naked, we'd swim in the canals. And like kids everywhere we'd flip baseball cards, pitch pennies, and play blackjack for pennies and nickels.

Sometimes we'd wander the streets, looking for yards that had apple or cherry trees in bloom. We'd snatch as much fruit as our hands could hold and, laughing with the pleasure of our mischief, run like hell, eating our stolen treasure back in the projects. Yeah, that was considered high adventure for us. That and chasing neighborhood girls.

When we'd scrap with one another, it was always a fair fight. No guns, no knives. It was a more innocent time then.

In those days, I wasn't really into boxing. Sure, I knew a few names of the professionals—like Rocky Marciano and Sugar Ray Robinson and the new guy, Cassius Clay. Maybe I'd catch a glimpse of them on newsreels or a thirty-second clip on TV. But I didn't follow the sport. Nor did the local paper, *The Express-Times* have much coverage of boxing. For the fellas from my street, the Philadelphia teams—the Eagles, Phillies, and 76ers— were Topic A.

Yet though I barely took notice of boxing's headliners, I ended up as part of the Wednesday-night bar fights, starting at age ten. The PAL would gather us kids to put on backroom matches for the various civic clubs around the Delaware Valley—like the Kiwanis and Rotary Clubs, and the VFW. All these organizations, not to mention the firefighters, had social clubs, and on Wednesday nights you would see us peewees whacking away at each other with oversize boxing gloves. It was regular entertainment for the older folks.

John Vogt from the PAL would drive to Fourth Street—a mostly black neighborhood—and pick a bunch of us up. He'd continue on through Easton, stopping in other neighborhoods until we had a carload. Off we'd go—my buddies Pooch Pratt and Butch Andrews, my brother Lee, and I—sometimes to clubs in Easton, other times as far as Bethlehem or Allentown. Most of us were black kids; a few were white. My mother never knew I was doing it. She wouldn't have approved, but there were too many of us kids for her to keep track of.

The bars were usually full of steelworkers or men from the paper mill and other factories. To me they were really like the bars I saw in the western movies at the State Theater downtown. Rough and tough and exciting. It was nothing like being in school or in the house or on the block. The atmosphere in those places felt seedy, and illegal, which probably it was since little kids were on premises where drinking and betting were going on. There was usually a lot of smoke swirling about and the rank smell of stale beer and whiskey. Sometimes there were a few bright lights over a clearing near the back of the barroom.

There was no ring set up in most of the bars. The people would gather in a kind of circle that might expand as the fighters scrambled to get at one another. Before I fought I watched the smaller kids box. While the bouts were on, it would get noisy and I'd stand there and look at the faces of the spectators. They were men mostly, but there were always a few women there too. More than a hundred people on big nights. Almost everyone was white. I saw their eyes brighten when a kid got hit with a solid punch. Sometimes they laughed at a fighter when he threw a punch, missed, and fell on his face. I didn't like it when they laughed. I never wanted anyone to laugh at me.

I fought in my white Chuck Taylor Converse All-Stars, *the* shoe back before there was Nike and Reebok and Fila. Your canvas-and-rubber "Chucks" were what you wore everywhere—school, sports, to go downtown. For my boxing trunks I had red shorts that really were a bathing suit.

Because I was big for my age, I usually fought the same kid, Barry Derohn, a white boy who was a little older and just about my size. Most of the time, we were both still standing by the end of the fight. If both fighters were on their feet after three rounds, the referee would declare the bout a draw, no matter how lop-sided the action might have been. But one night I caught Barry Derohn with a clean shot and knocked him cold. I can still see that right hand landing flush on the chin. When we got older, I'd see him around town and tease him about the night I gave him hell.

But let's face it: I was a boxing doofus, a kid with a jab and no idea of how to put punches together. I was unaware of the effort and serious training that went into making a polished fighter. Then again, when I was fighting those Wednesday-night three-rounders, the notion of doing it for a living was the farthest thing from my mind. I was doing it for the respect it got you out on the street . . . *and* for the free food that was our reward afterward. Sweaty and tired, we'd retreat to the kitchen for all the hot dogs, hamburgers, Cokes, and potato chips we could eat. For us free food was as good as gold.

I never thought much about the future then. I didn't have to because the life I was going to live was out there whether I thought about it or not. It was going to be a typical Easton blue-collar life, *if* I was lucky—a factory job, a family, weekends for drinking beer and playing poker or pool, maybe outfitting and driving my own stock car.

9

By the time I reached seventh grade at Shull Junior High, I was a hotshot football player. Seventh graders weren't supposed to play varsity football, but they made an exception for me. I was a starter as a defensive tackle and was second string at fullback. Football on the junior-high level was serious stuff. The games were well attended, and were officiated by uniformed, paid referees. The junior-high program was meant to be a feeder to the high schools, which were *damn* serious about the game. Like you read about football in Texas. That kind of serious.

There was one individual at Shull—a male teacher—who resented the fact that I was allowed to play as a seventh grader. Whenever he'd see me in the halls, he'd go out of his way to hassle me. I wasn't shy and would talk back to him, giving him a reason—at least as *he* saw it—to get physical with me. "You're not my teacher," I'd say, belligerently. And he'd slap me, throw me down on the floor, goading me to hit him back. I never did, even though at age thirteen I thought I could kick his ass. More than once he laid his hands on me, and more than once I complained about it to the principal. But the teacher was never reprimanded or even told to lay off. This teacher, it turned out, would be in the thick of a big jam I got into later that seventh-grade year.

See, a lot of girls at school liked me. But at the time there were two in particular—a white girl and a black girl—that I was interested in. I liked the white girl more, which seemed to bother the other one. She got angry at me one day while we were going to study hall . . . and, after we started name-calling, she jabbed her pencil at my hand. Hurt me. I got a little crazy and went after her.

Well, who should come along to break up our little skirmish but this teacher nemesis of mine. Once he saw that I was involved, he grabbed me and threw me down to the floor. When the assistant principal came by to investigate, the teacher laid the blame on me. By now I'd grown tired of the indifference of my teachers—and the jealousy and meanness of this particular one. I yelled, "I don't have to take this! I'm getting the hell out of here!" And I headed home, in spite of being warned that if I left the building they'd sic the cops on me.

"Go ahead," I said.

I didn't give a damn what they did. I walked out.

An hour later, I was sitting on the porch of my house when along came Jack Paul, the good-guy truant officer. When he reached Lincoln Street, I was sharpening and polishing a hunting knife. It wasn't a threat outright, but it sure was a clear signal of how I was feeling. Jack tried to reason with me, and told me he had to get me back to school. I told him that no matter what he said or did, I would never go back again. I sat there polishing this big knife, which, I'm afraid, Jack Paul suspected I was fixing to use on him.

I guess Jack felt he had no choice. He called the cops, who carted me off to juvenile jail. They put me in a cell that had a bed and toilet and locked me up at night. Word was I was going to be sent to reform school.

The first night in jail they had spaghetti for dinner and I ate a ton of it. When it came time to have dessert—ice cream—they ran out of it by the time it got to me. One of the older guys told me, "When the dessert's good, always eat it first. That way you know you'll get some." That made sense then, makes sense now. When I go into a restaurant, I still check out the desserts first thing. I've been known to eat my pecan pie and whipped cream before my lobster.

It took thirteen days to sort things out—thirteen days of killing time in the juvenile facility by playing cards, checkers, and Ping-Pong. Finally a court hearing was held, and my options were laid out. Quit Shull Junior High, I was told, and I wouldn't have to go to reform school. Otherwise . . .

Well, there was no otherwise. I was wasting my time in school, with teachers who saw me as incapable of learning and that one rat bastard who had it in for me.

So I quit school and went to see John DiVietro at the Jet car wash in Easton. Back then, I was tall and skinny and looked older than thirteen. I told DiVietro I was eighteen and needed a job. He hired me for the grand sum of a dollar an hour. At various times I'd wash the cars, wipe them down, or vacuum their interiors—whatever they needed me to do. Two hundred cars a day at $2.50 per car we did. I'd walk home with $8 at the end of each day.

At thirteen, I was no longer a kid, really. By now I was hanging out in bars, and driving back and forth to work in my own car, a black Ford that I bought for $50 from a friend. When that car conked out, I went up to a junkyard in Rieglesville called Upper Black Eddie's and bought an old car for $30 and fixed it up, the first of several cars that came from there. I'd fix them good enough to get me back and forth.

DiVietro was quoted years later as saying: "When Larry first came to the car wash, he was insubordinate. He used foul language. Always had a chip on his shoulder." True enough. I was a rough, tough kid who took no guff from anybody. You messed with me, I'd be right in your face. It was like the gunfighters in the Old West. Guys were always trying me and wishing they hadn't. I used to knock out a guy every weekend. There was always somebody to challenge you. I had streaks. Once I went forty straight weekends knocking out one badass or another.

One of my fights came at the Jet car wash. One of the bosses there, a big guy, thought he could flex his muscle with me. We got into an argument. When he grabbed me, I got him in a half nelson and just held him. We didn't move. Just stood there. I hit him a couple times in the back. When I finally let him go, he told me I was fired. A month later he hired me back.

Eight bucks a day for washing cars—figure it out. It wasn't a helluva lot of money. Pretty soon, I was hanging with guys who broke into parked cars and stole tape decks and radios. I must have stolen more than a hundred of them. I felt guilty every time, but it didn't make me stop. I used to hide the stereos in my closet. I sold them for $25 apiece and I even learned to install them.

Even though I did steal for a while, I wasn't doing armed robberies like some of the hard cases I knew. I never crossed that line. But some of the fellas that I hung out with did cross the line, and they paid for it. Like Vickie Strickland, who was shot and killed by the police. And Willie James Lee, who sassed a drug dealer he owed money to and was shot and killed for it. Another of the boys from the hood died from a drug overdose. What they all shared with me was a kind of code that existed on the streets. You didn't let anybody mess with you, or treat you like less than a man.

I'll give you an example. When I was fourteen, Father Barbato, who ran the St. Anthony's Youth Center, put me in charge of locking the place up. Well, this one night, I went to turn out the lights and there was a bunch of guys playing basketball, big guys, football players, seniors in high school. I asked them to leave, and one of them hit me and knocked me down. I got up and turned out the lights. The guy knocked me down again. It went on like that: me turning off the lights, the guy knocking me down. I took a whupping but kept getting up and in the end turned the damn lights off and locked up.

A few years later, I did something even crazier. A scuffle developed on the main street of Easton. It was a racial thing—blacks against whites. A bunch of guys came and got me. They told me that a white guy had run into this gas station, grabbed a shotgun, and screamed, "I'm gonna blow you apart!" At that, everybody started running.

I showed up and the guy was still there, holding his shotgun. I walked straight toward him, telling him: "Come on, punk. You ain't gonna do a damned thing." Kept walking toward him. Kept walking, walking. When I was close enough, I snatched the shotgun from him and then beat him up.

When you're a kid, your blood is boiling. You don't care about consequences. In the years since, I've thought about that incident a lot. What if the guy had shot? It was one of the dumbest things—make that *the* dumbest thing—I've ever done. Why'd I do it? Honestly, I don't know.

Like I said, I was no angel. I know how it feels to get in trouble with the police. I know how it feels to drink and get drunk. I know how it feels to smoke grass and get high. I did it all. You can't tell me about it. But say this for me: I worked for a living. From the time I was thirteen, I made real wages, working real jobs. A lot of the guys I ran with didn't want to do that. They wanted to hustle and to pimp. I always felt that you had to work for anything you got.

I worked. After the Jet car wash, I went over to the Kraft rug mill, $1.50 an hour. I'd stand there with a hose that sprays the rubber on the back of carpet. At the Ingersoll-Rand foundry in Phillipsburg, I made casings for the shells used in the Vietnam War. I worked in a clothing factory. I worked in a fur factory. Worked in a paint factory . . . and a quarry. And eventually I began driving a truck for Mort Levy's Strongwear Pants—$3.50 an hour.

It wasn't all work and no play. When I was sixteen, I bought a brand-new Plymouth Road Runner and tricked it out for the local drag strips. It was street legal, but I could drop my heads in a couple of seconds. I won a lot of races, got that thing up to 110 miles per hour in no time at all.

Some of the racing was strictly unofficial. But man, did I love to drag on the straight road alongside the Lehigh Valley railroad tracks. Take on all challengers until the cops came and told us, "Hey, get your ass outta here. If I catch you again, I'm gonna give you a ticket."

You wouldn't think fighting and racing stock cars had anything in common, besides both being dangerous, but they do. I learned from driving stocks that sometimes you had to take chances to win but you didn't want to do something stupid and kill yourself in the process. In other words, you had to pick your spots, not be too headstrong and foolish. In a tough fight, that's exactly what you have to do. Takes chances but be under control too. Believe me, it's easier to talk about than to do.

I began seeing an "older woman," Millie Bowles. She was all of twenty-two, six years older than I was. I lied; I told her I was twenty-two, like her. Millie was skeptical. But I persisted. I'd met her in one of the bars where I hung out. And when she mentioned she lived in the same projects I did, I began showing up at her door.

At first she'd turn me away, insisting I was too young for her. I said, "No, I'm a man. I'm twenty-two."

It wasn't until we had our first child, Misty, in March 1968, that she found out how old I really was. That was when I moved in with her.

In June 1969, we had another daughter, Lisa.

In between the births of my daughters, I got in big trouble with the law, even though I was truly innocent. Late in 1968, a riot broke out in Easton. It was a Saturday night and I was coming back from an Easton High School football game. As I got near Northampton Street, I heard a lot of noise and saw people smashing windows and looting stores. Sirens were wailing as cop cars raced through the streets. It turned out the trouble started in a restaurant when a white girl called some guy a nigger and spit in his food. A fight started and spilled out into the street, where it became a riot. There had been very bitter racial feelings in town ever since Martin Luther King was assassinated.

When I got closer, I saw my brother Lee running like hell down a narrow street. The cops were grabbing everyone black. I figured this was no place for me to be, so I took off after him. When I ducked into a small cross street, the cops saw me. They came after me in a car, and when I turned another corner into an alley, I ran smack into another cop, who had a shotgun leveled at me. I threw my hands in the air. He put the gun up against my stomach and said, "Move and I'll blow a hole in you." I looked into his face and knew he wasn't fooling. I tried to explain. He told me to shut the fuck up. I didn't want that trigger to go off by accident. I let him handcuff me and throw me in the car with other people.

The judge gave me a $365 fine and ordered me to serve thirty days. My sister Pearl tried to get me out on bail, but couldn't raise the money at first. After four days, she finally managed to get me out. Charlie Spaziani, the district attorney of Northamp-

15

ton County, looked into my side of what happened. Spaz, as everyone called him, had a reputation as a tough law-and-order guy. Plenty of times I'd heard blacks say he was a racist and that a black man could never get justice from him. Well, this black man did. I told him that I hadn't done anything wrong, and he checked out my story. Eventually he got me back my money and had my record cleaned up. Spaz and I didn't know it then, but we were going to be connected for a long time to come.

Word then came from Connecticut that my father had died up there in June 1970. I never found out exactly what the cause of death was or exactly how old he was, but I figured out that he was pretty young, probably in his early fifties. I always tried not to judge my father. I figured there were things about his life I couldn't understand. My mother cried. She never really stopped loving him.

Tough as I was as a street fighter, I still didn't think about boxing as a way of life. Not until Ernie Butler showed up in Easton.

Butler had been a professional fighter who'd started his career in 1944 in the Washington/Baltimore area, and he was still campaigning in the early 1950s.

He moved on to New York and fought a few big-name guys—like future lightweight champion Joe Brown (who'd knocked him out in five rounds in '47) and middleweight contender Rocky Castellani (who beat him by decision the same year). Though he fought regularly, it was for penny-ante purses, never enough to support himself. To make a go of it, Ernie had to moonlight as a New York City cabbie.

When I met Ernie, in 1968, he had settled in Easton, working for the prison system, helping parolees get jobs and giving boxing instruction to the cons. He also owned a shoeshine stand on South Third Street and would teach kids how to shine shoes, taking a percentage of what they made while working his stand. At night, you could find Ernie at the PAL, a small gym on Sixth Street, where as a kid I had played basketball, knock-hockey, and Ping-Pong. Evenings at the PAL, Ernie would teach kids how to box.

I ran into Ernie one day at his shoeshine stand. In later years, some writers had me acting cocky and telling this forty-four-year old ex-professional I'd kick his butt if he dared try boxing with me. No way. I was curious. Ernie Butler had been a fighter, and that made him a big man in a small town like ours. What would it be like to spar with a man like this? I wondered. What could he show me? Back when I was fighting for hot dogs on those Wednesday-night barroom fights, nobody had bothered to teach us the fine points of boxing.

Ernie invited me to come on up to the PAL, and one evening, I took him up on it. We started fighting slow and cautious before he began to quicken the pace. It didn't take long to see Ernie was in another time zone when it came to boxing skills. Yet as raw as I was, I showed enough, I guess, to prompt Ernie to say he thought maybe I could be something.

"If you're interested," he said, "I could show you things."

"Yeah, I'm interested."

"Okay," he said. "I'll teach you. But you got to listen. You got to remember I'm the boss."

Ernie believed in repetition and building from the ground up. He stressed the fundamentals. I was eager to get in the ring and beat on other guys. Ernie wouldn't have it.

"You're gonna learn how to box before I let you in the ring," he said.

Nine months went by. I learned. Learned by doing nothing but shadowboxing for the first two months, then hitting the heavy bag for two months. Ernie taught me balance, taught me to slip punches. Boxing was the last thing he let you do.

"If you listen to me, you'll win," he said.

I listened. He stressed the importance of having balance, and would demonstrate by having me push on his shoulder as he stood in front of me in a boxing stance. I pushed. I couldn't budge him. Ernie had balance. He taught it to me. Taught me how to stand, and how to move.

He would throw jabs at my face and see if I blinked. You blink, you might not see the next punch. He'd have you practice not

17

closing your eyes. One jab after another at my face, and watch whether my eyes stayed open.

He had me throwing sequences of punches at the heavy bag and reminded me constantly, "When you jab, keep both your hands up." This was a source of conflict between us. I always felt comfortable carrying my hands low. I thought I got my punches off quicker from that position.

"You're gonna get your ass knocked down," Ernie warned.

As the months went by, I was growing more antsy to get in the ring.

"You ain't ready," Ernie said. "I told you, you listen or you can hit the door."

I might not have liked it, but I listened. I wanted to learn this game and in Easton, P-A, Ernie Butler was the only way that was going to happen. Ernie knew a lot and taught it to me. All the classic boxing moves. All the combinations. How to slip the other guy's best shot. How to counterpunch. I wanted to learn and had some natural athletic talent too. Still, I wasn't all strung out on boxing. It was just something to do around Easton.

I never thought I would become a champion or that I would make a lot of money. Even later, when I turned pro, I didn't think about ending up with the heavyweight title, or even being ranked among the world's best. For me, it was just nice to have people around town know who I was. I fought because I was good at it and it gave me pleasure. People express themselves differently. Painters paint, writers write, dancers dance. I discovered I needed physical contact to let what was in me come out.

All the kids Ernie was training, me included, fought other amateurs from around the area, and we were all brave as hell. But when Ernie scheduled us to go against the big-city kids from New York and Philly, everyone quit. Except me. I went on up to New York to fight. And I won.

The tougher the competition got in the amateurs, the better I got. My jab was fast and accurate, and could hurt you. I knew how to snap the jab, and turn it over so when it landed it moved the other guy. Moved him and hurt him. For a lot of fighters, a jab is like a directional finder—something to navigate distance and distract the opponent. But mine came at you with bad intentions. I'd jab and then bring the right hand over the jab. Guys couldn't deal with that. I don't mind saying I was getting pretty damn good. I was like a young colt who thinks he's the best thing in the corral.

As my amateur career blossomed, I was working at the Ingersoll-Rand factory in Phillipsburg, grinding steel for $125 a week. I had my eyes on the '72 Olympics, training when I could. When I took days off to fight in amateur tournaments, I lost my pay. So I picked my spots. But when I did fight, I always won. My name was in *The Express-Times* pretty regularly.

I almost blew it, though. And it wasn't becoming a criminal and going to prison that nearly ruined things. Or that cop almost blowing me away in the alley. It was drugs. I was about eighteen years old, still at Ingersoll-Rand. Every week I'd buy two nickel bags of pot from a guy at the plant and then sell it by the joint, a dollar a joint. It meant fifteen extra bucks a week. I was an entrepreneur before I knew what the word meant.

Then I started smoking with a friend of mine named Junior Williams. I had known Junior since I was twelve. We used to go to school and play sports together. Junior graduated high school; he even had some community college. We started smoking every weekend. We used to smoke straight pot, but every time we did we always said we would give it up. Then we'd laugh and keep right on. It was bad for me because I was not training as hard as I should have. One day Junior came up with some hashish and said let's smoke it in a pipe. I smoked it and started hallucinating. I remember it like it was yesterday. It started at the pool hall. I stared at the table and mumbled, "That ball gonna go in" over and over. A million times. Couldn't stop. I'd think, "What am I sayin'?" but I couldn't stop saying nonsense things over and over.

Then I'd see myself stepping away from the pool table and I'd blank out and not remember how I got where I was going. Man, did that ever scare me. I saw my brother and said, "Lee, you got to take me home." He just cursed me out. I walked to the door, didn't remember getting there, but all at once I saw myself outside the door. Scared to death. Then I saw Willie Pratt, a guy I knew. I put my arm around him and begged him please to take me home. Willie told me there was nothing wrong with me. I heard very loud echoes in my head whenever I talked.

The only thing that could help me was running. I thought maybe I could run that shit out of me. I ran all over town. Up the hill, down along the Delaware River. Seeing myself going but now knowing how I got there. And little by little I started coming around. That's when I fell on my knees and said to God, "You get me out of this trick bag and I swear I'll never do it again."

I have never done drugs again. Never. Everyone in boxing knew—whatever else they said about me—that when you fight Larry Holmes you're going up against a fighter whose body and mind are not messed up with drugs.

Junior Williams? Junior had read about the forty acres and that mule that were promised after the Civil War. And he wanted them any way he could get them. Junior ended up dead in Atlanta, Georgia, with about a thousand FBI bullets in him. Running drugs. They said there was hardly enough of him left to put into the coffin.

It really made me stop and think about the turns life takes. Once Junior had been active in causes aimed at helping black people. But somewhere along the line he had lost the spirit of activism and become a me-first cat. Get for himself any damn way he could. Me, I get thrown out of school and end up heavyweight champion of the world, with a good family and more money than I'll ever need. If I'd have hung with Junior Williams, I'd probably be dead too.

There was only so much I could learn about boxing in Easton, P-A.

Ernie figured it was time to spread our wings. There wasn't a real talent pool here, so to find fighters to spar with we began traveling to gyms in Trenton and Philadelphia . . . and to the famed Gleason's Gym in New York.

Nowadays, Gleason's is located just over the bridge in Brooklyn, not far from the Brooklyn Navy Yard and the Jehovah's Witness international headquarters. It's adapted to this era of boxing chic, counting among its members numerous stockbrokers and women who do white-collar workouts, at the same time that your regular fighters train. It's a clean, nice place, twenty thousand square feet with six hundred lockers—light years from the Gleason's I stumbled into in 1970.

Back then Gleason's was on Westchester Avenue in the Bronx, and was run by an ex-fighter named Peter Robert Galiardi. Galiardi, who changed his name to Bobby Gleason to appeal to the predominantly Irish–New York fight crowd of that era, opened the place in 1937, and the minute you walked up a flight of creeking stairs into the gym you knew what you were there for. As Randy Neumann, another heavyweight who trained there, once wrote: "[The place] . . . needed a paint job and the wooden floors might have been taken from the *Mayflower*. A blind man with a sense of smell would have immediately known what went on there."

That's right. The place looked and smelled like a funky old fight gym. Gleason's was big-time boxing and it was a thrill to step inside and rub elbows with the professionals who trained there on the four heavy bags and two speed-bag racks (fighters brought their own bags) amidst a whole bunch of mirrors. Showers? Well, in the summer, when the neighborhood youngsters opened the fire hydrants to play under the spray of water, the water didn't always ascend to the second floor.

Gleason was a good guy, and if you spent any time around him, it was like taking a course in boxing history. 'Cause Bobby actually fought when the sport was illegal and guys got it on in barges or in the back rooms of saloons. He'd tell you how they legalized boxing back in 1911 with the Frawley Law and how the sport became even more legit in 1920 when the Walker Law provided for a state commission to regulate the sport. "Walker" was the mayor of New York, Jimmy Walker, who, according to Bobby, was a regular at ringside for all the big fights.

Gleason's quickly caught on in the forties when the hotshot fighters from the streets of the Bronx—guys like Jake LaMotta,

Mike Belloise, Phil Terranova, and Jimmy Carter—made it their place to train. Back when I was starting at Gleason's, there were plenty of heavyweights who worked out there, guys like Neumann, Pedro Agosto, James J. Woody, and Wendell Newton.

Sparring with them was a humbling experience, and often a painfully humbling experience. Wendell Newton, a big guy from Jamaica—the island, not Queens—hit me with a shot one day and suddenly it was like a bell was vibrating in my head. *D-rooooom.* A sound like that. My eyes went blank. Wendell saw I was gone and held me up to spare me the embarrassment of falling on my ass.

It wasn't always as bad as that. I had some good days. But from those guys I learned how far I still had to go if I hoped to become a pro someday. Even so, Bobby Gleason thought enough of me to talk about getting involved as a manager. He'd managed fighters before, including a world-ranked Cuban heavyweight from the fifties named Nino Valdez.

Gleason used to tell about Nino's membership in a voodoo cult back in Cuba. Whenever Valdez got beat, he'd jump on a plane to Cuba to do a kind of voodoo exorcism, a bloody ritual with beheadings of chickens and goats and lots of dancing. Bobby, who witnessed it once, said once was more than enough for him.

As fighters go, I was a late starter. Many boxers start out as grade-schoolers and have upwards of one hundred fights in organized competitions before they turn pro. I was around twenty when I began competing. Ernie's objective was to get me enough experience to have me ready for the '72 Olympics.

By '71, I was fighting in, and winning, Golden Glove and AAU competitions.

Then one day Ernie said, "Come on, we're gonna take a ride up to Deer Lake."

Deer Lake was maybe fifty miles northwest of Easton.

"What's up there?" I asked.

"Muhammad Ali—he's building a training camp."

CHAPTER
TWO

If as a schoolboy I paid little attention to the fight game, by 1971 that had changed. And Muhammad Ali was the reason.

He'd become the Elvis Presley of boxing. You just couldn't ignore him.

From the midsixties Muhammad was everywhere, talking his talk, spinning out his rhymes, mugging for the TV cameras, making people laugh. In the ring, he was one of a kind, moving with the grace of Sugar Ray Robinson while tattooing guys with blinding combinations. Heavyweights weren't supposed to be that quick, that graceful, and still be possessed of power that could knock a man cold.

With all his jive *and* that great talent, Muhammad made the fight business a marvelous entertainment. He hooked the marginal sports fan, who usually didn't bother watching boxing. With Ali, all the world was his stage. And for damn sure, he made the best of it. The man would predict what round he'd knock a guy out, and he'd back it up with his fists.

In March '67 he had knocked out Zora Folley in seven rounds at Madison Square Garden. Soon after, he had declined to step forward when his name was called for induction into the army. Remember how he said, "I ain't got no quarrel with those Viet Congs?" By refusing to be drafted he became a boxing outcast, suspended by fight commissions everywhere; and he was convicted by the lower courts for draft evasion, fined ten thousand dollars, and sentenced to five years in prison, pending appeal.

But as the war in Vietnam went on—endlessly, it seemed—the American public grew disenchanted with it, and the sentiment against Ali changed. Ali caught a break from the courts in June 1970 when the Supreme Court ruled that "conscientious objector" status was not restricted to those who were motivated strictly by religious belief, but applied equally to those who refused to serve for moral and ethical reasons. While Ali's appeal was yet to be decided, the ruling acted like a wedge against those who had worked strenuously to keep Ali from boxing again. By October 1970, Ali had come back to the fight game, stopping Jerry Quarry in three rounds, and in December he stopped Oscar Bonavena in the fifteenth and final round.

Even if Joe Frazier, who had become heavyweight champion in Ali's absence, whupped him in March 1971 in Madison Square Garden, busting his jaw with that sweeping left hook in the final round, Muhammad was still my hero. I looked forward to meeting him.

From his days as a fighter Ernie Butler knew Angelo Dundee, who trained Muhammad, and thought he might be able to persuade Dundee to let me spar with Ali. At the time, Ali's Deer Lake camp was under construction. Muhammad had bought land from a mink rancher named Bernie Pollak. The tract sat on a ridge in the Poconos, on Highway 61, looking down on a valley with farmland and pine forests. While the camp was being built, Ali was working out on Pollak's mink farm.

Well, we rolled into Deer Lake and discovered that Dundee

wasn't there. But Gene Kilroy, who ran Ali's camp, was. It turned out I was the right man in the right place. Ali had an exhibition for charity scheduled in Reading, Pennsylvania, thirty miles down the road. When Kilroy told him I was a fighter, Ali had me raise my dukes and react to moves he made.

"I'm gonna show you how fast I am," he told me.

He held up his hands.

"Want to see it again?" he said, with an impish smile.

He hadn't moved the hands, only pretended to. I laughed.

Then we began to shadowbox playfully. He'd make a move, and see how I responded. I guess he liked the way I handled his stuff, because he said, "Okay, kid, come on with us."

The sparring session was at the Reading PAL, and the place was packed. Another kid and I sparred three rounds apiece with Ali. Muhammad hit me with some good shots and gave me a black eye. In the dressing room after, he told me: "You're gonna be pretty good." He invited me to come up to Deer Lake and work with him whenever I had the chance to.

I went back to Easton on cloud nine. And why not? Muhammad Ali had given me his A-OK. As for the shiner, that was my badge of honor, my Purple Heart. I wasn't in any hurry to put ice on it. When folks saw the black eye and asked what happened, I told them proudly, "Got it sparring with Muhammad Ali."

Nobody believed me.

No matter. I began going up to Deer Lake on weekends (and whenever I could get time off from my job) and working out with Ali. I wasn't paid for sparring with him, but I didn't really care. I figured what better way to prepare for the Olympic Trials in '72 than training with "the Greatest," as Ali called himself.

And even though I wasn't on the payroll, Muhammad was very generous to me. I got to stay in the camp at no expense and Ali gave me brand-new Everlast equipment to replace the raggedy gloves, headgear, shoes, and skip rope I had.

The camp at Deer Lake was shaping up. A gym was built as well as a cabin for Ali. There were bunkhouses for his aides, four cottages for guests, and a corral for horses. Muhammad had had these huge rocks from the Ice Age hauled in and set down along the perimeter of the camp, each rock with the name of a great fighter painted onto it. A huge forty-ton boulder had Joe Louis's name. Another one had Rocky Marciano's across it. There were big rocks for Jack Johnson, Jersey Joe Walcott, Archie Moore, Sugar Ray Robinson, and Kid Gavilan. In the gym hung a floor-to-ceiling Leroy Neiman portrait of Ali.

Ali's camp was full of incredible characters, who in time became minor celebrities when the media "discovered" them. Kilroy was a tough Irishman, and Ali trusted him completely. Kilroy had left a marketing job with Metro-Goldwyn-Mayer to work for Ali when Muhammad came out of exile. Kilroy even wrote Ali's checks. Kilroy put himself into everything. Nothing could happen without him making it part of his business. Say I needed a head guard. Kilroy wanted me to go through him to get it . . . and not bother Ali.

Drew "Bundini" Brown was Ali's spirit man, the guy who kibitzed with and clowned with Ali. They were like a comedy team, Frick and Frack, Martin and Lewis. All kinds of routines. Bundini would pump Ali up, chanting phrases with his eyes bulging and sweat trickling down his face. Like when Muhammad was going to fight Buster Mathis, a fat heavyweight. Bundini began chanting, "Gonna fluster Buster." And Ali would answer, "Gonna flail that whale." And it just built from there. So much of Ali's famous rhyming came from him responding to Bundini.

Bundini had been a merchant marine and had spent twelve years traveling the world. He had hooked up with Ali before the Doug Jones fight in New York in 1963 and had stayed on as Muhammad's court jester. Bundini was the guy who gave me my favorite nickname. He called me "Big Jack," after Jack Johnson, the great champion, who Bundini said was built and fought like me—tall, with long skinny legs, and with fast hands, a good jab. I admired Jack Johnson too. Especially how he always spoke his mind and did whatever he believed he had the right to do. To this day, I still love being called Big Jack.

Another intriguing cat was Walter Youngblood, whose Muslim

name was Wali Muhammad. His job was to tend to Ali's equipment, and he did so without any fanfare. Ali would come to the gym, and everything would be laid out—gloves, headgear, protective belt, Vaseline, hand wraps, tape, spit buckets, water, mouthpiece, towels. Youngblood stayed out of the way. Did his job and, at night, disappeared, saying with a smile, "Got to take my medicine."

The routine in camp was you'd kill time after early-morning roadwork, and begin heading for the gym around 2:30. That's when Ali came to the gym to train. And that's when the sparring partners—guys like Ed "Bossman" Jones, Jaybar Brown, and me—would put in our time sparring with Muhammad. As each of us finished our allotted rounds, we'd move out on our own, hit the heavy and speed bags, skip rope, and shadowbox.

After the workout, I liked to hang out in the dressing room and listen to Ali jive around. He talked. He joked. He played tapes of Elijah Muhammad's speeches in which the white man was equated to the devil. Ali used to talk about that a lot. But the strange thing was he was more friendly with white people than blacks. I didn't understand how the white man could be the devil one minute and be best buddy the next. Not to mention that Gene Kilroy and Angelo Dundee, both whites, were two of his most valued members in the camp. Did I ask him about the contradiction? Nope. I was just happy to be there. I didn't want to ruffle any feathers.

Once we'd all showered, it was dinnertime. The food at Deer Lake was prepared according to Muslim rules. That meant when Lana Shabazz, Muhammad's cook, served you, there was no pork and that soul food was kept to a bare minimum. If you wanted butter with your corn bread, Lana would shake a finger at you and say, "Butter'll kill you. Animal fats, worst thing you can put in your system." She would say that live enzymes—whatever they were—were best for you.

After dinner, guys would sit around these long wooden tables talking boxing—mostly tales about the oddball characters and the weird things that had happened in their years in the business. I liked hearing Angelo Dundee tell about the days when he was coming up, in the late forties and early fifties . . . and the tricks he learned from the old-time trainers who hung around Stillman's Gym in New York.

See, the boxing business in the late 1940s was concentrated in New York in a way it has not been since. In those days, there were small fight clubs operating throughout the metropolitan New York area, with boxing cards six nights a week. Angelo carried the "spit bucket" for guys like Ray Arcel and Chickie Ferrara, some nights making as little as twenty dollars in those smoke-filled arenas while learning the little cons, the "edges" that sometimes make a difference.

He told about the night a fighter who had been knocked to the canvas looked to the corner for advice. Ferrara signaled him to stay down. The trouble was that Chickie was working the other guy's corner. By the time the cobwebs cleared in the floored fighter's head, he was a beat too late in recognizing his error, as the referee's count reached ten.

Another time, Angelo saw a fighter of Ray Arcel's score a knockdown. As the referee began to count to ten, Arcel mounted the steps to the ring apron with his man's robe. As the count reached seven, Arcel slipped the robe over his guy's shoulders, prompting the referee to speed up his count, which was Arcel's intention to begin with. The speeded count resulted in a knockout victory, over the other man's noisy protest. Years later, when he was on his own, Angelo did the same thing with a boxer of his, Bill Bossio, suckering the referee into a quick count that once again left the opponent complaining about being victimized by the official.

Whatever. That sort of quick thinking was invaluable in a corner man during a fight and was why, through all the upheavals in Muhammad's life, and in spite of attempts to poison him against Angelo by some of Ali's Nation of Islam aides, Ali always made sure Angelo Dundee was in his corner. Dundee had proven his worth practically from the git-go.

Remember the first fight against Sonny Liston in February

1964? Ali, known then as Cassius Clay, came back to his corner after the fourth round with his eyes burning, his vision impaired. He was in a panic. "Cut the gloves off," he told Dundee. "I can't see."

Dundee, convinced the condition was temporary, refused. "This is the big one, daddy!" he shouted. "Jab and keep circling until your eyes clear."

As the bell sounded for the fifth round, Angelo raised his fighter off the stool and pushed him across the ring. By the seventh round, the bout was over. Liston was on his stool, complaining of an injured shoulder, and Clay was the new world's champion. Dundee had guessed correctly that Clay had somehow gotten liniment in his eyes, which would wash out.

In Easton, I was telling folks that I was spending time in Deer Lake, working out with Ali. Most of them figured I was in Fantasyland, and discounted what I said. Then one day, after Ernie Butler asked Ali if he would come down to Easton and stop by the Northampton County prison, where he worked, and talk to the inmates, Ali climbed into his white bus and drove down to Easton.

The bus had his name in red letters across the side of it, so as we drove folks were beeping their horns at Ali, who would beep back and wave. He loved the attention, and kept us all entertained with poems and jokes. I remember him saying, "I'm so bad I rassle with alligators, tussle with a whale, handcuff lightning and throw thunder in jail. That's how bad I am."

At one point, I heard him talking to himself on the bus. He was saying, "I'm one bad nigger."

We went to the prison first. Everybody there was excited. Muhammad shadowboxed with some of the inmates, cracking them up by telling them, "I am the greaaatest . . . of aaaalllll tiiime."

But he also told them prison was a form of slavery for the black man.

"That's why they build these prisons—to keep you in slavery," he said.

Afterward, we arranged for him to speak at Easton Junior High

School. From the stage, he introduced me as a member of his camp. Then he amused the schoolkids with his poems, exiting the stage with: "I like your school, I like your style, but you pay so cheap, I won't be back for a while."

Ali's appearance in Easton ended all the doubts about my connection to his camp. All of a sudden, the jokers on the street corners who had scoffed at the notion that their homeboy Holmes sparred with Ali wanted to know what Muhammad was really like.

For me he was a graduate course in the manly art. For a guy who was aiming for an Olympic berth, I was awfully inexperienced. When I first showed up in Deer Lake, I had had about eleven amateur bouts. But through Ali I was sharpening my skills. Not that Muhammad would say here's how. Ali never set out to show me a move or a fine point. I learned by osmosis. I'd notice how the great man threw a punch, or executed a move, and it would sink in. Next thing you know I'd be mimicking Muhammad's side-to-side movement, his knack of turning the opponent in circles so that the guy could never set his feet to deliver a telling blow.

When I first began working with Ali, my approach had been more offense-minded; Ernie Butler had schooled me to slip punches and walk forward to lay some hurt on the other guy. Through working with Ali, I saw there was another way to go— that you could use your quickness and agility and avoid taking a lick while still having the opportunity to nail the opponent with your best shots. It was the art of boxing, a more defensive, safety-first approach. It wasn't long before that became my way of fighting too.

Ali had moves that were unconventional. For instance, he would lean back from punches, a no-no for traditionalists because it left the fighter vulnerable to the next punch. But while that thinking made sense for the average fighter, it simply didn't apply to an Ali, who was quicker and slicker than a heavyweight had a right to be.

It turned out I too had the sort of superior reflexes that most heavyweights don't, and it allowed me to adopt that method of avoiding a punch by pulling back.

Ali had another way of eluding a punch as he was circling. He would rotate his head and shoulders away from the punch, tucking his chin against his shoulder. At the same time, he would extend his arm and intercept the punch with his glove . . . and still be in position to fire back with the other hand.

These were moves that, as an amateur and more so as a professional, I found would work on my opponents. But *not* against Muhammad. He was hip to his own tricks when I used them and knew how to counter them. So I learned not to try them with Ali.

When Ali boxed, he was quicker with his punches when he held his hands low. That was a tendency I already had, and seeing that the great Muhammad Ali did it encouraged me not to change to the more orthodox way of holding my hands way up.

Ali's ways became mine, even when it came to conditioning. To tighten his stomach, he would lie on his back, roll up on his buttocks, and pedal the air as if he was riding a bicycle. I'd never done that before, but in Deer Lake I made it part of my training regimen.

Same for wearing boots when I ran, as Ali did. But that was one Ali practice that I would discover wasn't for me. The boots hurt my ankles and collapsed my arches. I tried putting padding in the boots, and it helped some, but eventually I did my roadwork in running shoes.

In later years, among other things critics would knock me for being a "carbon copy" of Muhammad Ali. As if that was so awful a model to emulate. Fact is, I did steal a trick or two from Muhammad, and did try to hit and not be hit, as he did. But so what? As it worked for him, so it eventually worked for me.

For a fighter to win an Olympic title is the equivalent of a civilian winning the lottery. Ever since the 1976 Olympics in Montreal, it's been the open sesame for American amateur boxers. That was the year that Sugar Ray Leonard, Howard Davis, and Leon and Michael Spinks won gold and then turned pro with multifight big-money TV deals and promoters eager to build their careers through cautious matchmaking. They were the chosen, the favored.

For instance, when Sugar Ray Leonard and Marvin Hagler appeared on the same card in Hartford in June 1977, each man scored a quick knockout. For his victory, Hagler (who had not been an Olympian) earned $1,500 in what amounted to his thirty-sixth fight as a professional. Leonard got $40,000 for the third fight of his career.

See what I'm saying? Olympic gold is the fast track to success. Ali took it when he was Cassius Clay in Rome in 1960. Joe Frazier (1964) and George Foreman (1968) saw their gold medals make their careers easier to launch than if they had been no-name guys. As the father of two baby girls, I was hoping to catch lightning in the jar. Win that gold and, wham, get me some real money.

By 1972, I'd won several eastern titles and was invited to Minnesota to compete in a tournament that was said to figure heavily in the selection of the U.S. boxing team. I made it all the way to the finals there, only to run up against a left-handed slugger named Nick Wells.

It marked the first time I'd fought a lefty. It threw my reactions off. I was hesitant and ended up being an easy target for Wells, who had good power. Good enough to give me the worst beating of my career and stop me in the third round. My first-ever defeat.

The way things unfolded, I had another opportunity against Wells in a later tournament in Texas. This time I managed to find left-handed sparring partners to get ready for him. Guess what? It didn't matter. Not one bit. The guy Wells had my number, and he beat me again. Badly.

But for a fleeting moment, it looked as though Larry Holmes might get lucky. That was when I learned that Nick Wells would be unable to compete in the Olympic Trials due to injuries. Something like that had happened to Joe Frazier in '64. Buster Mathis had been awarded the decision in their showdown fight.

But then Mathis broke his hand and, like that, Frazier was the U.S.'s man. He'd gone on to win the gold in Tokyo.

I was hoping to follow his example. In my mind, I was next best among the heavyweights, after Wells. But the amateur boxing establishment is a clique as closed to outsiders as a WASP country club is to blacks and Jews. The amateur officials often anoint the fighter they want, and short of their man being knocked cold he is virtually home free with his spot on the team.

The amateur officials wanted Duane Bobick as the U.S.'s heavyweight. He had, as Ali used to say of certain opponents, the right connection and complexion. Bobick was a white boy, a slow-moving heavyweight I figured to box circles around. But I began to have second thoughts about my chances when it was suggested I ought to drop down to the light heavyweight class. Word was that U.S. amateur officials wanted a white hope to represent America after all these years of black Olympic heavyweight champs. Almost the whole Olympic boxing establishment was white, and there hadn't been a white U.S. Olympic heavyweight since 1956.

I'm not saying it was *just* a black-white thing. It was more complicated. The amateur clique was partial to fighters who came from established programs with deep pools of talent. The trainers from those organizations were treated like insiders, and their fighters often got preferential treatment. For instance, the military was one of the traditional sources of Olympic boxing talent. That gave Bobick an even greater edge. Not only was he white, but as a navy quartermaster from Bowlus, Minnesota, he had the right affiliation too.

As for Ernie Butler and his tall skinny fighter, well, we were complete outsiders.

It's funny, but the same thing would happen to Mike Tyson, whose mentor, Cus D'Amato, was viewed with suspicion by amateur brass in 1984. The amateur establishment had anointed Henry Tillman as their heavyweight of choice, and Tyson would regard his pair of decision losses to Tillman—the eventual U.S. Olympic heavyweight—as political.

At first I thought of going along with the desires of the amateur officials and dropping down to the light heavyweight class. My weight was sinking anyway, due to the difficult schedule I had. I'd gone on the night shift at the Ingersoll-Rand mill so I could train in the daytime. Working all night and trying to do roadwork the next day had proved fatiguing. My weight, usually 190-something, had sunk to 182.

It quickly became clear to me that I would lack the strength to win as a light heavyweight. So I told the amateur brass I would stay at heavyweight. Trouble was, the whole experience was undermining my spirit. I felt the deck was stacked against me. Unable to get back to my correct weight now, I worried whether I'd have the stamina to do what I knew I could against Bobick—box circles around him.

Nor was my confidence boosted by what ole Howard Cosell had to say when he previewed the U.S. boxing competition on TV. I had seen Cosell before at Deer Lake but had never talked to him. Cosell would get Angelo Dundee to give him inside information about Ali and his opponent and then go on the air and parrot Dundee's thoughts as if they were his very own. At the Olympic trials at West Point, he did the same thing, only the man he parroted was Sarge Johnson, the only black man on the coaching staff. But Sarge was interested in pushing his own fighters, which was why Cosell told America that Bobick was our best heavyweight and that Larry Holmes wasn't worth a damn.

I tried to buck up against the bullshit. But when Bobick and I finally fought it became clear to me that I couldn't win this one. In the opening round, I leaned back from a right hand Bobick threw and slipped. Uh-uh, said the referee. Score that as a knockdown. When I told the referee that the punch hadn't even touched me, he dismissed my protest and signaled the fighters to get on with it.

In the second round, I was scoring with the jab, well enough to swell up Bobick's right eye. But Bobick was stronger than I, and used his advantage to push me toward the corners of the ring. I knew I didn't want to operate from there. A slick boxer like me works best from the middle of the ring. So I tied Bobick up. That's when the ref warned me for clinching. He warned me again in the third round. The next time I clinched he disqualified me. After 22 fights as an amateur—and a record of 19–3—it was good-bye Olympic glory.

Not that Bobick was any great shakes in Munich, where the games were held. The Cuban fighter, Teofilo Stevenson, knocked him out in his second fight.

In later years, it was reported that I had been cowardly against Bobick and actually crawled out of the ring in fright. As late as 1985, *The New York Times* was still treating that version as if it had merit: "He was a frightened boxer—the word often used was 'yellow'—whom people remembered as trying to crawl out of the ring against Duane Bobick in an amateur bout in 1972."

Where the story started, who knows. It wasn't true. But this much I can say for sure. For years after the Bobick fight, the boxing establishment—many of them relying on word of mouth—was under the impression that I had caved in against Bobick and shown a lack of heart.

It would be one of many obstacles I would have to overcome in the future. A future that now saw me, at twenty-two years of age, obliged to forget any dreams of Olympic gold and launch a professional career as just another guy.

CHAPTER
THREE

I didn't have any delusions about how far I could go in boxing.

Hanging out at Deer Lake for almost two years gave me a chance to see that lots of really talented fighters don't get anywhere. Most guys just pick up a few hundred bucks here and there. A degree of luck, I knew, could make a big difference in a fighter's career. I wanted to keep fighting. Since nobody else was interested, I had no choice but to turn pro in '73 with Ernie Butler as my manager. He said he could get me fights up in Scranton.

I now had a new and easier job, driving a truck for the Strongwear Pants Company. When I had worked in the steel mill in Phillipsburg, I had dreamed about driving a truck. Now that I was a truck driver, I found it wasn't nearly as ideal as I thought it would be. Things are almost never what you make them out to be.

Ernie Butler sought backers to put up money to launch my

boxing career. It had been done before. Ali had had the Louisville Sponsoring Group—a bunch of businessmen from his hometown who'd anted up about $30,000 to get things rolling and given their man a signing bonus of $10,000 and a guaranteed draw for his first two years of $333 a month against earnings.

Joe Frazier had had the Cloverlay Syndicate—a group of Philadelphians who put up seed money, about $20,000, and started off by paying Smokin' Joe $100 a week, a sum that would increase as the purses he earned increased.

When Ray Leonard was starting out, his attorney, Mike Trainer, remembered that he had borrowed money from a bank to launch himself as a lawyer. He decided to put together a group of backers that would lend Sugar Ray the capital to get started and would in turn receive 8 percent interest on the loan. Trainer got twenty-four people to kick in a total of $21,000 and then incorporated his man as Sugar Ray Leonard Inc. For his pro debut in February 1977 against Luis "the Bull" Vega, CBS-TV paid Leonard $10,000. Sugar Ray added $30,000 more from his share of the gate. The investors were paid back from the proceeds of his first fight and Leonard was in the enviable position of owning himself.

Mort Levy was my boss at Strongwear Pants. When Ernie Butler asked him if he would bankroll my boxing career, Levy said he knew too little about the fight game—he would need a professional opinion before being able to commit to that sort of project.

Levy knew a guy who knew a guy who knew Gil Clancy, the veteran fight manager and trainer, who had first made his name working with Emile Griffith, the welterweight and middleweight champion who had fought from 1958 to 1977—112 bouts in all. Clancy had also trained WBC middleweight champion Rodrigo Valdez and George Foreman. Levy's idea was for me to go down to New York, where Clancy had a gym, and work out for him. A kind of audition. If I passed muster with Clancy, well, then Levy would get involved.

On the day I rode to New York, I was sick with the flu. But I felt confident of making an impression on Clancy even if I was under the weather. Wrong. When I got back to Easton, Mort Levy told me that Clancy had concluded from four rounds of sparring that while someday I might be a contender, I would never be a champion. Clancy said I hadn't the quickness of an Ali, or the willfulness of Joe Frazier, or the punching power of either of them. Levy quoted Clancy as saying: "Holmes will make money, but he's not a great, great athlete."

That was enough to keep Mort Levy from taking the plunge.

"Look, Larry," he said. "I like you personally. But let's face it. If you got beat by amateurs, it's only logical that you'll get beat by professionals. Gil Clancy thinks you're not a future champion. My recommendation is to forget boxing and concentrate on making a living here. I wouldn't like to see you get hurt fighting."

"Well," I said, "it's a chance I got to take."

"Okay," he said. "You got your job here as long as you want."

Ernie Butler sounded out other local businessmen to see if they'd cough up enough money so I could concentrate strictly on boxing. None of them would put up a penny. Not one. If I was going to fight professionally, it was going to be without any real support.

In March '73, Ernie Butler and I drove to Scranton, Pennsylvania, a declining coal-mining community eighty miles north of Easton.

That night, at the 4,500-seat Catholic Youth Center, I would be making my pro debut against Rodell Dupree, a kid from Jersey City who had had six fights. Two charter buses from Easton, filled with family, friends, and coworkers from Strongwear, came down later in the day.

By the time the Easton contingent arrived, I'd had my medical examination and an early dinner. When it was time to go fight, Ernie and I headed to the arena.

Dupree came at me smokin'. What I remember is while I was fighting him off, a phrase kept going through my mind—the words repeating like a chant, or what those Hare Krishna people call a "mantra." The words were: "Come on body, don't fail me now. Three more rounds to go."

Each round, I'd adjust the remaining rounds as I repeated the musical phrase. Sometimes it came out, "Come on body, don't fail me now." Other times: "Come on feet, don't fail me now."

Obviously, I was worried about my stamina. This kid Dupree just kept coming, and I had to use my jab and footwork to keep him at bay.

But when it was over, my feet and body had done right by me. And I'd come away with my first victory—a four-round decision. Ernie paid me sixty-three dollars in cash afterward, of a one-hundred-dollar purse. We had the standard fighter/manager arrangement, which allowed Ernie to deduct 33⅓ percent of my earnings for his share. He had done that, and deducted the $3 he had paid for my boxing license.

That night I went back to Easton on one of the buses and celebrated my victory. The folks on the bus were drinking beer and smoking. I abstained. I didn't smoke then or now, and wouldn't become a beer drinker until the early 1980s. Even so it was great to be among friends and hoot and holler with them. We sang. We told dirty jokes. We were loud and jovial, and maybe a bit too crude for Mort Levy. He came up to Scranton on the bus that night, but for future fights there—and in the beginning most of my bouts were in Scranton—he took to driving up there on his own.

For the promoter in Scranton, Larry Holmes was a bargain. He could pay me a prelim fighter's meager purse and, with those two busloads of paying customers, come out way ahead. In truth, it was embarrassing to get so little to fight. These weren't the toughest guys in the world I faced, but they were tough enough. It wasn't like I was one of those Special Cases, who came into the game with a gilded reputation and was given a bunch of Mr. Softees to fatten my record on.

Take Art Savage, my second pro fight. Savage—who I later became friends with—was a rough and tumble son of a bitch, hitting on the break and after the bell. There was no way I'd have been in against a guy like that had I been an Olympic hero. But that hadn't happened, and now I had to deal with his questionable tactics. I put a little more mustard on my punches and stopped him in three rounds.

Folks back home read about the millions of bucks that Ali and Frazier were making and figured I was probably chasing down the real money too. What a joke. I just couldn't bring myself to tell them—not even my mother—how little those purses were. It was too humiliating. When people asked me, I'd smile and say, "I'm doing very, verr-rrry good financially." Made it seem like I was making thousands.

I'd like to tell you that in spite of my struggle back then, in 1973, I knew things would turn around—that someday I'd look back on those days with the satisfaction of a man who had overcome his difficult origins. I'd like to tell you that, but I'd be a damn liar if I did. I knew no such thing. I only hoped I could move up in the business and make some money before I got too old, too used up. I realized that this would be no easy feat, given the position I was in. I had no illusions about Ernie Butler. Ernie was trying—and trying hard—to advance me in the business, but he hadn't the clout or the influence to make it happen.

But chance is the X factor in any life.

And that spring, on a visit to Gleason's Gym, I would make a connection that would change my career. Through the door of Gleason's and into my life—bringing the bitter with the sweet— came a former numbers boss from Cleveland, now doing business as a fight manager. His name was Don King.

In September 1971, Don King had come out of Ohio's Marion Correctional Institution after serving a four-year term for manslaughter. King had been convicted of stomping to death a numbers runner of his who, he felt, had been shortchanging him.

It hadn't taken King long to get back in action. In his hometown of Cleveland he had befriended a boxing manager-promoter named Don Elbaum, a likable fella who had himself been a fighter for a while before turning to the business of boxing.

Through Elbaum, King became a managerial partner in heavyweight Earnie Shavers, who was said to hit harder than any man on the planet. Earnie was never a skilled boxer, but if he could land his right hand flush bad things would happen to you. At the time King became involved in Shavers's career, he went in as partners with Elbaum; a Youngstown construction man, Blackie Gennaro; and former major-league pitcher Dean Chance.

Impressed by King's razzle-dazzle patter, Elbaum talked him up to people in the business, even introducing him to Hank Schwartz, whose Video Techniques provided the satellite technology for most of the closed-circuit fights. King used the introduction to become an employee of Video Techniques.

Elbaum would discover that King was unconventional in the way he operated. Early on, King had turned up at Elbaum's office and set a briefcase on his desk. As Elbaum told people:

"It was eight o'clock and as King drops the briefcase and heads out the door, he says to me: 'Don't leave.' So I waited for him to come back. Eleven o'clock, twelve o'clock. I'm blowing my top. I get on the phone trying to reach him. I stayed all night. Eight A.M. he shows up. He opens the briefcase. It's filled with money. 'Where's my coat?' he says. He pulls money—big bills—out of one pocket, and then the other. 'Now I know I can trust you,' he said."

Soon enough Elbaum would learn that trust was a one-way proposition with King. By the time I met King, in the spring of '73 at Gleason's Gym, he had bought out Chance's share in Shavers and was beginning to undermine Elbaum's position, turning the fighter against him.

I knew nothing of these intrigues back then. What I knew was that King was a hotshot newcomer, a black man who was making an impact in the boxing business. King not only was involved with Shavers but also with heavyweights Jeff Merritt and Ray Anderson. He was a man on the move. You'd hear his name mentioned in Ali's camp, and Ernie Butler spoke of him from time to time.

That afternoon I sparred with Shavers, who was preparing for a June 18 fight against Jimmy Ellis. Ellis had won the WBA heavyweight title in 1968 and then lost it to Joe Frazier in 1970. My style was regarded as similar to that of Ellis, a boxer type who had been Ali's top sparring partner back when he was Cassius Clay. What that meant, I guess, was that we both were guys who relied on ring savvy . . . the scientific approach—move and hit and try not to be hit in return.

I worked three rounds with Shavers and held my own. Held my own against a guy who only months earlier had knocked out the clever Jimmy Young in three rounds. Given that Shavers had forty-three knockouts in his forty-four victories—he'd lost only twice—and was world-ranked, I was feeling pretty pleased with myself, thinking that maybe there was hope yet for Larry Holmes.

Meanwhile, Ernie Butler was talking to promoters milling around Gleason's, hoping that on the strength of those three rounds he could hustle up a fight for me. Easier said than done. Just because a kid looks good sparring doesn't mean he's the real McCoy. When you spar, it's with oversize gloves and protective headgear. And the fact that a guy looks like Superman in sparring doesn't mean he won't freeze up when it's the real deal—when the lights are on and the crowd is screaming for blood.

In those days, Don King's hair was normal: he hadn't styled it with that electrified look that would become his trademark. But in every other way, King was King. You heard the man well before you saw him, his voice booming as he walked into the room. And boy, could he make an entrance. He acted as though he was Mr. Shit on a Stick, a prime-time heavy dude, and damn if the guys loitering around Gleason's didn't fuss over him. Me, what did I know? I thought he was a famous celebrity, which he really wasn't yet, although no one had bothered to tell him.

When folks approached him, King, who wore an open-collar shirt and a blue-and-white plaid sports jacket, would ask them if they wanted an autographed photo. He had the photos in a shoulder bag. I figured he meant a photo of his fighter, Earnie Shavers. But King being King, an incureable egomaniac, it turned out he was giving away eight-by-ten glossies of the once and future baron of boxing, Don King his own damned self. I still have mine from 1973. He wrote, "Best Wishes, Don King." It was the beginning of a long and chaotic relationship.

That day Ernie Butler tried to interest King in me. But King stonewalled him. He thought he had a future champion in Shavers, more so after Earnie wowed the New York media by knocking Ellis cold in the first round of their Madison Square Garden match. King had neither time for nor interest in a prelim fighter of no special reputation. Not when he had a thunderous puncher like Shavers in tow.

That was typical of King. Over the next twenty-five years he rarely bothered with a beginner. He wasn't interested in growing a fighter. He wanted a boxer who could do business, like, right now. King's modus operandi was to latch on to proven commodities—sign 'em or steal 'em, whatever it took—and then get their money's worth while he could.

What kept me on his radar screen was the fact that one of King's associates, Richie Giachetti, thought I had the makings of a contender. He'd caught me working against Shavers and liked what he'd seen, and from that day he began badgering King to sign me.

Giachetti was a former fighter, a welterweight whose amateur career was followed by a short pro stint. Once he got married, Giachetti decided to open up an auto body shop—he was always pretty good at fixing cars. In '65 and while living in Cleveland, Giachetti plunged into stock-car racing, preparing cars for others to drive. That lasted seven years and Richie would call it "a break-even proposition."

By '73, he had quit car racing and gone into boxing with King. While Richie was the one who sold me to King, I always thought there was more to it than met the eye. See, from the get-go Richie wanted to be more than Don King's hired hand. Richie likes to tell people he saw from that first day at Gleason's that I had talent. Maybe. But I always thought it was more a matter of Richie wanting to have his own fighter to train.

43

Yet I'll say this about Giachetti. It was through his persistence that by the summer of '73—with my record 4–0—King finally offered to manage me. Hell, I was all for it. I'd seen how business was done while hanging around Deer Lake. The fight game was the Olympics all over again. If you weren't connected, you were screwed . . . no matter how talented you were.

The hitch was that the men in power had all the leverage. So when you signed it was going to be on their terms. I mean, you had your choice—fight in Scranton every few weeks for a couple of hundred bucks, or get bouts for real money by signing paper that would oblige you to your promoter for life, or for your career, which is about the same thing for a fighter.

I wasn't going anywhere with Ernie Butler. He had no power in boxing. I was almost twenty-four years old and dying in Scranton. And it really bothered me to see his 33⅓ percent coming out of my piddly-ass purses. No way in the world could he get me the fights I needed. Don King was going to take his cut too, but when all was said and done there would be more money in my pocket.

So on a day that summer, I went up to New York without Ernie Butler. At the office of the New York State Athletic Commission, I signed an agreement that made Don King my manager. Giachetti took over as trainer. As for Ernie Butler, King said he would work things out with him. Then, to cap our new arrangement—and to show me the clout he had—King got me a six-round preliminary bout at Madison Square Garden for that September.

It was a helluva step up from Scranton. I was thrilled, figuring at last I would get matches that would accelerate my career and put me in the big money. For months now I had been pretending to be a big man around Easton, dropping Ali's name whenever I could. To have a fight in the mecca of boxing—Madison Square Garden—well, that gave me a feeling of legitimacy . . . a sense that from here on I wouldn't have to play at being for real.

On the night of my Garden match, Richie Giachetti surprised me with a brand-new white satin robe. On the back of the robe

were the words "The Easton Assassin"—Richie's idea and the very first time the nickname was used. "The Easton Assassin" would remain my handle through the rest of my career. And though I became uneasy with the "assassin" part, I had no problem being identified with my hometown. The name stuck to me. When I'd walk into a casino in Vegas, say, people would call out: "Hey, it's the Easton Assassin." I liked it that I sort of put the place on the map.

My opponent at the Garden was Bob Bozic, a strong puncher who, lacking quickness, was a perfect foil for me. I outboxed him, keeping the jab in his face for six rounds as I won the decision. I felt great, like I was on my way. And with Ernie Butler working my corner alongside Giachetti, I figured everybody would end up with his fair share. Including me. Yet when King came around afterward, the money was a sobering $193. The lesson seemed to be that while I might have a connected manager, I was still Larry Holmes, just another face in the crowd.

Yet, with King I figured to have a better shot at meaningful fights. He could orchestrate that. Whether he would, well, that remained to be seen. It was on the likelihood of his making me a player in this game that I had signed with one of Don's corporations, Sportsville, only to discover much later how the contract was full of three-year options that tied me to King for damn near ever.

Had I been a more skilled reader, or been given better advice, I might not have ended up with such lopsided terms. Then again, what other options did I have? I was a virtual unknown. Nobody was knocking at my door, eager to make me a star. For now Don King was "it." None of this came as late-breaking news to him. He knew he had me by the short hairs. And had taken advantage.

By the terms of my new deal, I was ending up with only about half of my purses. As manager, King got 25 percent, Giachetti took down 12½ percent, and Ernie Butler 10 percent. King was also deducting nickel/dime expenses. I felt a lot like the little boy from 208 East Lincoln who'd taken to hiding his money in flowerpots, the better to avoid the grasping fingers of others.

Take what happened when King hired me to work as a sparring partner for Earnie Shavers when Shavers signed to fight Jerry Quarry. This would be the first time I was to be paid for sparring. Only problem was I never saw a penny. When I complained to King about it, he said he'd given the money to Ernie Butler. I guess Ernie felt he was entitled to keep it. I never put a stink on it; I just filed it away in my mind.

When Ali hired me to spar with him in preparation for his September '73 match against Ken Norton, I drew my line in the sand with Ernie. He claimed he was entitled to a cut of what I made as a sparring partner. I said the hell he was and said the same to King when he came sniffing around for a piece of that action.

In fact, Ernie had screwed up the original offer I had from the Ali camp. Ali had been willing to pay one thousand dollars a week for me to be a sparring partner of his, but Ernie—God knows why—said five hundred dollars a week would be fine. It compounded the growing sense I had that he was out of his element when the game got bigger than Scranton, P-A.

In any case, my life turned busy. When I wasn't in camp sparring with either Ali or Shavers, I was driving the truck for Strongwear and training in Easton on my own. The Shavers gig turned out to be shorter than anticipated. King had sent Jeff Merritt to camp to spar with Earnie too. A few days into camp, Merritt, who was six-foot-five and had a helluva left hook, got into a slam-bang sparring session with Shavers and busted Earnie's jaw. He didn't seem contrite about it either afterward. When I asked Merritt what prompted the fireworks, he told me that when he'd first come out of prison Shavers had whaled on him in sparring and busted him up pretty good. This was his payback.

That ran against the code of conduct for sparring partners. The idea was to work with the man whose camp it was—be less like an adversary than like a dance partner. Give him the kind of sweat he wanted. My philosophy was: Let him be what he wants to be, but never let him hurt you. That was how most guys who worked as sparring partners operated. But boxing is full of strange characters, and Jeff Merritt was certainly one of them.

I remember King sending him later to Ali's camp at Deer Lake, and giving Ali money to dole out to Merritt for his meals and incidental expenses. Merritt, who called himself Candy Slim—on account of he was sweet (or so he said)—waited until King left and then told Ali, "Gimme my goddamn money." Ali didn't care nothing about the money. He gave it to Candy Slim, who started plotting to return to Ohio, where King had his farm.

"I'm gonna go back to Cleveland and kill them prize black Angus cows of his," Merritt vowed. He was still steaming about King's holding out on his money. "Who does he think he is? I ain't no little goddamn kid."

Merritt hated King for being more attentive to Shavers. No matter what King did for him, it wasn't enough.

Merritt called to get flight information to Cleveland, and then drove down to Easton with me. On the way, we stopped in a drugstore and Jeff Merritt bought a bottle of Robitussin, the cough medicine. He liked to drink Robitussin to get high. He did that a lot in those days. Robitussin was his breakfast of champions. I was later told that the Robitussin they make today isn't as potent as the product Jeff Merritt used to slug down.

Anyway, we got to Easton, and Merritt asked, "Where can I buy pot?"

Even though I no longer did drugs of any type, I knew where the dealers hung out and drove him to a street corner, where a guy sold him three loose joints. As he smoked his joints, he kept talking about shooting "those goddamn black Angus."

I drove him to the airport later that day. I never heard about King's prize cows being assassinated. Maybe Jeff Merritt soothed his angry heart with another bottle of Robitussin. Who knows? Next time I saw King, I asked him whether he'd seen Merritt back in Cleveland.

"That crazy motherfucker—no, I didn't. But if I do, I'm gonna kick his ass."

I settled into the Ali camp. Life at Deer Lake was never without complications, due to the jockeying for position by the various members of Muhammad's entourage. Most of them had do-nothing jobs and spent the bulk of their time bitching. Bitching that this guy didn't do doodly and that guy didn't do squat, and how come Ali doesn't pay me more. Asked once what his brother, Rahaman, did, Ali had said, "I give him fifty thousand dollars a year for jiving and driving and that's not bad."

When they weren't complaining about being underpaid, they were doing their damnedest to take advantage of Ali. It was comical the extent of thievery—from outright stealing stuff to abusing the signing privileges Ali's guys had at a nearby convenience store. You were supposed to sign just for what you needed—fruits, snacks, a bottle of pop. But there were guys that loaded up bags of groceries and hauled them to girlfriends' homes. They just brazenly exploited Ali's generosity until Muhammad said no more and closed the account.

There was a lot of backbiting too. Once, when Ali's wife, Belinda, asked me how Muhammad was looking in training, and we chatted awhile, the camp grapevine had me putting the move on her. You had to be careful because there were some real weasels in that camp. The next time Belinda approached me, I told her I couldn't talk because of what was being said.

In those days, whenever a guy came into camp looking for a sparring job, Ali would say, "Get in there with Larry." What the guy did with me told Ali whether he could fight or not. I'd become Ali's best sparring partner. But if Ali thought he was using me, I saw it just the opposite. I was using him, learning my trade day by day from the master. And getting paid for it.

When Ali wanted a "war" in there, I could give it to him. We had plenty of those. Fighting all-out with Ali, I'd be right there with him, trading punch for punch. Which showed me I was becoming a good fighter. I mean a *really* good fighter, even if no one else but Giachetti knew it.

In November '73, I had my first big fight, on a Don King promotion in Cleveland. The opponent was Kevin Isaac, who, like me, had just turned pro. In fact, his first opponent had been Rodell Dupree, the same man I'd fought in my pro debut. Isaac was 2–0, but the way King's so-called advisers, Al Braverman and Paddy Flood, fussed about him, it was easy to see that Isaac was, in their minds, *the* prospect. Me, I was just a body for hire. That was just as plain by how they avoided me and by the snide remarks they made about me, word of which always got back to me. Boxing is a gossip's industry. The pipeline is always flowing.

I knew that there was no margin for defeat at this point in my career. A loss to Isaac and I could become the kind of Don King fighter he used to joke about:

"You would be like a needle in a haystack . . . haaaarrrrd to find. Hah hah hah."

More likely I'd become an opponent, someone the prospects would beat on their way up. I wasn't stupid. I knew that's how it worked. It's why I kept my job driving the truck.

Kevin Isaac dropped me in the first round with a right hand that landed flush on my temple. Wham, and I was on my butt. First time as a professional. Any time that Hollywood depicts a knockout it's always that shot to the point of the chin that does it. That's the movie cliché. But most fighters know it's the shot to the temple that knocks you off balance.

When I got to my feet, the referee was giving me the mandatory count of eight and then wiping my gloves. I remembered fighters at Deer Lake saying that after you've been knocked down you have the element of surprise going for you if you fire back with bad intentions. The other guy is usually open as he rushes in to finish you off. So if you keep your cool, you can get back in a hurry. Which is what I did with Isaac. I caught him with a punishing combination. The swagger went out of him like that.

In the third round, Isaac dropped his hands, just to relax a moment. He relaxed; I punched. Bang: a right hand . . . on time, as they say. I knocked him out. He was out cold for quite a while.

You think that raised my standing among King's stable of fighters? Not in the least. Suddenly I was tagged as a guy who couldn't take a punch. Never mind that I'd climbed off the canvas and put a licking on Isaac so bad that when I stopped by his hotel room later that night, he declined to open the door.

"Hurtin' too bad," he croaked from inside his room.

For me, the fight proved I not only could take a shot but that I had the poise to deal with adversity. Even when I was hurt, I had not panicked. I had kept my wits and improvised a plan. That was important. Lots of fighters just get in there and fight without having a clear idea of what they want to do.

Yet even with the victory, I was still odd man out. I'd only made $150 for beating Isaac, and still had no real allies in the King organization other than Giachetti. Braverman was no great supporter of mine. Just the opposite. He had a white heavyweight of his own, John "Dino" Denis, who had turned pro in 1972. Big Al was building Denis's record in places like New Bedford, Massachusetts, Bayonne, New Jersey, and, yes, Scranton, against the usual assortment of tomato cans. Christ, Denis's first three fights, all victories, had been against the same patsy, Henry Lawson.

Over the next few years, as King got busier and bigger in the boxing business, Braverman could have stepped in and smoothed the way for me. But he was more interested in seeing if he could get my butt knocked off, the better to clear the way for his boy Dino as the rising heavyweight star of the King menagerie. Braverman, a big, bent-nose kind of guy who moonlighted as, of all things, an antique dealer—he had a shop in New York City—later on would admit that he'd done his best to screw me up by matching me with guys he figured would beat me. At the time he confessed this to me, I was a success—in fact, I was heavyweight champion—so when he told me of his plot to mess me up he figured I would just kind of chuckle at the bald-faced shittiness of it. Instead, I looked at him and said, "Go fuck yourself, Al." And walked away.

See, I had had so much to overcome that it was not in me to forgive, or forget, the cruelty and indifference—the utter lack of respect—that was shown me in those early days. Boxing is a hard business. Not just in the bloodshed that occurs in the ring. The scheming and scamming that goes on outside the squared circle is every bit as nasty, and hurtful to a fighter.

In my case, there was so much to surmount. Even with a record of 7–0—and my improvement obvious when I worked with Ali—I was the invisible man. Mostly ignored. And when not ignored—scorned, ridiculed, dismissed. A negative dossier arose. It went like this: Larry Holmes will never go anywhere. The guy is built funny, with spindly ankles and thin calves that could never support a heavyweight's torso. Look at him, with that peanut head and imitation-Ali moves. Can't punch. Can't take a punch. Got no heart.

A mustard seed for a heart was how Jeff Merritt (who I sometimes sparred with) taunted me one time, picking up on the party line about Larry Holmes. Yup. It was gospel among boxing people that push come to shove, I'd run scared. The ghost of the Bobick fight still lingered. And even though I knew that rap on me was total bullshit, it bothered me just the same. Bothered me because it was part of the negative talk that could only stymie my progress in the business.

And for me this was a business—a chance to make money, a chance to build a life, the best chance I would have. Even now, working regularly with Ali and knowing from those daily sessions that I had superior skills, even now I had no illusions about becoming a champion and making millions of dollars. My goal was way more modest—make enough money to buy me a house in Easton and settle down there with a family.

But in 1973, you couldn't have gotten me to swear that even that simpler objective was within reach. Uh-uh. I was an afterthought to the one man who could fast-forward my hopes—Don King. It was pretty damn obvious. After I'd beaten Kevin Isaac and King had paid me $150, I'd asked if he could lend me another $50. He looked at me as if I was some smelly old bum and shook his head. Said he didn't have it. Which was bullshit. I'd seen him pull out a stack of hundred-dollar bills earlier to give Jeff Merritt a few bucks.

To know you have talent, if only you can get the chance, and to be denied the chance, well, that can sour a man. A fighter's time is brief. If he doesn't move up the ranks, he stagnates. Mentally and physically. A case of use it or lose it. Believe me, that can make a man bitter. Very bitter. I saw it up close and personal with another of Ali's sparring partners, Roy Williams.

Big Roy Williams was six foot five, 240 pounds, and could punch holes in people. But he was a fighter who'd never gotten the breaks, a fighter who had never had any of the sport's power brokers to maneuver him. The better fighters knew how tough he was and avoided him. What the hell. Why take the chance? Because he was an unknown, beating Roy Williams wouldn't advance your reputation. And there was a damn good chance that if the man landed one on the button, you'd end up in orbit.

Talk of bitter. Wooo-boy. Roy was nasty bitter. In camp, he hung by himself and had a permanent scowl on his face. One time, when he'd finally gotten a match, I'd gone to it and, from ringside, was rooting him on. And ole Roy had turned to me in the midst of the fight and from the ring shouted, "Shut the fuck up." Unbelievable.

But that was Roy Williams. Never happy. Perpetually pissed off about something, usually money. You'd hear him griping: "That motherfucker Ali should give me some more money."

The breaking point in his relationship with Ali came in Zaire, where Muhammad shocked the world by knocking out George Foreman. The night of the fight, Williams was to have been on the undercard against Henry Clark, and arrangements had been made for him to go to the arena with Ali and his group. But when Ali was late getting to the arena, Williams's fight was scratched and with it went the five thousand dollars big Roy had been assured of.

As he saw it, since Ali had screwed things up, Ali was obliged to come up with the five grand. "Give me my goddamn money, punk," he told him, back at Deer Lake.

Ali tried to ignore him, but big Roy wouldn't let up.

"You motherfuckin' pussy, pay up."

Ali decided to exact revenge in the ring. He ordered a ten-round workout—the bossman versus his angry hired hand. For Roy Williams, no problem.

"I'm gonna kick your ass, chump," he told Ali.

They went at it tooth and nail. Ali was trying his best to knock the man out. But Williams was giving as good as he got. And after every round, he'd growl: "Faggot, punk, pussy. I'll kick your goddamn ass."

Ali tried the rope-a-dope with Williams, coming off the ropes with a flurry of punches. But big Roy met him and slammed him back. It was a helluva session.

And afterward, there was Roy Williams glaring and muttering: "Faggot, punk, pussy."

Ali wasn't satisfied. He called for another ten rounds the next day.

Roy Williams ate good, slept good. And the next day, he stood toe to toe with Ali for another ten rounds, punching and cussing and giving no ground against the heavyweight champion of the world.

Well, that was enough for Ali. He gave big Roy his five grand and dismissed him—fired his ass.

Roy Williams was a bitter, bitter man, and it wasn't hard to see why. I felt as though I was in the same bag—a fighter who could easily get lost in the shuffle, more so as Don King, working for Video Techniques, began to put together the Rumble in the Jungle—Foreman versus Ali in Zaire.

As he became increasingly involved, he was unavailable to me, leaving the rest of his boxing operation to goddamn Braverman and Flood. And while I had Richie Giachetti pushing them to get me matches, I knew that at least until the Foreman-Ali fight came off, I was in the boxing equivalent of the Bermuda Triangle. Off the radar screen as far as significant fights were concerned.

CHAPTER
FOUR

As a fight manager, King had made an impact quickly with Earnie Shavers. But he had larger ambitions—he wanted to be the main man in boxing . . . and that had nudged him toward promoting. At the beginning of the year (1973) King had gone to Kingston, Jamaica, to watch the heavyweight title fight between the favored champion, Joe Frazier, and the challenger, George Foreman. He had gone to Kingston at the invitation of the Frazier camp but, being the great conniver that he was, he'd cultivated Foreman too, encouraging the challenger's dream of becoming champion while also making airport pickups for him when Foreman's relatives began arriving in Kingston.

The night of the bout, King rode to the arena with Frazier in a limousine that was escorted by siren-blasting police motorcycles, and took up his front-row seat in Frazier's corner. Over the years, I would hear him tell reporters what happened next.

"The first round," King would say, "George hit Frazier with

a devastating punch that sent Joe leaping into the air. Every time he'd strike Frazier, I'd move closer to the end of the row, toward George's corner. By the time the fight ended, a second-round TKO, I was in George's corner. When the fight was stopped, I'm into the ring, saying to George, 'I told you.' And George said, 'Come with me.' He took me to his room. Same thing. Motorcycle cops. Sirens blasting."

King would then pause a moment and say, pleased as punch: "I came with the champion, and left with the champion."

Years later, a reporter recollecting King's rendition of this tale would write in *The Ring* magazine:

What struck me, as I heard King narrate this tale, was his utter lack of irony. There was never a roguish twinkle in his eye, as if to acknowledge that what he was relating was about opportunism so blatant that in polite company one might think to mitigate it in the telling. Uh uh. He told his story as though the good fortune that had befallen him, through Foreman's savage victory, was his due, like taxes to medieval kings. The presumption that he was entitled—and that moral nuances could go screw—was never actually articulated. But it hung there like dust in a shaft of light, as I kept waiting for King to acknowledge the tawdry instinct he'd shown. But no, he was matter of fact about what he had done. And what I came away with was an insight into the industrial-strength egomania a Don King has.

Egomania, or what on the street corners of Easton we called "brass balls." King had himself a pair of brass balls, which enabled him to do whatever it took to get where he wanted to go. Bluff, threaten, plead, even cry real tears. Anything.

To get himself center stage in fight promotions, King had used his relationship with Foreman . . . and the color of his skin. He'd tracked Foreman down in Livermore, California, where big George was training at the time, and told him: "Come on, George. Give the black man a chance. Because I'm black, no one wants to give me a chance."

Foreman, who previously had turned down another promoter who wanted to match him against Ali, signed a blank piece of paper and told King: "Okay. Here. Get Ali to fill in the blank signature and I'll do it."

The hitch, of course, was money. Each fighter was to get $5 million—tremendous money for that time. King's mission—to find somebody to put up that sum—took him around the world, and saw him jump through all kinds of hoops until he found an African dictator, Mobutu Sese Seko of Zaire. Mobutu thought the spectacle of Foreman-Ali in his capital city of Kinshasa would be excellent for his and his country's image. Mostly his image, since he was in the process of stealing millions of dollars from Zaire's treasury for his personal use. And when he died years later, in 1997, the obits that recounted his life would invariably refer to his looting his country's treasury and leaving his people impoverished.

When King first told Hank Schwartz of Video Techniques that he'd gotten Foreman's signature, Schwartz was amazed. He told him, "If you got Foreman, your whole life will change." The change affected me. During the months of King's scuffling to get the fight on, I was in limbo, fighting keep-busy matches for no real money while continuing to work as a sparring partner and drive for Strongwear Pants.

Not all my sparring was with Ali. When Muhammad signed for the rematch with Joe Frazier for January 28, 1974, at Madison Square Garden, Ali needed sparring partners whose style resembled Smokin' Joe's. So while Bossman Jones, who was what we call a "face" fighter—a guy that comes straight at you—stayed on to help Ali get ready, I was of no use to him. My style was too dissimilar to Frazier's. On the other hand, my style was an awful lot like Ali's, which made me right for Frazier to work with. What the hell: I even leaned back from punches the way Muhammad did, which traditionalists said was dangerous. Fighters were taught to roll their head and shoulders to slip under punches. Leaning back exposed you in a way that left you more vulnerable

. . . unless you were quick enough, and clever enough, to dodge the punch.

The Frazier camp asked me to come to Philadelphia and work with their man for $375 a week. It was no problem with Ali. He understood: business was business. You went where the work was.

Smokin' Joe trained like he fought, on full throttle, all burners blasting. No matter what it was—shadowboxing, hitting the bags, skipping rope—he went all out. And that's how it was when it came to sparring.

Joe would walk into the gym and say, "Let's go. We gonna war today." And he wasn't fooling. Smokin' Joe sparred as if the whole world was watching. The man ripped that left hook like he wanted to bury it in you. He busted up my ribs—actually fractured one of them. And when I tried to get the next day off, his handlers wouldn't hear of it. The fight was too close, too important, to worry about my troubled rib. They needed to feed the beast his quota of sparring partners.

Joe liked to tease us, saying, "You guys can't carry my jock." One day, Jimmy Young heard him say that and then walked into the dressing room and came out holding a jockstrap. "You mean one of these?" Everybody cracked up, even Joe.

My career was stuck in place. I went back to Scranton in April '74 and TKO'd Howard Darlington in four rounds, and a month later in Scranton I scored a seventh-round TKO over a tough guy named Bobby Mashburn. With the victories, my record went to 9–0. Then, nothing. Nothing but get Ali ready for his match against Foreman, which was originally scheduled for September 25, 1974.

Get Ali ready and contemplate my future. With King haul-assing all over the world to make sure nothing went wrong with the Foreman-Ali match, I was out of sight, out of mind. And very concerned about it. I'd seen what had happened with Earnie Shavers. That December ['73], Shavers—who had been King's ace in the stable—had walked into a punch and been knocked out by Jerry Quarry in one round at Madison Square Garden. King took it personally—Shavers had let *him* down—and dumped his contract. If a guy like Shavers could suddenly become a nonperson in King's world, what did it say about me should I take a misstep?

Several weeks in advance of the September 25 date for Foreman-Ali, we flew to Zaire.

When we got to the airport, King wanted me to grab his bag. But Gene Kilroy didn't like to see a fighter be a bozo for King.

"Let him carry his own damn bag," Kilroy said, with King standing there.

That was King's mentality. He wanted to diminish his fighters—make himself more important, preferably at their expense. You notice how these days practically every King fighter, when he's interviewed after his victory, will say, "I want to thank Don King who blah blah blah." Think that's not calculated—that the fighter hasn't been coached to give all praise to Massah Don? If you do, I have some costume jewelry here you might want to buy.

Once we arrived in Zaire, Ali moved into the presidential compound in N'Sele, which was forty miles from Kinshasa. It was a plush setting, on the banks of the muddy Congo—lots of white stucco buildings on roads that ran over a thousand acres. Ole Mobutu had built himself a zoo on the grounds as well as an Olympic swimming pool.

In and around Zaire, the posters advertising the fight were in French, which the people there spoke, and they said: *Un cadeau de President Mobutu au Peuple Zairois*—A gift of President Mobutu to the Zairean People.

Ali was staying in a nice modern villa, which came with a full kitchen and a bathroom that had a shower. There were sofas and chairs covered in green velveteen. The floors had plastic gray tile. If you didn't look outside, you could have sworn you were in the U.S. of A. The sparring partners stayed in a nearby army barracks. You had a bed, a phone, and no TV. There were lizards everywhere. And I'm scared of lizards. Truth is, while Ali made himself right at home in Africa ("It's a great feeling being in a country operated by black people," he told newsmen), I was ill at ease there. The elements were out of whack. The air was smoky—seems like they were always burning trees and leaves there—and it stank. There was no sewage system there, so you had that bad smell in your face all the time.

But Ali . . . Ali was having a ball. While Foreman stayed in seclusion at the Inter-Continental Hotel, Ali was mixing with the people. I'll never forget what it was like going downtown in Kinshasa with him. People running out of their houses shouting, "Ali . . . *Boo-ma-ye*. Ali . . . *Boo-ma-ye*." English translation: Ali, kill him. Thousands of them shouting that.

With the press, Ali was his usual entertaining self, telling the writers: "George Foreman is nothing but a big mummy. I've officially named him 'the Mummy.' He moves like a slow mummy, and there ain't no mummy gonna whup the great Muhammad Ali. See, you all believe that stuff you see in the movies. Here's a guy running through the jungle, doing the hundred-yard dash, and the mummy is chasing him. Thomp, thomp, thomp. 'Oooh, help! I can't get away from the mummy! Help, help! The mummy's catching me. Help! Here comes the mummy.' And the mummy always catches him. Well, don't you all believe that stuff. There ain't no mummy gonna catch me."

And of course he had a poem for the occasion.

You think the world was shocked when Nixon resigned?
Wait till I whup George Foreman's behind.

Float like a butterfly, sting like a bee
His hands can't hit what his eyes can't see
Now you see me, now you don't
George thinks he will, but I know he won't.

I done rassled with an alligator
I done tussled with a whale
Only last week I murdered a rock
Injured a stone, hospitalized a brick
I'm so mean I make medicine sick.

In Zaire, Ali acted like he hadn't a doubt in the world that he'd whup Foreman. But I'd seen him back at Deer Lake, walking the grounds, deep in thought. Acting like the weight of the world was on his shoulders. My gut feeling was he was a bit scared. But that's not necessarily bad for a fighter. It's like Cus D'Amato, the man behind Floyd Patterson, Jose Torres, and Mike Tyson, used to say: "Fear is like a fire. If you control it, as we do when we heat our houses, it is a friend. When you don't, it consumes you and everything you do and everything around you."

The big problem for me in Zaire was the food. I didn't know what we were eating, but it was lousy. I went to Ali and told him I just couldn't eat it anymore. He said, "Eat with me, man." He had Lana Shabazz over there cooking his special diet. Ali's food was flown into Zaire. Here I was, thrown out of school in seventh grade, living halfway around the world and eating with the most famous person there was. My eating with Ali really pissed off the other guys in camp but I didn't care. I'd see later, when I was running my own camps, how tough it is to keep jealousy out and things running smoothly.

Eight days out from the fight, Foreman suffered a cut over his right eye while sparring. The fight was rescheduled for October 30. Foreman talked of laying over in Paris for a while, until he was cleared by doctors to begin training again. But the government of Zaire—fearing Foreman might bolt—refused to let him leave the country. They weren't nearly as concerned about Larry Holmes, thank God. I told Ali I'd had enough of Zaire. He gave me five hundred dollars for my work there, and I wished him good luck and headed back to Easton.

With millions of others, I watched him rope-a-dope Foreman for an eighth-round KO.

While Ali was being celebrated across the world for whupping big George, I was back in Easton, wondering when my time would come.

While Millie and I were no longer living together, I still had the responsibility of my two daughters. It was hard going providing for them with the scant attention King was giving me.

I had one more fight in '74, against Joey Hathaway on December 11 in Scranton again.

It's funny, when you're early into your career you don't think all that much about the other guy. It wasn't until years later, when a writer named Mark Jacobson did a profile on me for *New York* magazine that I got an insight into what it was like for some guys to go up against Larry Holmes.

Jacobson told how he'd gone down to Scranton to write about another fighter, Mike Rossman, who was on the card, and because of the scarcity of hotel rooms in Scranton, had ended up having to share one with Hathaway.

Everything [wrote Jacobson] *was fine until about three in the morning when Hathaway shook me awake. "You asleep?" he said, agitated. "They never told me this guy I'm fighting was good," Hathaway said, close to tears. "He's been working with Ali. Giving Ali hell! What am I gonna do now?"*

I tried to console the distressed heavyweight, but it was no use. He paced the room cursing his fate into the dawn light.

Nearly twenty-five years later, Jacobson told me that I'd knocked out Hathaway in the first round with . . . a jab. Truth be told, I didn't remember Hathaway or exactly how the fight had ended. But it was fitting that I'd put him away with a jab.

The jab was the punch that made me as a fighter. From the start, my jab got out there quicklike. It had the thrust of a snake's strike and, as I refined it through those hundreds of rounds with Ali, it developed into a weapon that could punish a man.

It wasn't just a pathfinder for the right hand, it was a hurting thing that could move a man backward and put a pained look in his eyes. When I first came into boxing, it was said no heavyweight could jab as well as Ali. Well, by 1975, I thought not only could I jab with Ali, but I was every bit the fighter he was.

When Ali was working really tough, he sometimes tried to taunt a guy. He had that way of throwing jabs and combinations and did that thing where he made his upper lip puff out and blew air out with each punch. He'd says things like, "Want this? Here! And this? C'mon, nigger." In rhythm to his punches. He did it to Bossman and Jaybar a lot.

It didn't work with me. Eventually, I got so I could anticipate almost every move he made. For instance, his jab. A lot of fighters tip off the jab with their left shoulder. Not Ali, though. But I detected a slight movement of his eyes before he'd let the jab go.

Saoul Mamby, a future junior welterweight champion, was a King fighter who spent lots of time at Deer Lake. Saoul, a friend of mine, said that if I wanted to test how quick I was, I should try to block Ali's jab with my left hand and then hit him with my right. I tried it, and discovered it worked, not once but again and again and again—a clear sign that I was now on Ali's level.

Mamby also hipped me how to avoid Ali when he tried drawing me into a clinch. As Muhammad would reach for me, I would duck his gloves with a rolling motion and then, with my nearest hand, push him to the side.

Everyone knew that Ali was not the world's greatest gym fighter, that he always fought his best fight when money and pride were on the line, when the whole world was watching. That was Ali. Still, I knew I could give him a hell of a fight, and in my heart I began to think I could beat him. There was no chance we'd ever fight, though, because he was seven years older than I was. Still, I dreamed about getting in there with Ali for the title.

Ali must have sensed my growing confidence. While in training for his March 24, 1975, bout against Chuck Wepner in Cleveland, I was giving him hell one day in the ring. That's when he suddenly turned to me and said, "I'm gonna kick your ass till you quit."

Ali said we'd spar without a bell—just keep fighting until one of us bagged it. So we went at it, a kind of macho marathon of a fight. I gave him all he wanted, and could have kept it up indefinitely. But I thought: What's the point? If he feels that he needs to prove he's better, it says a whole lot about how far I've come. I'm no longer the beginner standing in awe of the master.

Rather than embarrass him, I told Ali: "I quit."

"See," he said. "You ain't experienced enough to go this distance."

By now Ali, who was married to Belinda, had fallen for Veronica Porche. He'd met her at a press conference in Salt Lake City to promote the fight with Foreman. And he'd started seeing her on the sly in Zaire. By the time we hit Cleveland for the Wepner bout, I was his "beard"—showing up with Veronica as though she was with me . . . and taking her into the hotel. Veronica was not typical of the physical sort Ali was attracted to. She was tall and slender, and Ali loved big juicy women. If you asked him about it, he'd tell you: "You can feel 'em and hold 'em good."

Ali had guys in the entourage who got him women, but he was pretty good at chasing on his own. Once, when he was throwing a party in his hotel room, I showed up with a hooker I'd met. A real looker. Ali got big-eyed when he saw her. Well, I turned my back for a second, and that was the last I saw of her . . . or Ali. Ali was very good at that. He'd see something he wanted and would try to get it.

All the years I was with Ali, we only had words once . . . and it was on account of his messin' with the women. He was getting ready for a fight—I don't remember which one it was—but he wasn't training hard and was spending too much time with his women. I saw so clearly what was going on and said to him quietly, "Hey, man, you got to get more serious training for this fight."

He got real angry, like I never saw him with me before. He said, "Don't you ever tell me what to do." Shut me up real good. And I never said anything like that to him again.

On the night Ali fought Wepner, I was on the undercard against Charley "Devil" Green. Green talked big before the fight—how I had no heart, stuff like that. But like my ten previous opponents, he had a whole lot less to say afterward. I knocked him out in two rounds. Case closed, Charley Green.

From Cleveland, the Ali entourage drove to Chicago. There was a bank there owned by the Muslims. Ali went in and then one by one we were summoned. We each of us got paid and then would go to a teller's window to cash the check. Mine was for $2,500, and I was happy to have it. But for the others it was the usual gripefest. "Man, he got X number of dollars, and he don't do shit for the man."

For me, it was the last time I'd be part of the Ali circus. I'd decided I'd learned all I could as a sparring partner and that it was time to move out on my own. Ali understood and wished me well.

"You gotta do what you gotta do," he said. "But any time you want to come back and use the camp, come on back."

In truth, I think he was happy to see me go. As much as I knew about his style, and how to counter it, he was having to work too damned hard to keep up with me.

Whatever. We gave each other a good-bye hug.

In the years that followed, when we'd see one another, we'd always give a hug. Then Ali—Lord knows why—would tickle my ass and smile. I'd do it back to him. And we'd laugh. Even to this day, it's how we greet one another. Crazy, right?

CHAPTER
FIVE

Sprung free of Ali and no longer a sparring partner, I was under no illusion that my career suddenly would take off. That sort of thing was beyond my control. Richie Giachetti was working relentlessly to convince King and his two stooges, Braverman and Flood, that I had what it took and that when time ran out on Ali—he was thirty-three years old when he fought Wepner—I could be the man to keep King in the heavyweight-title business.

But Giachetti was still bucking up against those preconceived notions about Larry Holmes. Even King bought the bullshit. My friend Jerry Lisker, the executive sports editor of the *New York Post*, wrote about a visit to Deer Lake and his encounter there with King:

> *There were many members of the boxing fraternity who labeled Holmes a dog.*

"No ticker, no potato, a blue-ribbon bow-wow," they said, dismissing Holmes. . . .

I recall vividly the day King was at Ali's camp as the champ prepared for his historic 'Rumble in the Jungle' with then-champ George Foreman.

Holmes was putting in a lot of hot and heavy sparring sessions with Ali and looked sensational.

I asked King what he thought of Holmes. King smiled and puffed on his huge cigar.

"Dunno," King answered. "He looks pretty sharp, but . . ." And then there was a long pause.

"I hear he ain't got much of this," the promoter said, tapping his heart.

"They say he ain't too strong in the chin department either," he said.

I just shook my head. There was that same old label that had been stuck on Holmes.

"He looks pretty good against Ali," I answered.

"Yeah," King replied, "but Ali takes it easy on every sparring partner."

"Why don't you ask Ali?" I said.

King just laughed.

I had asked Ali and received some truthful answers from a truthful man.

Ali knew Holmes was good.

"Outside of me, he's got the best jab around," Ali said.

"Some say he's a dog, but it ain't true. In a couple of years he could make it. He just has got to get mentally tougher."

Others may have doubted me, but I was convinced my time had come, so convinced I'd left my job at Strongwear Pants to concentrate exclusively on boxing. The top guys in the heavyweight division—Ali, Frazier, Foreman—were growing old; I was growing better. All I needed was the chance to show it.

With the Foreman-Ali fight, King had had a chance to stand up before the media of the world and do what he does best—sell

Don King. He did a helluva job of it. In a public setting—and with his hambone instincts and endless patter—King was something to behold. He had that flair, always had. When he'd been in the numbers business in Cleveland, he'd operated like no one before him had. He once told me: "If somebody hit a number with me I made a production out of it. I would tell the winner to meet me in a public place, usually a bar, at a certain time. Then I would arrive forty-five minutes late, driving up real slow in my Cadillac. The wait always made people apprehensive, fearful I wouldn't show. They were thankful when I appeared. I would pull their winnings out of a brown paper bag, always in small bills, ones and fives. It made any amount of money look like a huge hit. 'Tell them who you won it from,' I'd be whispering in their ear as I counted out each bill individually. 'Tell them who you won it from.' "

Years later, as a boxing promoter, he would croon the equivalent to the boxing press: "Make me biiiig, boys. Make me big."

As a Cleveland "numbers czar"—the phrase the local press there used to describe him—and as a fledgling boxing promoter, Don wanted to be out there, front and center, and he had the bullshit to make people sit up and notice him. The Foreman-Ali fight—memorable as it was—made him big, big with the TV networks, which were a significant player in the boxing business then . . . before pay-per-view and HBO and Showtime overtook them. Where before the networks wouldn't return his calls, now they wanted to be in business with him.

For me his rise in prominence was a double-edged sword. His link to the networks gave him power, power that made it easier for him to reach out to fighters and sign them. That meant it was going to be tougher for me to get King to pay attention to me. But it also meant that if I could persuade him it was worth his time to back Larry Holmes, he now had the clout to make *me* big.

After having only three fights in 1974, I got busy in '75, fighting regularly in small-time settings *and* on the undercards of Ali's fights. I'd KO'd Charley "Devil" Green when Ali beat Wepner in March, KO'd Ernie Smith in three when Ali stopped Ron Lyle in Las Vegas in May, and stopped Rodney Bobick in six when Ali beat Frazier in their third fight, "the Thrilla in Manila."

For beating Bobick, who was Duane's brother and a better and tougher fighter than our '72 Olympic hope, I made five thousand dollars—my biggest payday by a lot. Funny how these things go. Duane Bobick as a professional built a winning record against the usual stiffs—at one point he was 35–0, with 30 knockouts—and then flopped in his big chances, a prime-time television fight against Ken Norton, who knocked him out in one round in '77 . . . and against John Tate, who also knocked him out in one round in '79.

After those defeats Bobick, who thought his problems were as much mental as physical, went to see a psychologist, Richard M. O'Brien, who told a reporter: "What we did over a period of several months was to gradually expose Duane to what he was afraid of. We did this with Duane in a relaxed state—close to hypnotized. I'd have him tense and relax each muscle and relax his thoughts, then go through the steps leading up to the fight— from his manager, Dave Wolf, phoning him, to the fight itself."

The process uncovered certain fears in Bobick. When the psychologist said the names of other fighters, he found Bobick reacted with more anxiety to fighters he'd never seen or fought than even to the names of Norton and Tate. Fear of the unknown.

"It showed," said O'Brien, "that the problem was not with the capability of the fighter but with what Duane imagined about the fighter. . . . There was also a fear of looking bad. Duane was fighting in order not to look bad rather than to win. His concern was all negative. Particularly in the first round. Once past the first round, his anxiety started to decrease and he'd fight. Some of his self-images were negative. Like, 'If I lose, I'm a bum.' We spent time arguing that out of existence. Sinatra is no bum if he hits a flat note. We arrived at the notion that boxing was not life or death. We put things in perspective."

When Bobick incurred bursitis in his shoulder, his mental snags were beside the point. He retired after losing to George

Chaplin in 1979. Strange how the wheel turns. Bobick, a man who had given me a bad name among the so-called experts, had had the fast track to stardom and blown it. Me? I was chugging along like the little train that could—damn sure that if I got the opportunities he had I'd seize them. *If*—and it was a big if—Don King would do right by me.

Among his fighters, King was viewed as a moneygrubbing me-first son of a bitch. Talk of tightfisted. We used to joke that if a guy came in here claiming to be Don King, there was only one way you'd know if he was telling you straight. If he doesn't walk out with ten dollars out of your pocket, he's not the real Don King.

The only thing free you got from Donald was words, the endless horseshit that was like the fuel he ran on. A guy once wrote:

Don King worked a sentence like a man hunched over a pinball machine.

For him, words were not discrete links that eventually coalesced into sentences and thoughts.

With King, the mother tongue was a hoop-de-doo of polysyllabics that went crashing and caroming against one another, a sprockety boing with lights flashing, all in the service of his latest (and greatest) deal.

Like that player poised over the pinball game, King had a way of humping the great Anglo language machine, of imparting a little spin here, a little emphasis there. He was a unique listening experience.

A word like "assiduous," for instance, would loll on his tongue . . . as-siddddd-u-ussss . . . as if it were the last peppermint patty in these continental United States. Other words went rocketing off like tin cans shooting down treacherous rapids.

The effect of this veritable—or as King himself might put it, this verrrr-i-ta-blllle cascade and pro-fuuuuuu-sion of words— was to keep a listener transfixed.

King himself liked the sound of these mildly mutated words he sent out. He took a delight in filling the air with them; occasionally his pleasure was such that a grin would break across his face and his body would shake from the top of his Dr. Zorba head to his size-12 shoes with that deep rumble heh-heh-heh that was his laugh.

Heh-heh-heh, oh God! he would say, the exclamation in a near falsetto, as though he were as damn near overcome as his listeners by the audacious concatenation of sound.

Man, that caught ole Donald's public act—his way of ramrodding words to gain his objective. When he was out in public, he knew how to work the room. He was good. Amusing. Damn near likable.

But in private, with his fighters—another story. I'd been busy in '75, fighting eight bouts and winning every time out. My record was 18–0, with 13 KOs. In December of that year, King had me in San Juan, Puerto Rico, fighting a ten-rounder on the undercard of a Roberto Duran title defense. I was matched against a veteran named Billy Joiner for a purse of one thousand dollars. In those days, Don would say he was going to pay me such and such, and that's what he paid me. It wasn't anything formal, no accounting or anything, just you'll get so much for this fight. I wasn't in a position to bargain. After the fight Don usually paid me off in bills he'd peel off a roll.

Just before the Joiner fight, King stopped by the dressing room with an unusual request. He said he wanted me to "carry" Billy Joiner to fill time before the TV fight would go on. In case you've never heard the expression before, when a fighter "carries" his opponent, his objective is to win the fight but prolong it by taking it easy on the man. I'd never been asked to do that before and wasn't happy to start doing it now.

In a fight, anything can happen, particularly with heavyweights—strong men capable of inducing unconsciousness if the right punch lands dead-on. You don't fool with an opponent. The idea is to disassemble him as efficiently as possible. My approach was more conservative than some. I was not reckless in moving to an opponent, or in thinking I could get him out with one punch. I probed for his weaknesses and slowly but surely worked them until he was ready for the kill.

When the fight started, I was trying to balance my need for victory with a desire to satisfy my promoter's needs. Well, pretty quick I found myself in a trick bag. Nobody had told Joiner to go la-de-dah for a few rounds. He was laying some serious licks on me. Right hands that hurt. Happened in the opening round and again in the second round. When I returned to my corner at the end of round two, Giachetti was steamed.

"This motherfucker's dangerous," he screamed. "He's a professional fighter. Fuck Don! Take this guy out of there, you hear me? Take him out of there!"

Richie was right.

I had no business playing footsy with a professional fighter. This was my career, my future. The hell with Don King. I began putting some hurt on Joiner in that third round. Jab, right hand. Jab, right hand. Take that. And that. And try this one on for size. Joiner fell. The referee counted, and reached ten before Joiner stirred. Good night, Billy. So long, San Juan.

When it came time to get paid, King asked me to step out in the hall, where, it turned out, he had a surprise for me. He said he was only going to pay me three hundred dollars. Why? Because I hadn't followed orders—hadn't "carried" Billy Joiner. I looked at him and thought, Is this guy kidding? But then . . . Don *never* kidded about money.

"Hey," I said, "Joiner was hitting me shots."

"You're a professional fighter," he said.

"Whose job is to win, not to worry about filling time."

"Well, I was going to pay you a thousand dollars, at one hundred a round. You only went three, my man. That means three hundred dollars."

"Bullshit. Rounds got nothing to do with the money. I want the goddamn thousand, motherfucker."

"You ain't gettin' it."

Back and forth we went, shouting and calling each other names. Finally, in a calmer voice, I told him it was right before Christmas and I needed the money so my kids would believe in Santa. Begrudgingly, he paid me the money he'd promised—one thousand dollars.

But the whole encounter was typical of the crazy adversarial relationship we had. It didn't matter that I had a record of 19–0 and talent that, if properly promoted, could benefit both King and me. He seemed not to care about anything but asserting his authority. King the big man.

It was like that comedian, Rodney Dangerfield. No respect. Whenever we went on the road, Richie and I always had to share a room. A pain in the ass. Two grown men living in cramped quarters. For damn sure it was a real crimp on having a woman visit. But when I tried to get King to give us separate rooms, he cried poverty. That was pure horseshit, and King knew I knew it. But that was the idea—let you know you were just another guy to him.

We'd talk, Richie and I. In '74, I'd tell him over and over that all I wanted was to get ranked and get out with maybe one hundred thousand dollars and my brains intact. I didn't believe you could beat the system. But by the end of '75, I'd begun to think bigger. I was feeling my strength as a fighter—twelve knockouts in my last thirteen fights. After more than three years sparring with Ali, I was ready for anybody. Richie knew it. And maybe Bundini. And Ali. For almost everyone else, I was this bigmouthed pain in the ass who thought he was better than he really was.

In boxing, the so-called experts take a look, make a judgment, and that's it. Mostly, they just see what they want to see. Of course, if you're a sparring partner for someone like Ali, you become an invisible man—they don't even see you at all. If you're looking good in there with him, it must be there's something wrong with Ali. They put you in a box, and that's it. The thing they almost never see is improvement. And, man, I was really improving. The fact that others refused to see it—well, that just gave me another reason to succeed.

I developed an attitude. Some said it was a chip on my shoulder. Call it what you want. By hook or by crook, I was going to damn well show people about Larry Holmes.

Things began to look up for me some.

On April 5, 1976, I scored a second-round TKO over Fred Askew in Landover, Maryland, which made me 21–0, with 16 KOs.

I was feeling good about life outside the ring too. There was now a woman in my life, Diane Robinson, who was making me forget a love gone wrong with another gal.

I'd met Diane the previous year when I gave a talk at Liberty High School in Bethlehem. She was in the twelfth grade. My brother Bob was dating her sister Wanda. I thought Diane was intelligent and attractive. I told her I wanted to see her. We began dating.

I liked her a lot but was more in a hurry than she was to get in bed.

I'd tease her: "Every time I see you, you never give me anything. If you want me, you got to give me something."

"Okay," she said, teasing back. "You can have it at the right time, the right place. And when I'm ready."

"I hope you're ready soon."

The next time I saw her she was not ready. Or the next time either. Or the time after that. Or the time after that.

I told her: "I might have to take it."

She said: "You'll have trouble."

Well, in time the teasing stopped and the loving began. A couple weeks after I knocked out Fred Askew, Diane and I were holed up at a motel in Bethlehem. I don't remember telling anybody where I would be, or giving out the phone number. All of which made it more than a bit shocking when the phone rang and Don King was on the other end of the line, telling me that in eight days I would be fighting again . . . on the April 30 undercard of Ali versus Jimmy Young against . . . oh, Lord, did I hear right— Roy Williams!

King didn't ask me if I wanted the fight, he *told* me. It was a summons to arms. Roy Williams on short notice. This was not the ideal way to meet up with that nasty son of a bitch. I hadn't been in serious training since beating Fred Askew, and, even though Williams hadn't been fighting much these past couple of years—one fight in two years—I knew firsthand he could hurt you if he hit you. I'd watched him work against Ali, and had sparred with him myself. What the hell: Williams had even beaten Jimmy Young, who was fighting Ali for the title. You didn't take Roy Williams lightly.

I couldn't afford a misstep at this point in my career. I sensed I was inching toward a breakthrough fight. With my undefeated record, I knew that very soon King would figure, what the hell—let's see whether he can go with the big boys. But when he came at me with Roy Williams eight days out from the fight, it made me uneasy. Real uneasy. Can you say "paranoid," boys and girls? Truth is I'd never trusted Don King . . . never saw him as a man championing my cause. Just the opposite, he always seemed to be trying to mindfuck me. I couldn't help but think that for reasons I couldn't fathom he was out to sabotage my career with Roy Williams.

I tried to argue that I wasn't ready—eight days was not enough time to prepare. He wasn't having any of that. To add insult to injury, he told me that for fighting Roy Williams on short notice he was prepared to pay me the grand sum of $2,500. Chump change.

"Ali-Young is a prime-time network TV fight," I said. "Which means you're getting mucho money. You should be paying me a whole lot more."

"That's the deal," King said. "Twenty-five hundred. Ain't no negotiations goin' on here."

Well, as the reality of what lay ahead sank in, I thought of improvising an injury in training to get out of the fight. You know. "Sorry. Hurt my back." Or: "Sorry, threw my shoulder out." But I knew Don King would find a way to get back at me. I didn't want to risk becoming that needle in the haystack—hard to find (heh heh heh).

Down the road, when the so-called experts looked back on my career, they would say the turning point for me came in March of 1978, when I fought Earnie Shavers in Las Vegas. The winner of that fight was assured the chance to fight Ken Norton for the WBC heavyweight title.

But the experts were wrong. Roy Williams was the turning point, the crucial fight of my career. Why? Because I fought a tough and capable professional with one hand and beat him. Early into the fight, I hit him on the elbow and felt a pain shoot through the thumb of my right hand. Bad pain. Pain that didn't quit. But then again, neither did Larry Holmes. I kept my cool and fought him the best I could, using my legs to stay out of harm's way while shooting the jab in his face. Jab jab jab. Pile up the points and watch for his right. When I threw *my* damaged right, I would turn my hand so that when I made contact it was with the outside of the hand.

From my years with Ali, I had gained enough ring cunning to know how to maneuver big Roy into my jab and keep him turning in circles. Keep a guy turning in circles, and he can't plant his feet and get real leverage on his punches. The other key was to avoid the corners of the ring, where Williams could trap me and get lucky with a shot.

I never panicked against Roy, even with the busted hand, just did what I had been trained to—boxed my ass off. When I threw the right, I could't really fire it with my customary authority. But I knew that if I punched in volume, the judges would score the fight in my favor.

The jab was my weapon of choice, and Williams was a sitting duck for it. I peppered him with it all night. Even though he kept his hands high, the jab was too quick for him.

In the tenth and final round, I had a scare. Williams knew he needed a knockout to win and late in the round connected with a vicious left hook to the body and then a right to the head. As Jerry Lisker would write:

Holmes was frozen stiff and immovable, as if his feet were nailed to the floor. Fortunately for him, the bell rang and the fight was over. The biggest win of his career was in his pocket.

In Holmes' dressing room, Giachetti finished off his 30th Hail Mary and Larry's brother, Jake, paced back and forth saying, "Unreal, unreal. Goddamn, I'm glad this one's over."

So was I.

Now had Roy Williams stayed active in the years leading up to our match, I might have caught hell that night. Roy Williams was the perfect example of a fighter beat down by the system. I respected Roy Williams as a fighter but marked him as another object lesson in the politics of the sport.

After fighting me, Williams had a few more fights and then dropped out of sight. Roy Williams never had a chance.

Back in Easton, X rays revealed that I had two cracks at the base of my thumb.

This was no big surprise. I'd come back to Easton with the hand doubled in size, even though it had been wrapped in ice immediately after the match.

The doctors put my hand in a small cast and said no boxing for three months. That meant three months with no money coming in, and medical expenses piling up.

Well, at that bleak moment Charlie Spaziani, the ex-DA of Northampton County, stepped up. Spaz, who had been advising me on some of the contracts King was asking me to sign, said he would take care of my medical expenses.

I was hoping King would step up and tide me over with a few bucks while the hand healed. But King kept ducking my calls. It didn't surprise me. Don King is the ultimate user/abuser. If he can't make a buck off a fighter . . . When I finally got through to him on the phone, King refused to help out. I tried to reason with him and somehow persuaded him to let me have two hundred dollars a week. *But* . . . King insisted the money would be regarded as an advance against future earnings.

I did the best I could to keep in shape, running a few miles along the Delaware River each morning and, when the cast came off, shadowboxing at the St. Anthony's Youth Center. I was trying to be sensible about the hand, and not use it too soon. So what happened? When the doctors finally cleared me to train again, the first time I hit the heavy bag hard—*boing*. Goddamn thumb broke again, the pain firing up my arm to the shoulder. A numbing pain worse than when the thumb was originally damaged.

Worse was what the injury did to me mentally. Finally, I was a ranked fighter—*The Ring* magazine had put me in their top ten ratings in '76 and *Sports Illustrated* in evaluating the up-and-coming heavyweights who might succeed Ali, had called me "the class of the young heavyweights." All that and, boom, I'd turned into a medical casualty, with no guarantee about when I'd be ready to get back in action. Time was going by and for me time was money—those six-figure purses seemed, finally, in range.

At Easton Hospital this time, four pins were implanted at the base of my thumb, and my arm was set in a cast that extended from my fingers to my shoulder. The doctors said just rest and let the damn thing heal.

It was a setback that shook me. I began telling myself, well, maybe that's it, and if it is—so what, it's a hard and unrewarding business anyway, with miserable lowlifes like Don King messing with you at every opportunity. As I look back, I was really preparing myself for maybe having to quit fighting.

I don't know an awful lot about psychology, but I've noticed one thing about the smarter fighters. They always acted and said things to convince themselves they didn't need boxing, that they could walk away from it whenever they wanted to. You see, the worst thing for a fighter is to have no alternative but to fight. I had a sample of it in the Roy Williams fight and didn't like the way it felt. That's when fighters get hurt. If I absolutely *had* to fight for a living, I could end up like a lot of other guys—broke and punch-drunk.

The way most fighters kept from thinking they were locked in was to convince themselves they could quit any time. Ali's technique was a little different. He acted as though he was bigger than boxing. Ali's approach didn't work because even though he could dictate terms for most of his fights, toward the end of his

career, when he needed the money, he took fights—and beatings—he shouldn't have taken.

Money is what professional fighting is all about, and it's the
way promoters control fighters. It's the carrot out there that the
jackass jumps for. Once you come to depend on purse money,
they own you. That's one reason I held on to my job during my
early professional years. I needed the cash, but it made me believe
I had an alternative and could quit if I had to. That's why I didn't
seriously think about being champ, or even a contender, because
if I had that for a goal and didn't make it, I'd be too hooked to
get out. So I kept telling myself, and Richie, that I wanted a
couple of nice paydays and then scram. And I believed that, at
least while I was saying it.

Because of the hand problem, the final seven months of '76 were
a black hole . . . a dead zone as far as my career was concerned.

But out of that darkness there was a ray of light—Diane Robinson. Diane hadn't been able to get over to the hospital from
Bethlehem, but she called me all the time and it was obvious that
she cared about me. Diane was different from any woman I'd
known—deeper and more caring.

One night at a drive-in, while waiting for the horror movie to
begin, as we sat in my flashy yellow Cadillac (for which Charlie
Spaz had cosigned) we had a serious talk. Diane questioned
whether we were really right for one another—she said that all I
talked about was being heavyweight champion, that it sounded an
awful lot like braggadocio and she couldn't help but wonder if in
all this talk of me-me-me there was any room for "us." As in, the
two of us.

I tried to explain that what she took for bluster was really my
way of dealing with the uncertainties of a business so hit-or-miss,
so unpredictable as to be a perpetual torment. To know I was as
talented as I was, and to be discounted by the experts and even
my own promoter, well, that required a constant resolve not to
let the bastards get me down. While they knocked me for this
and that, I had to fight the bullshit by saying aloud they were

wrong, I was right, and I was going to be heavyweight champ. While I was explaining all my defenses to Diane, they began to fall away, and we let our deepest feelings come through. That was the night we truly fell in love.

In my mind, Diane and I were going to get married just as soon as I got one of those big-money fights. I had a little money saved in the Lafayette Trust Bank. One big check would give us the cushion we needed. But my future depended on the thumb.

As the clock ticked down on 1976, the thumb healed. I was ready to fight again. But out there in DonKingland—nothing. No fights. Then one day Richie Giachetti called and said we had a chance at some big money without having to take on any of the top contenders.

"Don came up with one hell of an idea," Giachetti said. "And we're gonna hit big with it."

And that was how I first came to learn of the U.S. Boxing Championship Tournament for ABC-TV. It sounded good. In fact, it sounded perfect for me, a chance to be seen on national TV and make a fistful of cash fighting guys I knew I could beat.

But this supposed easy-money opportunity was like all those get-rich-quick schemes your mama warned you about. Not quite what it was cracked up to be.

CHAPTER
SIX

For Don King, adversity was the mother of invention.

After Ali had fought Jimmy Young in April '76, King became odd man out with the heavyweight champion.

Herbert Muhammad, Ali's manager, moved on to King's rival, Bob Arum, and allowed Arum to promote first Ali versus Richard Dunn in Munich in May '76 and then Ali–Ken Norton III that September at Yankee Stadium.

Arum would tell newsmen that King was 86'd when Herbert, who was the son of Elijah Muhammad, the spiritual head of the Nation of Islam, learned King was paying off people who worked in Herbert's office to spy for him. Arum claimed they were told to plant ideas with Herbert that would benefit King.

Others said King's outlandish ego was what troubled Herbert, and even King admitted to a reporter, "Herbert Muhammad discharged me because I was getting too many headlines. I got the headlines, but he got the bottom line."

Whatever the reason, by 1977 King had lost his grip on Ali and was bothered enough by it to remove the portrait of Ali that hung in his office on the sixty-seventh floor of the RCA Building. Don King was in dire need of a vehicle to rally the name of Don King. And that was how the United States Boxing Championship Tournament was born.

The concept was simple enough—a series of fights over a period of time to determine a so-called U.S. champion for each weight division, heavyweight on down.

To win that title, a U.S. champion would have to beat a number of opponents in a tournament format, the money increasing with each victory. Lose one fight, and you were history. Go all the way to the title and you'd end up with about $150,000, which sounded great to me.

Richie kept telling me the other seven heavyweights in the tournament were "guys we can beat . . . no problem."

Giachetti would have said the same thing had the tournament included Dempsey, Marciano, and Joe Louis. That was his job—to build my confidence. But in truth, I knew he wasn't just blowing smoke at me. The guys who had come into the tournament were not the topcats I was shooting for—the world-ranked fighters like Shavers, Norton, Jimmy Young. Nope. The heavyweight opposition I was looking at was a whole lot less to speak of.

For a marquee fighter, this ABC-TV tournament made no sense. The money was not serious enough to risk the chance of being beaten by some young turk like myself. A defeat was too costly for your established fighter. So the tournament became a perfect vehicle for young, hungry fighters, eager for a breakthrough in their careers . . . and the first taste of real money.

For ABC-TV, the concept worked too. King's tournament came at a time when boxing was getting great ratings. For its part, the network was assured of an extended competition that could attract sponsor dollars on an extended basis. And it figured that if you had fighters eager to make a name, then the matches would be aggressively contested, perfect to sustain audience interest. Over this extended period, the audience would develop a rooting interest in this guy and that one.

What's more, ABC-TV figured it would have the inside track on any fighter who might capture public fancy. What the Olympics did in exposing amateur fighters, the U.S. Boxing Championships could do for unknown professionals.

ABC picked Cosell to be the "voice" of the tournament. He was Mr. Boxing back then, identified with the Olympic boxing in Montreal, where our team had done so well. Most of the public thought Cosell knew boxing, so his job was to take them through the tournament, highlighting certain fighters as possible stars. Howard was a TV salesman, and he was there to sell the tournament to the public.

For Don King, the tournament was an ingenious way to keep afloat at a time when he was on the outs with Ali. Not only was he going to end up with lots of network money, but he'd convinced ABC-TV to give him complete control over the tournament. That meant he would pick the fighters, sign them to contracts, and hire the judges. That was not just putting the fox in charge of the henhouse. It was more like giving him the deed to the whole poultry farm.

King developed another clever twist—he figured a way to avoid having to pay a rental fee to arena owners. In the guise of being a great benefactor to our nation's armed forces, King persuaded the military to let him use their facilities to stage the competition. A chance for our beloved servicemen to be entertained, he said. Don King was astute enough to know patriotism is good business.

Which is how on January 16, 1977, I found myself on the windy 910-foot flight deck of the aircraft carrier *Lexington*—which had sent planes into crucial World War II battles at Okinawa and Leyte Gulf. The ship, anchored in the waters off Pensacola, Florida, was set up for three thousand navy people to watch the opening round of the tournament, which included a heavyweight bout—Larry Holmes versus Tom Prater.

Of the unusual setting, *The New York Times* wrote:

The Lexington, *oldest and smallest of the Navy's 13 aircraft carriers, is used entirely now for training purposes. But the elusive old warrior that sank 300,000 tons of Japanese shipping and earned the nickname "Blue Ghost" from Tokyo Rose provided an exciting backdrop for King's promotion. Five jet fighters had been parked on the flight deck, one of them in position on the catapult forward, and colorful international code flags hung from the bridge spelled out, "Welcome ABC" to those who understood.*

It was apparent that only torrential rain could have driven the production off the flight deck to the unglamorous hangar deck below. The cameras caught the flight-deck excitement despite unseasonably cold weather, with temperatures in the upper 40s and a 20-knot westerly wind from the Gulf of Mexico that raised whitecaps on Pensacola Bay.

Tom Prater was a kid from Indianapolis with a record of 17–3–1, including victories over Jody Ballard, later a sparring partner of mine, and over J. D. McCauley, an uncle of Buster Douglas who would go on to work Douglas's corner.

At first, when Richie told me I'd be fighting on a ship, I thought the ring would be tipping back and forth all the time. Wrong. Not only was it steady as she goes but that ship looked bigger than all of Easton. Yet the surroundings were strange for a fight, with all those sailors in white uniforms staring at me every place I went. Some of them called me "sir," a few even saluted me.

One who didn't salute was Cosell. To him I was still less than zero. When I saw him and jokingly said, "Make me big out there today, Howard," he responded with: "Can't do anything for you, Holmes. You just don't have the charisma." Howard was the king of the front-runners. It wasn't until I became heavyweight champion that he decided to call me "Larry."

Wouldn't you know that I couldn't get out of my locker room without King stirring up shit. Yup. He was up in arms that I wouldn't wear the "official" tournament robe, a red, white, and blue creation with the words "U.S. Boxing Championships" on the back. I had promised Diane I'd wear the two-tone purple silk robe, and trunks, she'd made special for me. I offered King a compromise: Diane's robe, his trunks.

"You don't wear that robe, I'm gonna disqualify your ass," King said.

"Get out of my face," I told him. "You wanna disqualify me, go 'head. I ain't fighting."

In the end, I wore Diane's robe.

I was not at my best against Prater. The layoff from the injury affected me. I saw the openings for my punches, but too often I was late in letting them go. No question, I had a bad case of ring rust. Add to that a certain degree of trepidation about busting up my right hand again, and what you got was Holmes Lite. Cosell made a point of letting the audience know I was not delivering.

"This kid just doesn't have it," he said. "He just doesn't have the punching power." Not that Prater was good enough to beat me. I took him in an eight-round decision, but knew I hadn't made the impression I was hoping to on the millions watching on ABC-TV.

On the other hand, I told myself, I was back again, and next time there'd be no ring rust—I'd show them the real Larry Holmes. I still felt there was no one in the heavyweight competition who was going to stop me. Kevin Isaac—hell, I'd already knocked him out. Braverman's boy, Dino Denis—it would be a pleasure to give him a good buttwhuppin' and then laugh in big Al's face. Who else was there? Leroy Jones, a kid from Denver, was undefeated, and could fight. So could Stan Ward from Sacramento. He had wins over Mac Foster and Jeff Merritt and was yet to be beaten. Scott Le Doux was a tough, experienced white guy from Minnesota, but, like the others, was beatable. I was looking forward to my next fight.

The purse for winning a first-round heavyweight match in the tournament was reported to be $15,000. That's how much the ABC-TV audience was told I would be getting. But King was double-dipping. Not only was he making money from ABC as

84

the tourney promoter—reportedly $250,000 with another $200,000 supposedly going to his "matchmakers," Braverman and Flood—he was cutting his share from my purse too. By now Ernie Butler was long gone. King had bought him out, in circumstances that embittered Ernie toward me. We didn't talk for years. With Ernie Butler no longer in the picture my purses were being divvied up like this: 25 percent to King, 12 ½ percent to Giachetti, and 12 ½ percent to Spaziani. That meant that my fifteen grand shrank to $7,500. At that, it still was my best payday to date, and I now had a chance for more like that in the next round of the tournament, against the winner of the Le Doux–Johnny Boudreaux fight.

Well, a funny thing happened on the way to that opportunity. On February 13 at the Naval Academy in Annapolis, Le Doux went ballistic when Boudreaux, who was managed by (surprise surprise) Paddy Flood, got a decision so questionable that even Cosell shouted in disbelief, "They gave it to Boudreaux!" Afterward an enraged Le Doux tried to kick Boudreax but missed and instead jarred Cosell's toupee off in front of a live audience. Poor Howard. He put that funky rug on backward momentarily before setting it right and proceeding with his interview of Le Doux.

Le Doux unloaded, claiming the tournament was rigged to favor fighters connected to King, Flood, and Braverman—that they had the judges in their pockets. While King denied the charges on air, ABC-TV was forced to begin looking into whether the tournament was as tainted as Le Doux said. The network had ignored earlier warnings that something was fishy from an in-house producer, Alex Wallau, who went on to become ABC's boxing commentator, and from other sources in the boxing business. The ABC execs figured they had a good thing with this Don King package—twenty-three hours of on-air boxing—and dismissed the allegations as untrue.

Big mistake. While the tournament slogged on for one more date, on March 16 from the gym of King's alma mater, the Marion Correctional Institution, ABC-TV was discovering what a corrupt tournament it had on its hands. It wasn't really the U.S.

Boxing Championships, it was the Don King and Cronies Tournament. Every fighter in the tournament had had to sign a contract giving King options on his future fights if he won the tournament championship. That way, whatever talent emerged was King's, thanks to the generosity of ABC-TV. It was because of those option clauses, and the 10 percent kickbacks from fighters' purses as so-called booking fees, that some good but independent-minded fighters like, say, Marvin Hagler wouldn't come into the tournament.

That wasn't all. As probers began looking at the ratings that Johnny Ort of *The Ring* magazine served up to justify the fighters included in the tournament they discovered Ort's records for some of the fighters were pure fiction, with phantom fights that never took place. It didn't help that investigators discovered that King had made a $5,000 cash payment to Ort, or that Ort would later admit receiving payoffs from managers of fighters admitted to the tournament.

One of the guys caught in the middle, as the exposé unraveled, was Cosell, and I have to plead guilty to feeling glee at seeing that pompous ole fool dangling in the breeze. Remember, when it came to boxing, Cosell tried to act like nobody since the Marquis of Queensbury knew more than he did. Besides that, he prided himself on being totally honest and a pretty good investigator. Now here was Mr. Tell-it-like-it-is announcing rotten fights like they were legitimate. Either way, he was a loser; if he couldn't spot the bad decisions or the corrupt setup of the tournament, so much for his expertise. If he could and didn't expose the fraud, then he was dishonest.

Every day now, news reporters on the case were digging up more and more details that showed how rotten the tournament was. Eventually, ABC decided enough was enough and pulled the plug. Pulled the plug before I could get a shot at the more than $100,000 I'd have made winning my division—money for Diane and me.

ABC did an investigation after announcing there would be no more U.S. Boxing Championships. That had me worried. I figured the blame would fall on King, leaving him so weakened that my career would suffer. But King turned out to be the original Teflon Don. Amazing. Nothing was pinned on him. Others felt the impact of all the scrutiny, but not him.

At *The Ring* magazine Ort was pushed out the door and the magazine's editor, Nat Loubet, resigned a while later. James J. Farley, the chairman of the New York State Athletic Commission, had lent his name as "supervisor" of the tournament in exchange for expenses and travel reimbursements. A bad move. For, in effect, he was vouching for the integrity of the event. When the corruption was revealed, he was suspended from the job by Governor Hugh Carey, and he never returned. King announced that Braverman and Flood no longer would be with the boxing division of his operation. But down the road, when the headlines had faded, both men would again be back with King.

ABC covered its corporate ass with a thick in-house report that insisted: "The evidence we have found relating to the allegations does not, in our view, establish conduct which would warrant criminal prosecution." However, the report went on to state that the arrangements between King, his aides, and the fighters "are clearly unhealthy. At worst they can provide King with a direct motive to manipulate the tournament. At best there is an unfortunate appearance of conflict of interest, which would subject any promoter to the kind of criticism that King has in fact suffered."

No one can say for sure the fights themselves were rigged. Mine certainly wasn't. Prater, limited though he was as a fighter, was in there trying like hell. It's possible Le Doux was right that the judges screwed him. Allowing King to pick the judges was dumb on the part of ABC. The judges had to be influenced by King's ability to hire and fire. And, wanting to be asked back again, they would—consciously or not—lean toward King's fighters on their scorecards. That was only human nature.

When the tournament went belly-up, I was quite depressed, convinced that my career would be stalled by the developments surrounding the U.S. Boxing Championships. I misjudged King's resiliency. Damned if he wasn't back in action quicker than minute rice. By May of '77, he had somehow convinced Herbert Muhammad to allow Ali to fight for him again. He delivered the Ali–Alfredo Evangelista fight to—believe it or not—ABC-TV. And soon after, he was promoting fights on other networks too.

My action picked up too. I stopped Horace Robinson in five rounds in San Juan, Puerto Rico, on a card headlined by a local hero, Ossie Ocasio, a fighter King seemed to be fawning over. Ocasio had turned pro only the year before and here he was, in only his seventh pro fight, getting the big schmooze from King, who figured, I guess, that a Hispanic heavyweight could do big box office with the Latino community. Black guys like me were an everyday commodity in the division.

I figured the only way King would realize my marquee value was to just keep beating everybody there was to beat—all his heavyweights of the moment. In the meantime, King's archrival, Bob Arum, like the rest of us in boxing, had heard that a federal grand jury in New York was looking into some of King's business practices. Arum must have figured the time was right to swoop down on fighters tied to King and steal them away. Exactly as King would have done had the situation been reversed. Anyway, one day Arum phoned me and asked if I would be interested in fighting a guy named Fred Houpe, who fought under the name of Young Sanford.

Sanford was managed by the X-rated comedian Redd Foxx, who had been a big boxing fan before deciding to take a shot with a heavyweight. Redd had labored for years on the Chitlin Circuit, one of the first black stand-up comics at a time when sketch comedy was very big in the places they played. Black folks knew him but it wasn't until 1972 that Redd went mainstream with the situation comedy *Sanford and Son*. Somehow Redd hooked up with Arum, who now offered me the fight.

The boxing grapevine at the time had King in deep shit with this grand jury investigation. Word was that any minute now, King would be indicted. If it happened, it probably would mean my contract with him was void and I could bolt to Arum, or anybody else.

There are always rumors flying around in boxing and at that

time, whether or not it was true, one of them was that Arum had sicced the government on King. See, before he became a boxing promoter, Arum had been with the Department of Justice under JFK's brother, Bobby Kennedy. The word now was that he was using his government connections to put the squeeze on Don. And it seemed to be working.

While I knew King was exploiting me, I was reluctant to make the switch to Arum. Not out of loyalty as much as habit. And maybe a susceptibility to his racial jive—the black solidarity line he ran on you, the slapping handshakes, the brother-this and brother-that. At the very least, I figured, I'd use Arum's interest to bid up my price.

King responded by saying he could stick me in against Young Sanford at Caesars Palace for ten grand. Arum countered with an offer of seventy-five thousand dollars . . . *if* I gave him some options. It was a helluva difference in dollars and cents. I was sure King would jack up his offer. Wrong. I couldn't believe he wasn't going to give in just a little. I told him he was leaving me no choice—I was intending to get married and start a family. I needed the money. That's when he got nasty.

"Don't you try to put a gun to my head just because I got these troubles," he warned. "Remember, I signed you when no one wanted to touch you. I gave you a chance when no one would."

Then, some of the starch went out of him and he damn near sounded like he was begging.

"You stick with me through this, Larry. And I swear I'll make it up to you."

Not good enough. I told him I couldn't bank his promises—I needed him to do something for me now. But King wouldn't budge. I think he saw Arum's challenge as a threat to his whole way of doing business. If he gave in to me, word would get out and other fighters would be in his face, turning his world topsy-turvy. King was used to sticking it to fighters. He couldn't live with the idea that any one of us could change his take-it-or-leave-it approach. Then he wouldn't be Donald King, would he? He'd be a mere partner.

So . . . the guy pointed his finger at me and warned me don't mess with him—he had a valid contract and, if he had to, he would enforce it. He'd make damn sure I wouldn't fight for anybody. Ever.

I sounded out Spaz about what-next. Spaz told me that I could challenge the contract I signed with Don and that I had a pretty good chance of winning on grounds that I originally signed under duress. I couldn't read well and never really understood all that I was agreeing to. Spaz thought a jury would regard King's business practices as unethical, if not actually illegal, and this might be the best time to challenge my contract if I really wanted out.

But . . . the legal process, he warned me, was time-consuming and I risked having my career stall out at precisely the moment I was on the brink of big-time big-money matches. And what would I have in Arum but another promoter with options on me, just like King did?

Still, I couldn't help but think about that seventy-five thousand dollars and the jump start it would give Diane and me on a comfortable life.

So I went back to King and again tried to get him to up his offer—to at least be competitive with Arum. Hell no. He still wouldn't give me the kind of money that I should have been getting, particularly after he'd blown my shot at some real dough with his Mickey Mouse "trickerations"—a favorite word of his—on the U.S. Boxing Championships.

He was cold as ice about what could have been but assured me that he would get me the fights that counted, for big money and eventually a world title. Talk is talk and, when it's coming from Don King, it's even less. Given the pressure the feds were applying to him, there was no guarantee he could deliver jackshit for me. Back and forth we went until King once again asked me to agree to fight Young Sanford for ten grand. I thought about that fancy office of his, the sixty-seventh-floor penthouse in the RCA Building, and knew he was fullashit that he couldn't pay me more. I told him I was going to talk to Arum again.

Well, I never saw King's face get the way it got, like he was in pain. His eyes turned cold and empty. He said, real quietly, "If you do, I'll have your legs broke."

I didn't take that as an idle threat. King had gone to jail for punching and then stomping a man to death on a Cleveland street, kicking him in the face even as the poor bastard was defenseless. That was in 1966. Earlier in his life, he had shot and killed a man who was part of a trio that had tried to rob one of his gambling houses. Justifiable homicide, the county prosecutor said.

In public, King had the knack of being amusing, of making people think of him as a P. T. Barnum kind of rascal. Like with his hair. He would tell people: "My hair is like an aura from God. It is like Samson's hair. But forget the hair. Ask me about my genius. They tell me to be cool, Jack. Not to make waves. I am the wave." It was bullshit that didn't quit. But I knew that King was no cartoon—that there was a whole lot of evil bully in him. Even so, no scare show of his was going to make me back down. I refused to sign for the ten grand. But I left believing I had better think seriously about protecting myself. The first thing I did when I returned to Easton was pick me up a .22-caliber Smith & Wesson.

Over the next few weeks, I was on ready alert. Sometimes, even while I was doing my roadwork along the Delaware River, I carried the gun with me. My brother Jake was armed too, and was watching my back wherever I went. And wherever I went, I took precautions, eyeballing the street when I left my house or stepped out of a restaurant late at night.

Meanwhile, Giachetti was trying to mediate. Not easy. Neither King nor I was in a bygones-be-bygones mood. Richie insisted that in spite of what I'd heard, King was going to beat his legal problems and I'd want to be in his good graces when he did. But of course Giachetti was not an impartial party in this mess. He relied on King for his wages.

Once again I went to Spaz, whose loyalty was strictly to me.

He advised me to stick with King, not because King was fair with me but because I was too close to a title shot to risk delaying things. Every day that went by was a day I lost as a fighter.

So in the end, swallowing my pride, I went back to King, took the ten-grand offer, and kicked Young Sanford's butt in Las Vegas. TKO 7. Redd Foxx was ringside, cheering his man on. But in the city of lost wagers, Redd crapped out. Too bad. Redd was a good guy, and a friend. Like me he'd come up the hard way, ignored by the establishment and shunted to the side. Here he was, finally a big success after all those years, and he would have done just about anything to get himself a good heavyweight contender. There I was, just hoping for management that really appreciated me but stuck with people who treated me like dirt. I couldn't help thinking how Redd and I deserved each other.

After the fight, Redd came by and saw me with my mother. She was crying. "Why you cryin'?" he asked.

" 'Cause I'm so happy."

"Then what do you do when you're sad?"

Ibar Harrington was next. A big white guy who was supposed to be a puncher. Trouble was he could never lay a glove on me. I was just too quick for him. Now you see me, now you don't . . . and take *that*, bam, a right to the face. I kept pounding him, made a mess of his face, spurred on by the trash talking that Harrington's trainer, Angelo Dundee, was doing. Angelo was shouting: "That nigger ain't shit. Kick that nigger's ass." It was exactly what he had shouted when he'd worked Rodney Bobick's corner. I guess Angelo thought it would psych his guys up. I can't speak for them. But it was a hell of an inspiration for me to hand out a beating. See what a great trainer can do for a fighter?

CHAPTER
SEVEN

Paddy Flood once told a writer: "Young heavyweights are as un-predictable as some 3-year-old horses—and they eat a lot more . . . You never know what's comin' next. One punch and it can be all over. You never know what's going to happen to their hands, never know when the eyes will go. They rip open easier—heavy-weights."

Flood was right. When two big men whale away at one another anything can happen. I'd experienced the chance misfortune of my hand going bust against Roy Williams. It was a moment that underlined the need to get the money while the money could be had.

Yet as New Year '78 came in, here I was—the man that *Sports Illustrated* had ranked as the best of the young heavyweights in '76—and I was still waiting to be recognized. Still waiting for the big-money fights.

There were a few in the boxing press who didn't deny me my

potential. Like the columnist Jerry Izenberg, who knew I could fight. When he asked me how I felt about being on hold, I told him: "Man, where is Norton, where is Ali, where are any of them? I can't make them fight me. If it don't get any better I'm going over to Ali's house, pull him out in the yard, kick his butt to show I can do it, and then quit the whole damned business."

Well, it didn't get to that extreme. For it was at that time that my break finally came. If you could call fighting Earnie Shavers a break. I had no choice. I'd waited too long to get a fight that mattered. If it had to be Earnie Shavers, so be it. I was ready.

The circle had closed. Five years before, I was an eager amateur, climbing into the Gleason's Gym ring against this world-ranked puncher and feeling thrilled to have survived three rounds with him. Now he was all that stood between me and my chance at the heavyweight title.

Outside the ring, Shavers was one of the most likable guys in all of boxing. And he was my friend. Over the years, we'd sparred a bunch of rounds and hung out together. I'd found him to be an unassuming kind of guy with a nice sense of humor. Earnie was easy to be around, but push come to shove—make no mistake, he was all man.

I remember one time a bunch of us were playing cards in a Cleveland hotel room and, with thousands of dollars on the table and Earnie riding a winning hand, one of the guys tried to claim a mixed deal on account of an accidentally exposed card. Earnie wasn't buying the bullshit. With one of his big-knuckled hands, he picked up the money and with a glare that might have made Sonny Liston envious, said: "This money belongs to me. Anybody says different, come and get it." Nobody said different. Not Jeff Merritt, not me, nobody.

That was, like I say, unusual for him. Most times you couldn't find a more peaceable guy. Earnie never put on a macho front. Earnie was Earnie, a regular kind of guy. The fact that he was now the man I had to whup to live the dream that was so long in coming . . . well, that didn't change how I felt.

I was never one of those fighters who had to hate the opponent.

Certain guys needed that—needed to make the other man out as the enemy. Marvin Hagler was like that. Take the time when Hagler met Roberto Duran, a fighter he'd always admired from a distance. Duran made the mistake of observing they were about the same height, then saying to his manager, Luis Spada—in front of Hagler—"I almost tall like Marvin. I fight him." Hagler, who up to then had been real friendly with Duran, gave him this squinty-eyed look and turned his back. Once Duran became a potential opponent, forget about being friends.

When Sugar Ray Leonard faced Hagler, Leonard drove Hagler nuts by being so complimentary in press conferences. He would talk of Hagler being a great champion, a credit to the fight game. Blah blah blah. Hagler didn't want to hear that. He would have preferred Leonard say he was going to knock his block off and that Marvin Hagler was overrated. Hagler got so annoyed with Ray's glib stroking that he bolted the press tour they were on. It didn't fuel the game face he needed when he fought.

Back in 1987, before Hagler fought Leonard, Arum told a reporter: "You know how fighters two, three years after they fight become friends. Not Marvin. Believe me, Marvin Hagler still hates every one of his opponents. If [Vito] Antuofermo comes into the room, he won't talk to him. Duran? Forget it. [Mustafa] Hamsho, he can't stand. It's not for effect. With him, it carries over forever. If he sees Tommy Hearns, he won't go near Tommy. 'Get him out of my face. What the hell is he doing here?' 'Marvin, the fight's over.' 'The hell it's over.' "

Me? I wasn't like that. I saw opponents, not enemies. Much as I admired Ali, I didn't like how he hurt and humiliated opponents of his in the ring. He did that with Floyd Patterson and George Chuvalo and Ernie Terrell. I don't know what got into him those times. If that's what they mean by killer instinct, I was glad not to have a big dose of it.

The fight with Shavers was set for March 25, 1978, in Las Vegas. King had sold the match to ABC-TV, and even though it was not a championship bout the network was showing it in prime time. Shavers was the reason for that, not me. Earnie had gained star power when he had extended Ali to fifteen rounds the previous September in a closely contested bout that was awarded to Muhammad.

Earnie Shavers gave you a lot to think about. Mainly it came to his punching power. Of all the fighters I ever fought, nobody could punch harder. Not Tyson, not Gerry Cooney, not Ken Norton. Shavers's punches numbed your bones. Those other guys hit hard. When they landed, their punches hurt. But Shavers was in a league all his own. Shavers was, as Jerry Izenberg once described him, "a righthand puncher who could hit you in the neck and break your ankle."

My job was to keep him from hitting me with a clean shot. To do that, I planned to jab and move in a way that would keep Shavers turning, turning, turning. The jab would break up his rhythm and have a cumulative hurting effect—if I was lucky it would puff him up around the eyes or open a cut. It was important to have Shavers turning because that meant he could not plant his feet to get the most leverage on his punch.

While Shavers was ever-dangerous, his record showed that most of his knockouts had come early in the fight. Earnie's reputation was that his stamina diminished as the bout went on. Jimmy Young, who was a boxer type like me, had taken Shavers ten rounds and gotten a draw. Ali had extended him to fifteen rounds and gotten the decision. I knew that in the early rounds I'd have to be particularly careful not to get hit by Shavers's best shots.

There was one other crucial consideration—my right hand. I'd been knocking guys out with that hand, and Shavers's chin was not granite. Quarry had knocked him out. So had Ron Stander, a very ordinary heavyweight. But . . . I still felt some nagging doubts about whether my right hand would stay intact over twelve rounds. It would be a long night if the hand went bust early in the fight. I'd gotten away with it against Roy Williams. I had doubts I could do it against Shavers. You needed to let a puncher like him know he couldn't come at you with reckless abandon— that he would pay for it if he did. On the other hand, I was hoping to parcel out my power shots early. Fighting a good opponent always means trading off risks.

Two weeks before the bout, I headed out to Reno to finish my training. When I got there I found out we were staying at the Mustang Ranch, a brothel that was legal in Nevada. Whoa! I hadn't known that it was that kind of setup. When they'd said "ranch," I'd figured it was like a Western-movies ranch. Well, it didn't take but a look at the line of prostitutes that showed you themselves to know that this was not conducive to the fighting spirit. Not by a long shot. My sparring partner, Jody Ballard, and other guys in the camp stayed there, but not me. I moved to a regular hotel. The only time we all met was at the gym.

The guys at the Mustang Ranch lived it up. The owner of the place, Joe Conforte, had been a longtime boxing fan and was now manager of a heavyweight from Colombia named Bernardo Mercado. Mercado was hot at the time—undefeated in twenty fights, with seventeen knockouts. Before the year was out, though, Mercado would lose a lot of his glitter, suffering back-to-back knockouts to John Tate and Mike Weaver.

Anyway, at the Mustang Ranch how it worked was you bought tickets that enabled you to have sex with the women. And Conforte . . . because he liked fighters just gave the guys in my camp free tickets. For them, it was like being on the VIP pass at Disney World. Joe gave me free tickets too, but I hadn't come to Reno for sex. I was there for business. Serious business.

From Reno it was into Vegas for the fight, staged at Caesars Palace. Before I went out to the ring, King stopped by the dressing room to wish me luck, as only Don King could. What he said was, "If you don't make it this time, Larry, don't worry too much. You're a young man. If it doesn't happen today, you'll get your chance eventually."

Pretty uplifting, right?

But I knew what he was up to. For King, Larry Holmes wasn't the commodity that Earnie Shavers was. So King, in his premeditated way, was trying to break my focus and send me out to the ring in a tizzy, worried about losing. Worried about losing because me losing was exactly what Don King wanted. With another fighter, maybe it would have worked. But I was on to this bushy-headed horseshitter. No way I was going to let him undermine my confidence.

I understood why he preferred Shavers to win. The guy was better known, a marquee name that would be easier to sell down the road. Me, I was a long way from being recognized. As Pat Putnam had written in *Sports Illustrated:* "Larry Holmes is 28 years old, 6'3" and 210 pounds, one of those heavyweights who seems vaguely familiar. For six years, he has been fighting pretty much out of sight against mediocre opponents, men going nowhere or coming back from there."

That certainly sounded like the definition of a "hard sell." And given King's me-first mentality, it didn't require a whole lot to figure why he wanted Shavers over me.

The funny thing was Shavers had warned me about King, way back when I was a sparring partner for him. Warned me: "Watch out for him and Giachetti." Earnie was going good then, but he'd seen what trickerations Don King was capable of. And *I* had seen how disposable fighters were to King when Shavers had been knocked out in one round by Jerry Quarry and King had treated him as if he were contaminated, unloading the managerial contract he had on him. But when Earnie resurrected his career, King was there to get full promotional value out of him.

When the bell rang, I circled Shavers, hitting him time and again with the jab. I had size and reach on Earnie, as well as speed, and my objective was to use them for all twelve rounds. I had figured Shavers would follow the slugger's formula for fighting guys like me, by working his way in and banging me to the body. The saying was: Kill the body and the legs will go.

But Earnie had decided to headhunt—to look for one punch that would finish me then and there. I didn't mind. It was easier to "read" him when he fought with that bombs-away approach. I just stepped clear of the blows.

I was moving side to side, creating angles from which I could punch him and retreat. In and out. Stick and move. You don't want to stand still in front of a big puncher. That gives him time to zero in on you and set his feet for maximum leverage. With a guy like Earnie Shavers it was all about angles and distance.

Even when Earnie got inside and I drew him into a clinch, I was careful. If Shavers could get his right hand free, he could hurt you. Earnie was a bull moose in those clinches, pushing you off so that for a passing moment you were exactly where he wanted you—at arm's length of his right hand. He did that to me— shoved me back onto my heels and hit me with a hard right hand that stunned me. Lucky for me, I was still easing backward when the punch landed. Even though I was hurt, I fired back to give him pause about pursuing me and give me time to clear my head. From that moment, every time Shavers hit me with anything, I made sure to pay him back double.

I was on my game this night, fighting as well as I ever had. Even Cosell noticed. Friends told me later that he was saying: "This is not the fighter I have seen pre-vi-ous-ly. This per-for-mance by a for-mer-ly lack-luster boxer al-most strains cred-i-bi-li-ty."

For him maybe it did. Not for me. I knew that some night I would bring before the public the vintage Larry Holmes, the guy who had dueled with Muhammad Ali in those private sessions back at Deer Lake. Against my toughest opponent yet, I did just that. I beat on Shavers like a tom-tom, hitting him with rapid-fire combinations even while I was moving backward.

A lot of guys lose effectiveness when they move backward. Me, I always fought better moving away than coming forward. I was six-foot-three and had long arms and the ability to pull my head back out of reach. I could do all that and still put enough on a punch to drop any guy who thought he could get lucky just walking in on me.

The big advantage to fighting that way is that you're not walking into punches very much. When Ali lost his legs and had to stand in front of an opponent, that's when punches began to take their toll on him. My legs lasted me a lot longer and really kept me from being too beat up.

For twelve rounds against Shavers, I did what I wanted to—beat him to the punch and then moved away so he couldn't make my head spin like the poor girl in *The Exorcist*. In fact, by the end it was Shavers who was in jeopardy. In the final round, I hit him with an overhand right. Earnie's right knee buckled, but he managed to keep himself upright. I was on him like white on rice, ripping a barrage of nine straight punches before the bell ended the fight.

I knew I had won, and won big. Even my big-mouth detractor Cosell was saying so on national TV. The only thing that gave me pause was whether King might have any influence on the judges. I was thinking about what he had said to me before the fight—that I was young enough to wait awhile for my title shot. Was he trying to tell me something?

As we stood there awaiting the decision, Richie kept repeating: "You got it, Big Jack. You got it."

I kept mumbling, "Please don't let them take it away from me."

The decision was announced. Judges Harold Buck and Joe Swessel gave me every round and scored it 120–108. The other judge, Dave Moretti, had it 119–109.

Just what lay ahead was a bit clouded in the immediate aftermath of my beating Shavers. See, the month before, on February 15, 1978, Ali had blown the title, losing in a shocker to Leon Spinks—a fifteen-round decision.

Spinks and Ali both had agreed that the winner would meet Ken Norton, who had become the mandatory challenger on the strength of a November 1977 victory over Jimmy Young. But Spinks's promoter, Arum, knew there was a lot more money to be made fighting Ali again.

And on the night I beat Shavers, word was that Arum was going to tell the WBC they could take their belt and shove it—he and Spinks were going to do what made economic sense for them. In other words, give Ali a rematch.

The WBC, it was said, would respond by declaring Norton the champion.

In that case, I would be the opponent. I would be fighting

Norton for the WBC heavyweight title. Spinks and Ali would be fighting for the WBA title.

It was just a bit fuzzy if that was how it would all shake out. But as *The New York Times* wrote: "Amid all the jurisdictional confusion, the one bit of clarity that emerged today was that Holmes was a visible and attractive new figure in the heavyweight picture. Against Shavers, he displayed speed, a certain amount of power, and the ability to take punches."

I'd like to tell you that when I went to sleep that night, I dreamed of heavyweight-title glory. Sorry. Not so. When you've been the boxing equivalent of the kid with his nose pressed up against the candy-store window, it's hard to forget the bullshit you've had to get through. That night, strange episodes from my life came back to me. In all of them I was the object of insult and humiliation. Did it have anything to do with the fact that when King got through carving up my purse, all I had for this prime-time network-TV fight was fifteen thousand dollars? You figure it out.

CHAPTER
EIGHT

Four days after I whupped Shavers, the WBC made it official.

Ken Norton was the new WBC heavyweight champion. By proclamation.

I was ready to snatch it from him, in the words of the E. F. Hutton commercial, the old-fashioned way. And earrrrn it.

King announced Norton-Holmes for June 9, 1978, in Las Vegas. ABC-TV would televise the match in prime time.

Norton was going to get $2.7 million, considerably more than the $1.5 million he had earned beating Jimmy Young. I would be paid $300,000, of which I could expect to end up with maybe half. But that was okay. That would give me a financial safety net—the kind of money that would enable me to think seriously of marriage and a family.

As for Norton, at that point he was one of only three men to defeat Ali—Smokin' Joe Frazier and Leon Spinks were the others.

Ali's trainer, Dundee, had this assessment of him: "Fights like Archie Moore—peek-a-boo with his arms across his face. Best punch is a left hook to the body and head. With his right he slaps with an open glove. I call his style a stutter-style, and he's so big and strong, you got to take it to him. Good fighter. Dangerous."

That caught Norton pretty good. Strong. A bit awkward. A body puncher. Of all the men I'd been in the ring with, other than Ali . . . Ken Norton would be my toughest opponent.

I thought back to the night in '76 when Norton and Ali had fought at Yankee Stadium. They'd packed the place—people everywhere, in the ringside seats, and out there in the bleachers and grandstands. I remember looking out at that scene from the Yankee dugout and telling a reporter: "Ain't it funny. Here are all these people spending all this money to see two guys fight and I can beat both of them and nobody knows who I am."

Before arriving at the stadium, I had gone to dinner with the *New York Post*'s Jerry Lisker at Costello's on Forty-fourth Street. The bartender watched us come in and said to Lisker, "Who's the basketball player?"

I shook my head and smiled.

"Until you're the champ nobody knows who you are and nobody cares," I told Lisker.

Well, now I could begin to change that. All that stood in my way was Norton.

Norton had come to boxing by accident while a marine enlistee at Camp Lejeune. Feeling he ought to have been a starter on the base football team but for the fact that the man playing ahead of him was white, and an officer, he'd quit the team and gone out for boxing. He became a three-time all-marine champion, won the '67 Pan-Am Games, and turned pro later that year.

He found it hard going as a pro. Fighting mostly on the West Coast, by '73 he had built a good record, 29–1 with 23 KOs. But like me, he had no recognition or money to show for it. Raising a young son (Ken junior, who became an all-pro NFL linebacker) by himself, he felt so desperate, he told one reporter, that "I actually considered robbing a liquor store. Or a supermarket. When a man is desperate enough, when he has a family to feed and no money, I guess he'll consider anything."

Then in March '73, Norton got his break—a fight against Muhammad Ali, at the time an ex-champion, for fifty thousand dollars. That genius Cosell beforehand called it the worst mismatch in boxing history, a disgrace. That afternoon Norton broke Ali's jaw and won the fight, and changed his life.

Afterward, Cosell told him: "Kenny, you made me look silly."

"That's okay, Howard," Norton said. "You always look silly."

Five years later, as I was looking for the good life, Norton had it, through big-money fights against Foreman, Quarry, Ali (three in all), Duane Bobick, and Jimmy Young. . . . *and* movie roles in *Mandingo* and *Drum*. He had a ranch house in the exclusive La Dera Heights section of Los Angeles and a garage in which he parked his eggshell white Cartier-edition Lincoln Mark IV Continental, customized Sting Ray, customized van, white Silver Cloud Rolls-Royce, and 1978 Ford station wagon. On order was a fifty-thousand-dollar Clenet.

But the only thing he had that I wanted was the heavyweight title.

The last time Norton and I had been around one another was when he fought Young the previous November. Remember Ibar Harrington? Well, I fought Ibar on the undercard of Norton-Young and got about as much attention as a freckle on a flea's ass.

Norton—another story. With his V-shaped torso and his Hollywood look-at-me airs, eyes swung to him every time he moved through the casino. Whispers would follow. Psst. It's Ken Norton . . . it's Ken Norton . . . Ken Norton.

Now he was WBC heavyweight champion by decree, given the title so that Don King could get back into the heavyweight title business. Over the next twenty years, King's good ole boy, Jose Sulaiman, president of the WBC, would repeatedly be King's accomplice, making rulings that screwed fighters unaffiliated with

King or fighters trying to slip the contractual noose Donald had around their necks.

Jose was a pisser, always so earnest in his explanations of why his WBC was taking such and such an action that would turn out to be so damn sweet for King. You listened to the little señor and you sometimes could swear he worked himself into a trance—to the point where he came to believe his bullshit . . . that was how sincere and believable he seemed. But the political games he played on King's behalf were sleazy and consistently to King's advantage.

There was the time in the nineties when WBC junior middleweight champ Julian Jackson was trying to break away from King's contractual stranglehold. At the time Jackson was recovering from a detached retina and Sulaiman used that as his reason not to sanction him for a return to the ring. The way Jose talked it he sounded like Mother Teresa in his concern for the fighter. Then Jackson agreed to go back to King and the detached retina became a nonissue in a damn hurry. Sulaiman reinstated Jackson quicker than you can say co-conspirator.

The world got a real insight into how transparent Sulaiman and King, working as a tandem, were when both of them tried to steal the heavyweight title after Buster Douglas had won it by knocking out Mike Tyson. The sweat on Douglas's brow was hardly dry when the WBC and the WBA, the governing bodies at ringside that night in Tokyo, responded to King's protest by announcing that they were suspending the result of the fight because of a so-called long-count controversy over Tyson's knockdown of Douglas in the eighth round.

The threat by the governing bodies to strip Douglas of the title he'd plainly earned created such an uproar that the WBC, based in Mexico City, and the WBA, based in Maracay, Venezuela, retreated pronto. Sulaiman later would testify in an American court of law that while he threatened to strip Douglas of his title he didn't really mean what he said. You know, his English— she not so good.

Whatever. Sulaiman had made Norton the paper champ and Norton was to have his chance against me to prove whether he deserved it. Norton told newsmen that while his handlers called him "champ," he was not yet taking the word to heart.

He told the press: "Holmes is a very good boxer, he has a very good jab. The way he beat Shavers, I realized I had underestimated him. I thought Shavers would take him out, but Earnie threw only one good shot. He threw nothing short, no flurries, only one punch at a time. I don't know whether Earnie couldn't get off or Holmes kept him off balance."

I went to training camp at Grossinger's, a Catskills resort ninety minutes or so north of New York City. A month out from the fight, I'd already sparred one hundred rounds. When I was in there with my sparring partner, Jody Ballard, I'd pretend he was Norton.

"Come on, Norton," I'd tease. "Show 'em what you got. Can't you move your head? These are my folks, mine! Show 'em. Don't want to do it? I'll do it then."

And I'd fire away with both hands.

When a newsman asked me about it afterward, I told him: "This is show business. The people like it. They want to hear what the next champion's got to say. I like people and I like to talk. Norton wouldn't do this. He says nothing in a workout and when he's finished he don't want anybody around him and he don't want to be touched.

"I don't like Norton. He thinks he's better than people. Sometimes he comes down off his high ladder, but most of the time he thinks he's too good."

In fact, Norton *had* come to bug me. It started as the usual prefight jive that promoters work up to create the appearance of a grudge between the fighters. When the public thinks the fighters really have it in for one another, supposedly that makes them more eager to buy tickets to the fight. So promoters—or more accurately their PR guys—concoct these scenarios to encourage the notion that we're mad as hell and not gonna take it anymore.

King had a fellow named Bobby Goodman working the publicity on the fight. And Goodman, along with Giachetti, was baiting Norton, telling him that I thought all the gold jewelry he wore—his gold rings, gold watches, gold necklaces—was tacky. Well, Norton went for the bait and told them: "Holmes is ignorant."

That touched a raw nerve. I hadn't forgotten how I'd been treated as a schoolboy . . . and the stigma of being regarded as a dumb black boy. Even though the whole thing was manufactured, I still got pissed that Norton said I was ignorant. Norton compounded the insult by calling me "Pinhead" and acting as though I was a peon compared to the great Norton.

Yeah. Norton had a grand opinion of Ken Norton, and walked around as though he was the prince of boxing. God's gift to the world. In later years, Norton and his NFL son would stop speaking to one another, about which a writer would comment: "You've read how linebacker Ken Norton Jr. stopped talking to his ex-fighter dad, Ken Norton Sr. Probably struck you as extreme. That was the reaction I had. Then I met the Norton who boxed. Trust me: given your druthers, you wouldn't talk to that pompous Norton either."

I knew what he meant. Not that I was working myself into a lather about Norton—you know, like a Marvin Hagler might have. It just registered: I don't like the son of a bitch. And that was it. I was still intending to go about my business as I always had, and not personalize this fight.

Then . . . six days out from the fight, suddenly I had a lot more to worry about than what Mr. Shit-on-the-stick Norton thought about me. In a public sparring session at Caesars Palace, I felt a pain shoot through the biceps of my left arm as my elbow collided with the elbow of a sparring partner. The muscle hurt so much I couldn't straighten it out. I knew I had a problem, but I also knew enough not to let on to the media that were watching. We wrapped up the workout and headed up to my room.

I was plenty worried. It was one thing to have a defective right hand, as I'd had against Roy Williams. I'd been able to survive with that. But it was unimaginable that I could do the same deprived of my left. Not against a fighter as physical as Ken Norton.

Up in the room Giachetti packed the arm in ice. Then we headed for Desert Springs Hospital, where Dr. Anthony Serfustini and a physical therapist named Keith Kleven looked me over and decided I'd torn tissue in the biceps.

"How bad is it?" Giachetti asked.

Bad enough, they insisted, to postpone the fight.

"For how long?"

"Four months."

When I heard that, I told them: "No way. What can you do for me now?"

I'd been too long waiting for this chance to kiss it off just because of a little pain. You could never be sure that the opportunity would reappear.

Kleven was eager to enhance his reputation by working with Larry Holmes. Say this about him: Kleven knew his business. He used deep massage, iced the damaged arm for hours at a time, and used an hour of ultrasonic hot-water treatment twice a day.

Kleven advised Giachetti to call in Dr. James Garrick, a Phoenix specialist who worked with pro football players, to see what he thought. Giachetti said we would keep things on the q.t. until Garrick examined me.

The next day Garrick told Giachetti I could fight if I wanted to.

"When the fight starts," Garrick said, "his arm should be one hundred percent. It's later the trouble will come. In the late rounds, he will lose six percent to eight percent effectiveness. And if he gets hit on the tear he could lose as much as forty percent."

That night Giachetti said he wanted to postpone the fight.

"No," I told him. "We've come too far, worked too hard. A lot of people are counting on me."

There were a few guys in the boxing press—Dick Young of the *New York Daily News*, Michael Katz of *The New York Times*, and Ed Schuyler of the Associated Press—that knew my routine and were suspicious why all of a sudden I was just shadowboxing and not doing any more sparring. We just said we'd peaked and didn't need the work. Although I felt some pain in the biceps, once I got it loosened up I could do what I had to with the arm.

I know I'm ready to fight when I get real cranky and little things start bothering me. Like I'll get on Richie for not having my water bottle ready. Or I'll get ticked at Jody Ballard for giving too much private information to the press. I don't really want to act like a prima donna, but I get like a tightly wound spring. Most fighters I know behave the same way just before a big fight.

There's another thing that happens, a strange, almost otherworldly experience. I find that at unexpected times, while I'm daydreaming or dropping off to sleep, I get this feeling that a punch is speeding toward me. Honest to Christ, without thinking I'll duck, or even respond with a counterpunch. It's the kind of crazy thing that maybe you've seen aging ex-fighters who are thought to be punch-drunk do. I can't control it, and at times don't even know I'm doing it. Diane told me that just before the Norton fight, I almost knocked her out in bed.

Two days before the fight, I told the news guys that if I won I planned to jump into the swimming pool with my boxing gear on, and that my handlers would do the same in their civilian clothes. The sentiment was that I wouldn't have to bother. Norton was an 8–5 favorite.

On that same day, I showed up at Norton's workout, and got into one of those shoving matches that are intended to pump up the promotion. It did.

NORTON-HOLMES . . . REAL GRUDGE FIGHT was the headline to Dick Young's column, in which there was Norton again calling me a pinhead.

"That's not a nickname, it's a fact," Norton says. "Just check the pictures of the Neanderthal man in any book, or the Cro-magnon man, and compare them to the shape of Holmes' head."

Holmes promises to change Norton's appearance come Friday night.

"Can you imagine me landing 70 or 80 punches a round on Norton's beautiful face?" he said after his workout. *"The movie studios will be calling me up to make* Mandingo, *and they'll be using Norton for mummy pictures after that."*

But finally all that was over with, and it was fight night.

Coming down the aisle to the ring, I was wired. Part of me felt nervous, part of me exhilarated to be center stage, knowing millions of peole would be seeing the fight on network TV, prime time.

Once I climbed through the ropes, I made sure to loosen up my arm. Kleven had worked on it in the dressing room and I was trying to keep it from knotting up. We were indoors at Caesars Palace, in what they call the Sports Pavilion, a 4,500-seat arena, and the heat was intensified by the TV lights. All to the good for my arm.

Norton followed me into the ring.

The announcer introduced both of us to the crowd. Then the referee, Mills Lane, called us to center ring for his instructions. Lane, who would become prominent years later as the referee who disqualified Mike Tyson in the notorious "ear-biting" match, was a hard-nosed little guy, an ex-NCAA welterweight champion at Nevada-Reno. After a pro career that saw him go 11–1, he'd gotten his law degree and, settling down in Reno, Nevada, gone on to become a Washoe County prosecutor and then a no-nonsense judge known as "Maximum Mills." I came to appreciate the way Lane took control of a fight without being intrusive, and over the years I'd ask the commissions to select him to officiate my fights.

On this night, as Lane gave his instructions, Norton was glaring at me, but I just looked at a point below his eyes. That staring game was Mickey Mouse. I wasn't about to encourage it. Instead I let my mind go blank, not hearing a word of what Lane said.

But when Norton and I touched gloves, I was back in real time and ready to go.

I believed that Norton, like Shavers, was made for me—and that when he came at me I would harpoon him all night with the jab. I expected his straight-ahead aggression to make my job easier. I anticipated that, like the moth attracted to flames, Ken Norton would impale himself on my jab.

But I hadn't anticipated Norton's strength. Not until I was in the ring with Norton did I get any sense of how strong he was. Not only was he strong, he was in terrific shape and knew how to corner me and keep me from using my legs as easily as I had against other fighters. The expression is "cutting off the ring"— and it means limiting the other fighter's footwork, his movement.

Norton didn't show much of that until the fight was into the sixth round. Up to then I'd been having my way, simply outboxing him. I had the quicker hands and I was painting him with the jab. The judges gave me four of the first five rounds.

But when Norton came on, he came on strong, punching to the body. They were punishing shots whose objective was not only to weaken me but to take away my mobility. Body shots could discourage the fancy footwork. But I wouldn't let that happen. Even though he was pounding the heavy artillery to the body, I managed to stay on my toes and keep moving.

In my mind, I was still landing more through those middle rounds than he was, but the judges saw Norton landing the heavier punches. *The New York Times* account said:

> *Jab, jab, jab, went Holmes, but Norton ignored the leather and charged into the challenger, landing one punch for four or five, but by far the heaviest punches of the night.*
>
> *In the seventh round he opened a cut around Holmes' mouth.*

The judges gave Norton five of the six rounds from rounds six through eleven. They were hard damn rounds. Norton hit me some good shots, to the body and the head, and a couple below the belt. When he went south of the border a second time, I told him to quit it.

"Fuck you," he said.

"Fuck you too," I told him.

Like I say, I thought I was winning—and winning big. But the reality was otherwise. After eleven rounds, Norton had a narrow lead on the scorecards. I was unaware of that, of course. But I knew that the established fighter, the household name, tended to get the edge with the judges. And that was Ken Norton. I was the new kid on the block. I knew I couldn't let up.

I remember talking to Ali once about being able to tell how good a fight is when you're in it. He told me that sometimes you imagine you're doing things you aren't really doing, and when you see the tapes afterward, you're disappointed. But when the other guy is fighting well and when you're staying right there with him, you almost always know you're in a really good fight. Of course, most of your focus is on what you're trying to do, but you can tell from the crowd at the end of each round that it's a good fight. This was the best fight I was ever in. It was one of the best fights a lot of people ever saw. THE BEST FIGHT SINCE MANILA was the headline that would run with the column written by *New York Times* columnist Dave Anderson. I could feel the crowd's excitement.

The fight that it reminded me of was the first Roberto Duran–Sugar Ray Leonard fight, when Sugar Ray—one of the best boxers there was—decided to prove he could punch with the puncher. As my bout with Norton wore on, I was slugging with him more and more, boxing him less and less. Lucky for me, my arm was relatively pain-free. The contest had become a battle of wills, a question of who wanted it more. A ring war. I never felt more alive than when I was fighting my best against a truly good fighter.

At times like this, when I was on top of my game, I swear I had a sixth sense that enabled me to see things before they happened. It was that way with Norton more than in any other fight. I could see his punches coming before he knew he was going to throw them. Same with my punch. I saw it land before I let it go. It was almost like I'd fought this same fight before. It was scary, but I loved it.

By the twelfth round my jab got reinvigorated, and in the thirteenth I hit Norton with so many overhand rights in succession that one ringside observer wrote, "[Holmes] appeared to be hammering a nail in Norton's head." We traded heavy leather in the fourteenth, and when I returned to my corner, Giachetti told me I had the fight won and that I should stay away from Norton in the fifteenth and final round.

That did not sound right to me. Norton and I had been to hell and back. I was hurting; I knew he was too. From the crowd I could sense the excitement in the air, a buzz that said they could barely wait for this final round to unfold. Stay away from Norton?

That seemed a tactical mistake. For in a fight waged with the fury both of us had shown that would look like retreat, and give the officials reason to award the last round to Norton.

While I thought I was ahead in the scoring, I couldn't be absolutely sure. Tired as I was, I couldn't just go on the defensive in this final round. If I wanted to be the champ, I'd have to show the officials I deserved the title.

I thought to myself: I'm going to fight this man; he's got to be every bit as tired as I am.

See, there comes a time in a fight when you have to ask yourself, "Should I or shouldn't I . . . go that extra mile?" The devil's working on you. One part of you is saying yes, another no. One part of your body is telling you, "I'm tired of taking these shots." But another part is saying, "If you have the heart of a champion, now's the time to show it." Physical ability is not enough. The inner man is what counts.

As the fifteenth round began, it turned out all three judges had the fight dead even. Unbeknownst to Norton or me, the WBC heavyweight title would go to the man who wanted the final round more. And that final round would go down in boxing history as a classic. In fact, when *The Ring* magazine held its seventy-fifth anniversary awards dinner in 1997, the fifteenth round of

113

Norton-Holmes would be one of the three nominees for the greatest round ever.

What made it great, I suspect, was that we stood at center ring and, bone tired though we both were, for three minutes we took our best shots. Norton landed early, hurt me, and had me in some trouble, at one point knocking my mouthpiece so high into the air that the infield fly rule could have been called. But somehow I found the strength to revive, firing back at him as the crowd roared. Suddenly it was Norton, not me, who was looking like Raggedy Andy. And that's how it went, down to the final bell, two adults beating on each other as thousands of people at Caesars Palace went bonkers.

Over the years people would ask me about that fifteenth round—could I sense how thrilling it was? Simple answer: No. I was tunneled into my objective: win the fight. But when the final bell rang, and the crowd sprang up out of their seats, I knew this had been a helluva fight even without hearing the roar that went up. I had nothing but admiration and a kind of affection for the man who had just tried to knock my block off for fifteen rounds. I learned more about what makes Ken Norton and me tick than if I had sat down and talked to him every day for a year. It has to do with being tested to the limit and coming out of it worthy. When I went over to Ken Norton, put my arms around him, and said, "Great fight, man," I was really saying he'd won my respect as a fighter and a man.

I was drained physically and emotionally, and grateful to have survived the bout. My thumb was still in one piece, my biceps muscle had held up. Blood was still flowing from a cut inside my lips that would need eleven stitches to close. But thank the Lord I didn't have to experience those heavy-handed body shots of Norton's anymore.

But . . . what did it all amount to? Would I be world champion or a guy that had merely come close? A decision was upcoming that could completely change my life. Please, God. Make it me.

The crowd grew hushed.

As the ring announcer, Chuck Hull, read the scores, I rested my head on Giachetti's shoulder. Chuck Hull said that judge Harold Buck had it 143–142 . . . for Holmes.

Lou Tabat scored it 143–142 . . . for Norton.

And finally, Joe Swessel—143–142 . . . for the winner and neeeewww champion, Laarrrrry Hooooollllllmes.

By a single point I'd won it!

Suddenly the ring filled with people who were all over me, hugging, kissing, calling me that sweetest sound of all: champ. Damn it, I was heavyweight champion! Richie was embracing me. My brothers too. And here came Diane at ringside, smiling and crying at the same time, as she tried to get through the crowd and into the ring.

And wouldn't you know King would be right in the thick of it too. Acting as if he couldn't be happier—a big-ass grin on his face as he slapped me on the back and kept saying: "I knew you could do it, Larry." What a lying sack of shit. Had Norton copped the decision, he'd have been over in Mandingo's corner, telling him he knew *he* could do it. Mr. Came-With-The-Champion-Left-With-The-Champion.

Now here was Cosell, the microphone shaking in his hand, as he, like King, pretended to be pleased as punch to share my moment of glory while he interviewed me. For me, he was another of the so-called experts who had treated me like garbage on the way up. Another one of the so-called experts I'd overcome. Remember the mustard-seed heart? Well, the next day's headlines would say things like HOLMES' RAW COURAGE BEFITS HIS CROWN (*New York Post*) and HOLMES REACHES TOP ON COURAGE IN 15th (*The New York Times*).

As Cosell stuck that microphone in my face, I said, "See, Howard. I told you. I told all you experts the kind of fighter I was. None of you believed me. You believe me now, Howard?"

Maybe it sounded like gloating. I didn't mean it to be. My heart was bursting with pride at what I had done, and a bit of defiance, I suppose, at the long odds I'd overcome. At twenty-eight years old, walking a long and bumpy road, I had beat the damn system. I had beat the front-running phonies like Cosell and King.

It was a mob scene, fighting our way to the dressing room. For a while, I lay down on a padded table there and breathed deeply. Mike Marley, a young reporter from the *Las Vegas Sun*, asked me what I felt.

"I got a good feeling," I told him.

Then, with my security man, big Bob DiGuilio, who'd once been a bodyguard for Robert Goulet, leading the way, I did what I had promised: I led the gang, maybe fifteen of us, into Caesars Palace's swimming pool. Jumped in with my boxing trunks on and whooped it up. Cham-peen of the world. My brother Jake jumped in in his street clothes, and Giachetti did too, both of them clutching and waving the green-and-gold WBC belt that Norton wouldn't be able to use anymore to keep his trousers up.

Even the reporter, Marley—who would go on to cover boxing for the *New York Post* and, in the nineties, go to work for Donald King—even Marley jumped in with all his clothes on. Jumped in and got a story in the next day's *Sun* by doing so: SPLISH, SPLASH ON A FRIDAY NIGHT.

> *Unfortunately the sports writer's pen wasn't waterproof* [Marley wrote]. *Holmes showed that he was. The group bulled its way to the elevators and they went to Holmes' 10th floor suite.*
>
> *Behind closed doors, the champ was nude except for a small towel over his shoulders. He was in the whirlpool bath, letting the water work on his aching limbs.*

That was when King sent one of his flunkies to get me. Seems like Donald was upset because I'd missed a postfight press conference for our dunk in the pool. And though I told him I knew nothing about the press conference, he seemed to be in a chest-bumping mood. He was gonna show me who wore the britches in this boxing family.

He was especially worked up about that celebration in the pool.

"You're the heavyweight champion of the world," he said. "You can't go around doing bush-league things like that."

He kept on and on about how I'd have to change the way I

behaved, lecturing me as if I was a troublesome child. He said it was his job to shape and control my image. I had to learn to carry myself like a true champion. My own instinct was to be myself. I wasn't a bum or anything. I was a decent man and a good fighter. I had earned my title. That should have been all the image I needed. I knew what King was up to. He was trying to show that, WBC title or not, he was still in charge. What he did with his little power play was rain on my parade. On purpose, I thought.

I decided to get away from the creep as soon as I could and booked a flight back to Easton for the next day.

At the airport, a few people thought they recognized me.

I told them I was Larry Holmes, heavyweight champion of the world.

This puzzled them.

"Heavyweight champion? Who did you fight?"

"Ken Norton."

"Ken who?"

It was the same for the folks on the airplane.

"*Who'd* you beat? What about Muhammad Ali?"

"He's not champion anymore."

"You beat him?"

"No, Leon Spinks did. They're fighting the rematch in September in New Orleans."

Talk of being brought back to earth. The thrill of victory was undercut by the ghost of Ali. I understood now that it might be a while before people would look at Larry Holmes as the best heavyweight around. It might even take my fighting the guy, if he were to beat Spinks in the rematch.

Years later, when Ali had that Parkinson's disease, he told me he'd always envied me for one thing.

"What's that, Muhammad?" I asked, curious.

"You know the smartest thing you ever did, Larry?"

I shrugged.

"You stayed in your hometown. Man, you were smart. You got a place where you feel you belong, where you have your people.

Me, I can go anywhere in the world and people will know me and make a fuss, but I don't really have a hometown no more. I really miss that."

He was dead right, of course. And if I needed any supporting evidence, it was what awaited me when I arrived at the airport in Allentown. As the plane descended, someone observed that there were lots of cars parked below. I didn't look down because just being in a plane always made me feel strange, and looking at the ground coming up toward me was too unsettling.

As the plane landed and then taxied to its gate, I could see hundreds of people standing on the roof of the airport, waiting, it turned out, to greet me.

I didn't know it, but immediately after the fight, Easton had spontaneously erupted, folks leaving their homes and the bars in which they had watched the fight and heading downtown to the square where a huge stone Civil War obelisk, topped by a bugler boy, stood. The joke around Easton was that some nights the city was so quiet you just waited for the damn bugler to blow.

Well, the night I whupped Norton was not like that. Car horns sounded and drivers flashed their headlights. People congregated at The Circle, as the town center at Northampton and Third Streets was known. The crowd grew and grew. Those of my brothers and sisters who had not gone to Vegas were mobbed by well-wishers. Friends told me there had been nothing like this since the end of World War II was declared.

Well, a day later—the day I arrived back home—it was even bigger, grander. At the airport, there were thousands of fans who'd come from all over the Delaware Valley—from big cities like Bethlehem and from small towns like Deer Lake and Pottsville. A few came from as far way as Harrisburg and Reading. They were joined by local politicians, as well as some of my brothers and Mom. It was amazing. The crowd chanted: "You're the champ" and "We're number one." As I disembarked from the plane I waved to the people and, making my way to the limo that an Easton car dealer had provided, signed hundreds of autographs.

In the open limo with Diane and my family, I rode at the head of a motorcade along Route 22, back to Easton. Along the roadside all the way to my hometown were people standing and cheering. Many of them were wearing buttons that said, "Larry Holmes—The Easton Assassin." I loved it.

It hit me that for the last two years, ever since I won the Roy Williams fight, I'd told everyone around here I was going to be the heavyweight champion of the world. It was my way of convincing myself I could do that . . . and be that. Folks used to duck me because they were so worn out by me telling them the same thing over and over. The truth was that until I was in that crowd and saw the familiar faces, winning the championship wasn't a reality.

If the ride along Route 22 was a wonder, what was awaiting me in Easton was even better. The people had come from Brown's Hardware Supply and the Sportsman's Cafe, and they came from the ivied homes up on College Hill. My neighbors from the South Side were there too. All of them were jammed thick in and around The Circle and, as our motorcade reached town center, they chanted, "La-rrry, La-rrry, La-rrry." Those sitting in their cars blew their horns. I saw signs that said, "Welcome, Larry Holmes" and "Welcome back, Champ." I felt more then than when I got the decision in Las Vegas. I was so happy I thought I was gonna cry. But I kept my emotions in and just waved. It wouldn't be right for the heavyweight champion to be crying.

I associated each face with some experience. Faces I worked with. Faces of bosses I'd had and their families. Faces of politicians. Faces of old teachers and cops. Faces I made deliveries to, shined shoes for, washed cars for. Faces of guys I drank with, girls I fooled around with. The face of an uncle of mine who had blown big money betting *against* me when I'd fought Shavers and Norton. Yup, I saw my whole life up to that point in the faces around me. I knew there could have been nothing like this if I came from a big city. I was glad I had stayed a small-town boy.

In The Circle they had set up a podium, but to get there we

had to stop the car and get out and walk because the crowd was too thick to drive our way in. When I finally got to the podium, I turned to the crowd and waved.

"I feel real good," I said. "This is all worth it. If fighting hard and becoming a champion means this is what you come home to, man, I'll fight forever. Thank you very much."

It's kind of ironic that the same newspapers that reported HOLMES GOES HOME IN TRIUMPH also reported how Ali had just embarked on a twelve-day goodwill visit to the Soviet Union, accompanied by Veronica and several friends.

Ali *was* a man of the world, and me, I was never more comfortable than when I was in Easton.

I had a little chuckle as I read the item about Muhammad's Soviet tour. The paper said, "Asked if he intended to tell the Russian people he was the greatest, Ali responded: 'I don't think that I'll have to tell them I'm the greatest boxer in the world.' "

Used to be I thought. Used to be the greatest in the world. At thirty-six Ali was just a shadow of what he had been. I knew it and maybe he did too. But the truth was that the shadow of Ali would, I now realized, obscure Larry Holmes and whatever he accomplished.

Ali had become a legend. In time, maybe the public would take to me. Who could say? For now, I would just carry on, do the best I could. Fight whoever Donald King chose to put in front of me, and get my money's worth for sweat, blood, and tears. I was a champion, and in boxing that was when a man could really cash in.

Weird, isn't it? You're a so-so baseball player, football player, basketball player, they pay you a cool million . . . and more, sometimes lots more. You have a lousy season, it doesn't really radically change the dollars and cents or your standard of living. A .260 hitter drops to .220, he's still gonna be paid handsomely. There are standards, built into the game, established through a players' association and through labor wars with management.

A fighter's career—another story. Step into the wrong punch and your chance at the big bucks can go up in smoke. You can go from a champion to a perpetual opponent in a blink, your purses shrinking to chump change. It's a free-market system run by merciless promoters who only give you what they have to . . . and not a penny more. And for us poor ole pugs, there is no Jimmy Hoffa getting into promoters' faces and demanding that we be treated fairly. Uh-uh. It's every man for his own damn self. And most of us, pitted against bloodsucking sharpies like Don King, are way overmatched.

A guy once said that boxing was closer to seventeenth-century buccaneering than any other business enterprise these days. I could buy into that real easy after five years with the Long John Silver of the game, brother King. Not only was he out to bleed you dry, he also thought he could run your life like a plantation massah.

It was only weeks after I'd become champion when King phoned and asked me to stop up to his town house in New York to talk business. That was just a smoke screen, it turned out, for what he really wanted to discuss. Which was how Larry Holmes was behaving since he won the title.

See, when newsmen asked me about what made me a fighter, I would say, "Money."

Now King was telling me, "You can't tell these people you fight for money. That's not what they want to hear. What they want to hear is that you love the sport, that it's an athletic challenge to you, that you fight for pride. They want to hear that you would fight even if you didn't get paid for it. I don't want to hear you say you fight for money anymore."

Listen to this son of a bitch. While money wasn't the only reason I fought—other things did count for something—I sure as hell would never have risked body and limb in the ring without it. I couldn't be so bogus as to say otherwise. And who the hell was Donald King to talk about the spiritual values of boxing? This guy didn't do squat when it came to boxing unless he could fatten his own pocket. It was okay for Don King to turn fighters into slaves and to profit from their sweat, but it wasn't okay for Larry Holmes to say what drove him to fight? The hell with that.

I told him he was my promoter, concerned with finding opponents for me and the money I'd need to fight them, and that he should butt out of the rest of my life. Was none of his concern. I knew that you had to assert yourself with King or he'd think he could do and say whatever he damn well pleased.

A few weeks later, I went down to San Juan, Puerto Rico, where King was promoting a match. We were meeting to discuss a bout against Alfredo Evangelista, my first title defense and likely an easy one. I didn't mind a Mr. Softee like Evangelista after the war with Ken Norton. Truth is that most managers and promoters like to "milk" the title—take advantage of being a champion by getting solid money for low-risk matches. Some of them do it as long as they can get away with it. In my mind, I was eager and willing to fight the best contenders out there, and prove I was the *real* heavyweight champion. Me, not Leon Spinks Jr., that gap-toothed fool. Me, not Muhammad Ali, should Ali regain the title in the rematch.

Anyway, the night of the fight in San Juan, I was at ringside with Giachetti when King, who was sitting upstairs, summoned me. "Immediately," his flunky said, as if I was some toady of King's. Well, when I got upstairs, I lit into King, in front of his WBC amigos, Sulaiman and a bunch of them.

"You can't treat me like a piece of crap, Don King. I don't have to come down here to Puerto Rico waiting until you snap your fingers and I'm supposed to come running like a dog. I'm the heavyweight champion of the world. I'm the one who takes punches in the face coming a hundred miles an hour, and you treat me like this!"

And I turned and took a walk on him.

I knew that as long as I had to do business with Don King, I would be in a war of nerves with him. I couldn't let him win or he would destroy me.

CHAPTER
NINE

Life changes when you're heavyweight champion.

For one thing, the money gave me breathing room for the first time in my life.

While the Sportsville contract now had Giachetti as my manager, that was on paper only. In boxing, a promoter like King is not permitted to promote and manage the same fighter. At least in the United States. In England, it's different. They allow the kind of double-dipping that King was doing by having Giachetti front for him as manager. The reality of it was Giachetti was my trainer and was paid as such.

King still took 25 percent of my purses, and Giachetti and Spaz each got 12 ½ percent. That meant my $300,000 purse for winning the title was reduced to $150,000. The IRS took its whack and that left me with $75,000.

I stuck the money in the bank. I was always afraid to blow the dough.

My first title defense was in November '78 against Alfredo Evangelista, who had been born in Uruguay but launched in Spain as a boxer. Evangelista, who was the European heavyweight champion, had gone fifteen rounds with Ali back in May '77. He was, like most European boxers, a stylist with no real punch. Those fifteen rounds with Ali, though, were like a credential for him, certifying him as legit enough to fight me, on network TV. ABC-TV execs could feel comfortable with a man who stood a chance of going the distance, enabling the network to shoehorn all their commercials in for the 50 million viewers expected to watch.

To me, Evangelista also had financial considerations attached. With whatever was still left of the $1.5 million purse that was due me, I would have the means to buy my mother a home and to set up housekeeping with Diane.

By the time I arrived in Vegas, Ali had regained the WBA title from Leon Spinks and was saying he expected to hold the title for six to eight months and then retire. Maybe. Maybe not. Knowing Ali like I did, I figured it would be hard for him to abandon the spotlight. All that attention was as natural to him as the air he breathed.

Whatever. Evangelista had gone fifteen rounds with Ali, and boasted that he had never been knocked out. After I fought him, he could no longer claim that. I knocked him out in the seventh round with a right cross from which he did not recover for nearly a minute.

Ossie Ocasio, the Puerto Rican heavyweight, was next, in March '79, and he wasn't much harder. I was a bit more leery, because Ocasio was awkward—punches came from strange angles—and he had a lot more power than Evangelista. But he was also too plodding to get out of the way of my jab. I was hitting him with it like a woodpecker drilling holes in a telephone pole. In the seventh round, I even knocked Ocasio down with a jab. At this level of boxing, guys are supposed to be too tough to floor with a jab. But damned if he didn't fall.

When he got up, I nailed him with a straight right and down

124

he went again. I knocked him down a third time, and still Ocasio managed to pull himself up. That's when Giachetti shouted at the referee, Carlos Padilla, "For God's sake, stop it before Larry kills him!"

But Padilla was braver than any of us. He asked Ocasio if he wanted to continue. Ocasio said yes—most fighters do. It's up to the referee to have enough sense to know when it's time to protect the boxer. Padilla, unfortunately, lacked that.

It took two rights and a left to send Ocasio down again, and this time Padilla finally got smart and stopped the fight, prompting *Sports Illustrated* to observe:

> *If Padilla hadn't called a halt when he did, the only way Ocasio would have made it back to the corner would have been on a stretcher. . . . There was no excuse for letting the young and inexperienced Puerto Rican take that much punishment. He was being paid $250,000 to fight, not to be demolished.*

It would not be the first time in my career when Giachetti or I would try to prompt the ref to step in and save the other man a beating. I always saw fighters as colleagues, decent guys using their bodies in a hard way to make a living. I hadn't the bloodlust some guys do, who actually enjoy beating their man to a pulp. For me, it was a competition, sure . . . but one with the logic of preservation. If it was a hurting business, it didn't have to be stupidly so.

Remember the film *Chinatown*, that tale of 1930s Los Angeles?

There was a moment in the film when John Houston, a millionaire businessman, says to Jack Nicholson, a private eye: "You may think you know what you're dealing with. But believe me you don't."

Nicholson smiles and says, "That's what the district attorney used to tell me in Chinatown."

"And," says Houston, "was he right?"

As right, it turns out, as Houston was in suggesting to Nicholson that there's often more than meets the eye in the affairs of men.

Well, I was reminded of that soon after the Ocasio fight when my brother Bob, realizing that King was ending up with as much money as I did from my fights, said it shouldn't be that way. He insisted that as the "talent" I should be getting the lion's share of the profit.

Bob was taking business courses in night school, learning how businesses were supposed to work—the law of supply and demand, stuff like that. I tried to tell him that it bothered me too, that I wasn't getting my full share, but any comparison between the fight game and a legit business was crazy. Boxing, like Chinatown, was inscrutable to an outsider.

But Bob persisted.

"You're the fighter," he said. "You're the product—the heavyweight champion of the world. You deserve a seventy percent or eighty percent share of your purse at least."

Bob is like me, he's got a one-track mind when it comes to fairness. And like me, he gets to be a pain in the ass when he thinks he's right.

We were sitting in a restaurant one day when the subject came up again . . . just as the coffee arrived. I started reaching for the sugar when I suddenly saw a way to explain things to Bob . . . and to me.

I took one of those sugar packets the waitress brings and said to Bob: "Look, King puts the sugar in the packet and gives it to me. I deserve more sugar, a lot more, but that packet is all I get. But it's also more sugar than I ever got before, more than I ever thought I was going to get. If I bitch too much or cause too much trouble or just plain stick up for what is fair, I might not even get that sugar packet. Bob, I got no power yet. What I'm going to do is collect and save as many of these packets as I possibly can, until my pile of sugar packets gets real high. I'd be a fool to think of the sugar I don't have because that could screw me up royally and make the sugar packets stop coming. Someday I might be able to take on the system, but for now I'll just keep collecting what the man gives me."

On principle, of course, Bob was right. The fight game was screwed. And even as a champion, the stench still reached my nostrils.

The thing that really got under my skin when I became champ was all the "favors"—the handouts and kickbacks and payoffs that were expected. Not that it was superbig bucks. But it grated on me just the same. The thing about it was that everybody was, like, "So what? That's how we in boxing do business."

There were writers who made it clear that they'd write good about you if you took care of them. "Taking care" usually meant picking up tabs for dinner, hotel rooms, things like that. It could mean cash payoffs too. For instance, it came out that King had given gifts and gratuities to a *Sports Illustrated* writer at the time of the U.S. Boxing Championships and in turn had gotten a favorable story on the tournament. When the magazine's editors discovered what had gone down, and even though King claimed the money he'd given was a loan, the writer—a talented guy having personal and money problems—was forced to resign.

Richie made a point of keeping the press happy. He thought it helped in getting "good ink"—and establishing the right image with the public. In that he was an echo of King. The way I saw it, it was all a total crock. There was something completely wrong about "the right image" if you had to pay for it. Whatever money was spread around was done through Richie and Don. I stayed out of it.

One of the biggest scams was the tickets for title fights. In the fight game tickets to big fights were treated exactly like hard cash. Main-event fighters, the managers, and promoters got plenty of "comps." Most of them went to family and friends, but there were usually tickets left over. Depending on the fight, they could be sold for hundreds of dollars. Or they could be exchanged for other valuable items, favors, or services.

There are guys who made a living hustling comps and then

scalping them. An old black guy they called "L.A. Flip" was a famous character you'd run into in Vegas. He's dead now. One time I needed a few extra seats for a Duran fight, and they were going for six hundred dollars. Flip had some, and even though I always helped him out over the years with comps, the old son of a bitch charged me eight hundred dollars. I said to him, "How come you're holding me up after all the times I helped you out, man?"

"Law of supply and demand. You want 'em or not?"

If it was someone else, I might have thrown a little scare into him, but Flip was around eighty years old at the time.

If a fight at one of the big hotel-casinos didn't sell out, King came around and told me I had to buy up some of the tickets. I know he did that with other fighters too. My guess is that he had an agreement with the casino that he'd buy some of the unsold tickets, but then he passed the expense on to the fighters. And because of the price of tickets, sometimes it could amount to more than a hundred grand. You didn't really have a choice. You don't say no to Don. Naturally, because those tickets are so valuable, they find their way into strange places. Some get scalped in the casinos, some out on the streets.

As champ, from time to time I'd be strongly "advised" to put a certain someone on my payroll. The adviser might be a big shot on a boxing commission or an officer in one of the sanctioning organizations. I was told at various times that by hiring Archie Moore or Jersey Joe Walcott or Beau Jack, I'd be helping myself a lot. It could be for just a single fight or for longer. Those are the kinds of favors to friends that tend to get remembered when close decisions come up in a fight.

Dick Young, the sports columnist for the *New York Daily News*, was a very powerful man in the press. He wrote good stuff about me in the early days. Not a lot of it, because I wasn't the champ, but it was always favorable. He told me one day that I'd really be helping myself a lot if I hired a certain woman to be my press agent. This woman was Young's lady friend. I knew her and liked her. She was a good press agent too, so I had nothing against hiring her. But for whatever reason, King didn't want her in the picture and that was that.

Well, with that Young's columns about me began to change. Eventually, there was never anything good, and some of the stories were downright nasty. He said I wasn't much of a fighter. He said I was stupid. He said I was a racist. And none of those things were there before I refused to hire his friend.

Even though I didn't like the nickel-and-dime graft that went on, it didn't surprise me. I'd seen it ever since I began working for Ali. Everyone in the fight game knew that's how things worked—dirty hands washing other dirty hands. And I sure wasn't ready to blow the whistle on it. I was no hero. I was ready to fight for what was right only up to a certain point, and that point was very clear—it was where my little sugar packets could be affected.

Even though I was champion, Ali still loomed. His retirement was rumored, but that didn't change things, really. When people thought of heavyweight boxing, they thought of Muhammad. I didn't resent him for that, but I did want to carve out my own niche, I did want the respect and attention that traditionally came to the heavyweight champion.

Sometimes I thought there was a kind of backlash against me because I was not Muhammad Ali. Even after I'd beaten Norton for the title, there were some in the press that made me out as a kind of bargain-basement champ, not worth the world's attention. There was one columnist, an Atlanta-based writer named Furman Bisher, who had written in *The Sporting News* that I was the "oops champion"—in other words, a kind of accident. Looking at the heavyweight division after the Norton fight, he wrote: "Then what do we have? Probably the only champion who never threw a punch except in self-defense." He was referring to me.

Or if he has [Bisher continued], *the other fellow waved back. The surprise is, after watching the fight from Las Vegas, that Holmes has knocked out 19 people. Of course, his victims included*

the immortal Howard Darlington, Bob Mashburn, and Joe Hath-
away, et al.

The thrust of his column was that I was a pitty-pat fighter, who ran rather than stood and fought. And this was *after* he saw the fight against Norton, which still ranks all these years later as one of the great action fights.

What are you going to do? Bisher was not a guy who followed boxing but rather a columnist who wrote about all sports. You know, one of those experts who knows more and more about less and less. And while the guys who covered boxing on a regular basis—Katz of *The New York Times*, Putnam from *Sports Illustrated*, Lisker and Izenberg from the *New York Post*, Young from the *New York Daily News*, Schuyler from the Associated Press—had given me my due, Bisher represented the marginal fan who knew boxing by its broad strokes, which in 1979 still meant Muhammad Ali.

Because of that I was eager to be in action as much as possible. If there had been a time when I'd only hoped to snatch a couple of paydays that would allow me to live a comfy middle-class Easton life, that had changed. Now that I had the title, I wanted more. I wanted to be seen as one of the great heavyweight champions in the sport's history.

No question, I was only now beginning to register on the public. At airports and out on the road, people would recognize me from having been on network TV. And while some of them might know who I was, others would get that look on their face, like: I know he's *somebody*, but . . . who? I'd be mistaken for other fighters and even guys from other sports. *Holmes, right. Ernie Holmes, Pittsburgh Steelers.*

That was okay. I figured I was in this now for the long run. And in time people would know me; I'd get my just dues, my "props" as they say out on ghetto streets these days. I'd get it by fighting regularly, and against the best fighters out there.

There was some question, after I beat Evangelista and Ocasio, if that was what I really had in mind when it was announced that

I was fighting Mike Weaver next. Weaver was not considered much of an opponent, even if he looked great, with a V-shaped Muscle Beach body—forty-four-inch chest, thirty-two-inch waist—that had led to his nickname of "Hercules."

But Weaver's record of 20–8 with 12 KOs suggested he was second-rate. In his very first two fights as a professional, he had been knocked out by and then decisioned by the same opponent, Howard Smith, in 1972. In the years that followed he had lost to both Bobick brothers, Rodney and Duane, and to Larry Frazier and Billy Ryan, who were not exactly household names in boxing.

Only the previous year, both Stan Ward and Leroy Jones had beaten him. But a managerial change supposedly had set him straight and Weaver had reeled off five straight knockout wins, numbering among his victims Ward and Bernardo Mercado, both reasonably good fighters.

Hercules' spotty record, the networks felt, made him unsuitable for prime-time exposure. The networks passed on the fight—the first time a world heavyweight championship fight would not be shown on home TV since Ali-Norton III in September '76. Instead a cable-TV newcomer to the sport, Home Box Office, stepped up and bought the television rights to the fight for practically pocket change—$150,000.

The fight would be on June 22, 1979, at Madison Square Garden. As the boxing business went, the Garden as the site of a heavyweight title fight was unusual. The big fights, then like now, routinely went to Las Vegas, Nevada, where the tax bite on fighters' purses was far kinder than in New York State. There hadn't been a heavyweight title fight at the Garden since the first time Smokin' Joe Frazier and Muhammad Ali went at it, in 1971.

But King had put the fight in the Garden because it was good business for Don King. See, earlier in the year, the new guy running the Garden, Sonny Werblin, had hired King to revive boxing at the arena that used to be called the "mecca" of the sport decades before.

Werblin didn't know diddly about boxing. Once, when he was

talking the sport with a reporter and the reporter mentioned the names of several fighters, Werblin's face clouded over and he said to the man: "How do you remember all those damn names?"

Between the lines what he was saying was that boxing was beneath him, a gutter sport. But Werblin was too much a businessman to let personal taste interfere with his profit margin. He knew boxing could fill the seats in his building. And so he did what had worked for him in the past: he went for the big name.

When he was a showbiz talent agent, he had seen what could happen when your agency had stars like Jack Benny and Johnny Carson.

When he was running the New York Jets football team in the 1960s, Werblin had paid $411,000 for a three-year contract, unheard-of money at the time, for Joe Namath to be his quarterback. A Super Bowl team was, eventually, the result.

Once installed at the Garden, he had fixed up the Ranger hockey team by bringing in a new coach–general manager, Fred Shero, and two Swedish stars from the rival World Hockey Association, Ulf Nilsson and Anders Hedberg. Through the addition of these big names, the Rangers went from being a collection of sluggards to a bona fide team that got to the finals of the Stanley Cup playoffs. Werblin didn't know too many "damn names" in boxing, but he knew Don King's because King was a genius at self-promotion, working overtime to make himself bigger than his fighters. And in most cases he was. Werblin had hired him on a nonexclusive basis to restore the Garden's reputation as a boxing presence. And King figured putting a heavyweight title bout in the Garden would make him look good with Werblin and the Gulf & Western corporate big shots that at the time owned the Garden.

Never mind that Larry Holmes might have done better, financially, had the fight gone to Vegas. For Don King boxing was not about the fighters; it was about taking care of K-i-n-g. As I told the press: "I'm not getting a guarantee, just a percentage at the gate, maybe $500,000, maybe $750,000."

King put his own spin on it, making me out to be a kind of riverboat gambler:

"He's putting everything on the line. He's risking losing the championship and remember—'upset' is the largest word in the dictionary when it comes to boxing. More than that, he's risking his $3 million fight with Earnie Shavers in September. No one has ever come into the Garden and risked a championship without a guarantee.

"But he wants to be a fighting champion and he wants to be the people's champion. And he knows New York is the greatest city in the world for media. If it comes out of New York, it comes out ten times bigger than anywhere in the world."

While training for the fight, Weaver, who was getting $50,000, acted like a man who wasn't intimidated by the idea of going up against Larry Holmes.

"I think about winning the title," he told reporters. "I think about the things that come with it, about walking the streets and hearing people say, 'There's the champ.'

"Holmes is a good fighter, not a great one. I believe I can beat him. Hercules is a myth, I'm not."

Whatever he was, Weaver gave me a hard time on fight night. He was helped by my having been hit by the flu a week before the bout and having used antibiotics to beat it. The antibiotics made my body sluggish. I felt strange, dreamy.

Weaver added to that feeling by hitting me with some big punches in the fourth round, stunning me.

"Come on, Big Jack. Wake up!" Giachetti shouted from the corner.

But I was just plain flat. No spring in my legs, little snap in my jab.

When I came back to the corner, Giachetti started insulting me.

"Goddamn it, let's go," he said. "You look like shit out there. What the hell's the matter with ya?"

In the fifth round my left eye began swelling shut after being thumbed by Weaver, and I couldn't see him very clearly for a while. He took advantage by hitting me on the ear with a hard right hand. I didn't go down from the punch, but it hurt like hell and then I heard these echoes in my head. Every sound, even my own heart beating, had a spooky echo to it. It was frightening out there, not seeing clearly and hearing strange sounds in my head.

Between rounds Giachetti reduced the swelling around the eye, pressing it with his thumb and ice. Gradually my vision cleared. My eardrum was punctured, so the echoes stayed.

The sight of me getting whacked around shook Diane. She ran from her seat to the ring steps in a panic. I looked down and told her to pipe down and go back to where she was supposed to be.

An underdog who puts up a scrappy fight often gets the sympathy of the crowd, and many among the 14,136 paying customers at the Garden started rooting for Weaver. By the eleventh round, he had me against the ropes and was pasting me with some good shots. Chants of "Weave-ah, Weave-ah" rang out through the building. It looked like I was in big trouble.

But that's when I reached down and found an answer. I unloaded an uppercut to the head that dropped Weaver onto the canvas and left him sagging against the ropes. His legs were split awkwardly, the way a hockey goalie looks after the puck has whizzed past him. The referee, Harold Valan, began counting.

By now I was exhausted. Between the flu and what Weaver had been doing to me, it had been a hard night's work. Damn hard. As I retreated to the neutral corner, I was hoping like hell that Weaver wouldn't beat the count. But he did . . . barely. And then the bell ending the round sounded a few seconds later and Weaver headed back to his corner on shaky legs.

After eleven rounds, I was up by a few points on the scorecards of all three officials, including Valan's. In those days in New York, the referee scored the fight along with two judges. But for what was billed as a tune-up for a big-money showdown with Earnie Shavers in September, this had been a whole lot more work than I'd anticipated. I was determined to end it in the twelfth.

At the bell starting round twelve, I saw Weaver had not fully recovered from the knockdown, so I let the punches fly. Forty-four seconds into the round, Valan threw his arms around Weaver and it was all over. Valan told the press: "He couldn't defend himself. He didn't know where he was. I even asked him if he was all right and he couldn't answer."

Thank God, it was over. Weaver had hit me with some serious leather. It had been a war in there. During the fight, I had told him at one point: "Man, I'm going to kill you for my [championship] belt." And he had answered, "I'm gonna get it."

He hadn't failed for lack of trying. That record of his, now 20–9, gave a false impression of the kind of fighter he was. Weaver wasn't especially clever in the ring. But he was strong, and he could punch. It didn't surprise me when less than a year later, in March 1980—nine months after Ali announced he was retiring from boxing—Weaver pulled off a shocking upset for Ali's vacated WBA title. In the fifteenth and final round, far behind on the scorecards against John Tate, Weaver connected with a powerful right hand that dropped Tate dead in his tracks. Boom—one punch and that was it. Fifteenth-round knockout.

But he hadn't been able to finish me. The important thing for me was on a difficult night I rose to the challenge and kept my title. There was something in me—a will, a hunger—that could not be stopped. It took over even when I didn't really want to fight, and it got stronger whenever I got hurt. My sugar packets would keep coming. My share of the purse was $250,000 of the $400,000 announced to the public.

As for Diane, when she reached the dressing room, I told her in a croaking voice—Weaver had hit me in the throat: "You were scared. I told you, never get scared unless I'm scared. And if I'm scared that will be enough for both of us."

I was well aware that HBO's audience of 2 million subscribers and the 14,000-plus at the Garden hadn't seen Larry Holmes at his best. Some in the boxing press thought I had taken Weaver for granted. They didn't know about the flu and antibiotics problem. I had kept that to myself.

Just the same I wanted to make an impression in my next fight, a rematch against Earnie Shavers. The last time we had boxed it had been to see which of us would fight Norton for the title. This time the heavyweight crown, my WBC belt, would be at stake.

Shavers had fought his way back into contention earlier in the year, on the night I beat up Ocasio in Las Vegas. On the same card, Earnie had knocked out Norton in one round, instantly regaining his star status.

You didn't have to be Einstein to know what the deal was when you fought Earnie. Earnie was no ballet dancer. He was the heavy artillery of his weight class and Lord help you if that right hand of his landed. He had fifty-five KOs in sixty-six fights. That he'd knocked out Norton, who was industrial-strength tough, told me what I knew already, from sparring with Shavers at $145 a week and from fighting him previously. I didn't want this guy hitting me.

But the prospect that he *might* was enough to bring ABC-TV back aboard. The network would televise the bout, which was set for September 28 in Las Vegas, prime time. My purse? Two-point-five million.

Earnie was sure that this time the result would be different. At the news conference to announce the fight, he told me: "A few more weeks, man, and you'll be mine."

"No way, brother," I said. "I beat you once, and I can do it again. I know you too well. Nothing you can do I haven't seen before."

That's when he held up his right fist and grinned. "But you been lucky. You ain't never got trumped by this five of clubs."

Well, that five of clubs seemed an idle threat through the first six rounds. I was having my way with Shavers. Earnie had never been nimble on his feet, which made him a target for a guy who could move smartly and jab. As he came in, Earnie was lunging to get at me, and throwing wild, looping punches . . . Western Union punches . . . telegraphed from way out and easy enough to avoid. Not only avoid but counter with rapid-strike combinations that by the fifth round had his left eye starting to close. Then, in the sixth, I hit him with a flurry that opened a cut over his right eye that bled profusely and would require twenty-seven stitches afterward.

Round seven. You could see Earnie was hurt bad. I liked the guy, and didn't relish giving him a beating. What for? Let him take his $300,000 purse and go home. Like me, Earnie had had it hard when he was young—picking cotton and working for the Baltimore & Ohio Railroad and on assembly lines for Republic Steel and General Motors. What was the point of his taking a beating?

As we maneuvered in center ring, I told him: "I'm beating you up, man. Don't keep taking this, Earnie."

At that moment, I saw an opening for my uppercut and let it fly. That's when I saw a blinding flash. I was sure a photographer's flashbulb had gone off right in my eyes. But no . . . Holy Christ, I was down and struggling to get upright. My legs felt like Jell-o. Above the roar of the crowd a voice in my head was screaming: "Get up. Get the fuck up! He's taking your championship. Your championship."

I got to my feet at the count of five, and began jumping up and down to clear my head. The news accounts described my eyes as being glazed.

The referee, little Davey Pearl, gave me the mandatory eight count.

After the fight Pearl would be quoted as saying: "An ordinary fighter would have stood there dazed and helpless, waiting to be knocked down again. But as stunned as he must have been, Holmes reacted the way a smart seasoned fighter should."

In fact, rather than stand right by Pearl, I began moving away from him—in doing so, putting more distance between Shavers (standing in a nearby neutral corner) and me. That would buy me precious time—the time it would take for Pearl to walk over to me to wipe my gloves. . . . the time it would take for Shavers to take those few extra steps to get at me. Face it, I was in survival mode, doing every damn thing I could to gather my wits.

Well, Earnie came at me like a wild rhino, knowing this was as good a chance as he'd ever have to be heavyweight champion.

My thinking was strictly defensive. Hold him, grab him, don't let the son of a bitch hit me again. As he threw wild rights, I managed to draw him into a clinch, and when Pearl broke us, I tied Shavers up again. I felt his strength as he tried desperately to shake me loose so he could punch again. But I was hanging on for my boxing life. When the bell rang, I made my way back to the corner.

Giachetti broke an ammonia capsule under my nose, then slapped cold water on me to awaken my senses. Freddie Brown, the assistant trainer, broke another ammonia capsule.

"Look at me," Giachetti said. "Go out there and double jab. Hit and move. Move to the right, keep away from his power. Do you hear me? Do you?"

"Yeah."

"Tell me back."

I repeated what he had said.

Earnie Shavers was thirty-four years old on the night we fought, and fortunately for me he now began to show it. The right hand that knocked me down was Shavers's last hurrah. By the eighth round, he was showing signs of fatigue. Round by round, he became more and more exhausted as I potshot him. By the eleventh, he was falling back into the ropes, his arms at his sides. He was struggling to keep upright. But somehow, he would will his way into the battle again and come at me. By now I was turning to Pearl, and with my eyes asking him to stop the fight. I just didn't want to hit Earnie Shavers any more. His right eye was a mess. He was out of gas.

Pearl stopped the fight momentarily to inspect Shavers's eye, but decided he could continue. I hit Earnie with two more punches and the referee finally waved me off. The fight was over.

As Earnie stumbled back to his corner, I followed him, put my arms around his shoulders, and told him: "I love you. You're a great fighter. You're a man."

That night as I walked through the casino at Caesars Palace, and acknowledged the congratulations of the people, I noticed in the air-cooled lobby three huge cutouts of Shavers, me, and

Don King which had advertised the bout. I also noticed that King was the central figure, and loomed larger than either of his fighters.

So much you put up with to get to the top of the mountain.

Not just the jive bullshitters like King, looking to seduce and then reduce you as a man.

Simply put: it was hard damn work. But you know what? I loved it. I loved the sweat and toil, loved the early-morning runs in Vegas, Giachetti driving the rented Lincoln out toward the rust-colored mountains west of the city, where Sahara Boulevard narrowed to one dusty lane in the desert.

I'd get out of the car and kid my brother Jake, who would do roadwork with me: "Come on, Jakey. God wants you to feel the pain with me."

In training, I was in my world, in charge, whether in the early phases in Easton or out in this *Treasure of the Sierra Madre* desert that was where we ran.

Training was hard but it was good. No one could tell me what to do or how to do it or when. And I was with other fighters, guys like me who understood what was going on in the ring like no one else did. Mostly they were fighters I was comfortable and friendly with.

In the ring I was in touch with my deepest instincts. And I usually liked the way my reflexes felt when they were sharp. I guess you could say that was how I expressed myself. I even liked the way the gym smelled, the smell of sweaty, honest work. I felt clean inside and out after a hard workout. And it always felt good afterward just to hang around and eat with the other fighters, talking about fighting or just messing around.

I suppose being heavyweight champion made it easier to feel that way. I suppose all the hard work would have felt different if like, say, Roy Williams, I hadn't gotten my shot. It was, when you came down to it, easier to feel at ease with the hard wages of a boxer when you could look at it through the rose-colored glasses of a champion.

One day I was a nobody, with next to nothing in my savings account. Now I was a fellow they were very happy to see at the Lafayette Trust Bank.

Your life changes.

Two days before Christmas '79, Diane and I were married.

I bought us our first house on Gordon Drive in Easton for eighty-five thousand dollars. A trilevel home—four bedrooms, two bathrooms, a fireplace, a porch, and a nice yard. I was proud of it.

I also bought Mom her own place. This was a little trickier because she wanted to be near her friends in the projects. But I managed to find a half-acre tract nearby and built her a home there with three bedrooms and two baths. Price: sixty thousand dollars. A nice little place she would feel comfortable in.

But she no sooner had moved in than she got worried sick. Seems like her know-nothing friends from the projects began buzzing in her ear, saying that Don King would steal all my money because he was a sharpie and I was a seventh-grade dropout. And that would leave her, according to these neighborhood gossips, out on the street.

I told her: "Mom, your house is all paid for. No one can take it away from you."

She believed me, but only until the next genius told her different.

Finally, I went to the bank vault, got out the deed, stuck it in her hand, and pointed to where it said, "Paid in Full."

But I understood exactly how she felt. If you haven't had anything for so much of your life, making do for your family with welfare payments and Salvation Army clothes, when you finally have something really valuable, you believe that someone can come along and take it away.

When you've been where the Holmeses of Cuthbert have, Easy Street sounds too good to be true.

CHAPTER
TEN

Muhammad Ali, Muhammad Ali, Muhammad Ali.

With 1980, increasingly I was hearing Ali's name as a potential opponent.

Even as I was beating Lorenzo Zanon in February (KO 6) and Leroy Jones in March (TKO 8), the rumor mill was flogging the notion that Ali—grown fat and sassy in his retirement, and graying around the temples—would be coming back. Coming back to show his old sparring partner he was still the topcat, still the show.

In the year and a half since he'd regained the title from Spinks, I'd run into him at fights, and at various boxing functions. He didn't look like a guy who wanted to fight again. Where once he had been matinee-idol handsome—or "pretty," as he liked to say—now he was all chubby cheeks and hair prematurely gray for a thirty-eight-year-old man. Not to mention he weighed fifty pounds more than when he had boxed.

And while thirty-eight was young for a man, it was old for an athlete and taps for a fighter.

Ali was my friend. I loved the guy. And I loved teasing him once I had the title. I'd tell him that if he came back I'd whup his butt like I did when we sparred.

He'd say, "Ma-a-a-n, Larry, I never showed you my best stuff in the gym just in case I ever had to lay it on you someday."

I kept hearing the rumors he would fight again, but I didn't really believe he would get himself back in shape. What's more, I'd noticed even before he retired he was beginning to slur his words and pause a lot. I figured he'd noticed too, and wouldn't want to tempt fate. But then again, Ali was, like a lot of fighters, a sucker for that spotlight. A fame junkie.

Since his retirement, Ali had kept in the public eye, touring the world. In Russia, he met with Soviet leader Leonid Brezhnev. Later, U.S. president Jimmy Carter sent him to Africa on what *Time* magazine would call "the most bizarre diplomatic mission in recent U.S. history." Carter wanted Ali to explain our position on boycotting the 1980 Moscow Olympics—Russia had just invaded Afghanistan, remember?—to African leaders . . . and persuade them to join with us in boycotting. Well, the news reports that followed indicated the trip was a bomb—that Ali was out of his depth.

Would he, or wouldn't he . . . come back?

I wasn't eager to fight him. I felt he was shot as a fighter and all I could do was inflict hurt on him, give him a beating that might be injurious to his health.

I sure as hell wished there was another fighter out there with the marquee magic Ali had so I could make the big dough. But the best names were gone. Smokin' Joe had retired after Foreman beat him a second time, in June '76. Foreman? He had lost to Jimmy Young in March '77 in steamy San Juan and, while thoroughly dehydrated and delirious and feeling close to death, claimed to have had a spiritual vision in the dressing room afterward. As he told a reporter: "I couldn't see anything. It was like being hopelessly lost at sea. I thought: 'This is it. I'm dead.' There was a horrible smell and a feeling of loneliness. Then it was like a giant hand pulled me out—I wasn't scared anymore. I had collapsed onto the floor, with people all around me, my brothers Roy and Robert, my trainer Gil Clancy. They picked me off the floor. 'It's okay,' I told them. 'I'm dying. But tell everybody I'm dying for God.' "

Big George took that vision as his cue to become a preacher, and by 1980 he was out there on the streets, speaking the Word.

Leaving me without any box-office names to fight. The best of them—Norton, Weaver, and Shavers—I had already beaten. Where was the serious money going to come from?

Enter Harold Smith.

In November 1979, Smith, a Los Angeles–based newcomer to boxing promotions, had knocked on the door of my hotel suite in Las Vegas.

I was in town to watch Sugar Ray Leonard fight Wilfredo Benitez for the welterweight title.

Don King happened to be in my suite when Smith knocked. Seeing who it was, Donald told Smith to take his black ass and be on his way.

Smith wouldn't leave; he said he wanted to talk to me.

I was busy inside the suite and could hear but couldn't see them arguing back and forth, in the language of the streets. It got loud and nasty and eventually Smith left.

Later, Smith, who was a tall athletic man—a 4:10 miler at American University in Washington, D.C—told me he had left only because King had waved a pistol at him.

Boxing guys bullshit, but maybe Donald did pull the gun. A few years later, in 1987, he would try to enter the ring at the conclusion of the Leonard-Hagler fight, a Bob Arum promotion. When Arum, who is white, saw him, Arum grabbed King and a scuffle ensued. When a black Caesars Palace security guard intervened, King became angry and indignant and called the guard an "Uncle Tom." It was reported that while King and Arum wrestled, a gun fell out of King's pocket.

In any case, that would not be the last of Harold Smith in my life. As King's name had been bandied about at Deer Lake and beyond in the early 1970s, so was Smith's at the start of the 1980s. My pal Saoul Mamby, a fighter I'd known from the Gleason's Gym days, roused my interest with this tale:

Mamby said that one morning the phone had rung in his Bronx apartment and Smith was on the other end, asking him to stop by his office to talk business. Mamby, who had just won the WBC junior welterweight title in February '80, grabbed a pencil to jot the address, thinking Smith was in New York.

But no, Smith wanted him to leave immediately for the airport and fly to L.A.

"Just go to the airport; your ticket will be waiting," Smith told him. "Oh . . . and bring your woman if you'd like."

When Saoul got to the airport, he stood in line and the ticket agent asked his name. He told her and there was a pause, so he figured: "Typical boxing bullshit." But no . . . it turned out he was flying first-class.

Mamby had been fighting since 1969 and for most of his career had been promoted by King. And even though he was a champion, he had never flown first-class before in his life. In L.A. there would be a limousine to meet him and an offer from Smith he couldn't and didn't refuse: $75,000 for one fight and another $75,000 in cash as a bonus. Mamby flew back to the Bronx $150,000 richer than when he left. It wasn't quite Michael Anthony from the 1950s TV show, dispensing a million. But damn, it was plenty good.

Word was out that Smith was doing for other fighters what he had for my friend Saoul—paying them big money to fight for him. I figured if that was the case, then for sure he would be knocking on my door again. So I looked into just who this Harold Smith was. And since his boxing organization was called Muhammad Ali Professional Sports (MAPS), I checked him out with Ali. Ali said he had first lent his name to Smith a few years before for Smith's track-and-field promotions, and again later for his boxing ventures. In return, Smith agreed to pay him a percentage of the net profits of MAPS-sponsored events as well as personal-appearance fees. Ali told me Smith met all his payments and that he had had no problem with Harold Smith.

It seemed to me that Smith was doing what King had done when he persuaded Foreman to let him make the fight in Zaire—he was using black solidarity patter and the promise of big cash to attract the sport's big names. Compared to King, Harold worked at a lower pitch. King was loud and forceful. Harold was smooth and relaxed. In August '79, Ken Norton and Scott Le Doux fought to a draw in a MAPS promotion. Norton, who had been knocked out in his previous fight by Shavers, got $100,000, Le Doux $15,000. Tommy Hearns fought for Smith a month later in Los Angeles.

The scuttlebutt intensified that Smith was willing to give huge piles of cash that he sometimes brought to fighters in pillowcases or shoe boxes if they would sign with him. When Le Doux lost to Mike Weaver by decision in November '79 in Bloomington, Minnesota, Michael Spinks was on the card in a cofeature, knocking out Marc Hans in one round. Two hours later, as Spinks's promoter, Butch Lewis, would recall, strange developments occurred.

"The fight was over," said Lewis. "I'm in my suite. Here comes Mike, knocking on the door. He says to me, 'What's going on here? And he tells me about Harold Smith. Harold Smith took him a briefcase with $250,000 in cash with a contract sitting on top. We go look for Smith. Smith's in the lobby. Grinning. With a cowboy hat on."

By Lewis's account, Smith's grin disappeared when Butch told him where he could stick his briefcase. Well, just as I expected, Harold Smith was back at my door in March '80 when I fought Leroy Jones in Vegas, offering me $1.3 million to fight Scott Le Doux.

"I'll give you a couple hundred thou in cash," he said. "You don't mind cash, do you? And one-point-one in a letter of credit."

"Sounds good to me," I told him.

Somehow Don King got wind of Smith's arrival and came storming up to my room as Harold and I were walking out.

"What are you doing with my fighter?" he demanded.

"I'm offering him Scott Le Doux for more money than you'd ever give him," Smith told him.

King called Harold a "scumbag," and they went at one another with name-calling. They were ready to fight; people got between them.

As Smith and I went down in the elevator, King told him: "I'm gonna walk your ass down." Meaning: I'm gonna get you. But King's little scare show didn't seem to faze Smith.

Later, King had me come by his room.

"This guy's a criminal," he said. "Nobody knows where his money is coming from. Stay away. You want Le Doux, I got the fight for you."

King made the Le Doux fight for July 7, 1980, in Bloomington, Minnesota, and guaranteed me $800,000—half a million dollars less than Smith was offering. I agreed to the fight. I figured if I tried bolting King, he wouldn't take it lying down. I was in the prime of my boxing life. Maybe Smith could pony up more than King for fighting Le Doux. But if I went for it, for sure I'd end up in court going up against King's high-priced lawyers. To defend against them would cost me plenty and might even eat up the difference between what King thought was fair for fighting Le Doux and what I could get out of Harold Smith. Was it really worth it?

Well, the question got pushed to the limit not long after when Smith phoned me in Easton and asked if I would meet him if he flew in on his private jet. It was May 1980. I remember the date because it was just after Diane gave birth to our daughter, Kandy. I said sure. At the time I had an office in the Alpha Building, one of Easton's oldest, right on The Circle in the center of town. The office had no air-conditioning, and the day Smith flew in turned out to be one of the hottest days of the year. I asked Charlie Spaz to backstop the meeting, knowing that the way Harold operated

I might need to have on-the-spot legal advice as well as a reliable witness.

Then I did something on impulse. I phoned Don King in New York and let him know his nemesis, Harold Smith, would be meeting with me shortly in Easton. Talk about pissed. King ranted and raved, and said I'd be sorry—Harold Smith, he insisted, was bad news. Besides, hadn't he, Don King, done right by me, guided me to a title and kept me out of the hands of the sharks? Lordy, Lordy: the man could say some far-out wild and woolly stuff when he was under siege.

"I don't have time to argue with you, Don," I said. "Harold will be here any second. I just didn't want to do anything behind your back."

That part was true. But it was also true that I wanted to put a little squeeze on Don and make him competitive. Mostly I wanted to worry his ass.

"Don't be signing anything," he said. "I'm on my way."

Smith showed up in a stretch limousine that I saw pull up from my office window. He had two sexy women with him and a man he referred to as his business associate. They waited behind while Spaz, Harold, and I went into my inner office.

Smith got right to the point. He was prepared to pay me $5 million to fight Muhammad Ali, $2 million of it right here and now if I signed an agreement giving him promotional rights.

The talk was that Ali was thinking seriously of unretiring so that he could fight me. Smith said that if he was unable to get Ali's signature or for any reason the fight fell through . . . that $2 million was mine, free and clear. He'd pay me the other $3 million when Ali agreed to the fight. Spaz poked at his offer with a few legal questions, but the deal was the deal. Five million to fight Ali, as sweet an offer as had ever been made to me.

I was sweating profusely and stepped over to the window to cool off.

"That's a lot of money you're talking about," I told Smith. "How do I know your money's any good?"

That's when Harold dipped into his pocket and pulled up two peach-colored checks.

"Larry," he said, "here are two checks drawn on the Wells Fargo Bank, each for five hundred thousand dollars. If they don't clear, we don't have a deal. Your lawyer will tell you that. What have you got to lose?"

Harold Smith waved those checks with obvious pleasure, savoring my reaction. At the sight of those two peach-colored beauties, I was damn near salivating. The sweat was trickling down my cheeks and along my rib cage.

The room grew a whole lot steamier when Smith made his next move.

"To show you the confidence I have in you, Larry, that's not all I'm offering."

He now laid on my desk a lightweight leather case that opened up like a pillowcase and exposed the contents—piles of cash, old bills in denominations of twenties and fifties and hundreds.

"Here's a million dollars, cash, if you agree," he said.

Michael Anthony had finally made it to my doorstep, and he was a black man. He was Harold Smith, and it was a helluva show. I'd never seen so much hard cash in all my life. Even Spaz, usually a cool cookie, was bowled over. His eyebrows soared north, he was speechless.

Man, was it hot in that office.

I was shook. I won't pretend otherwise. I stalled Harold with questions about this and that, waiting for King to show up. I had no doubt he was driving like a maniac at this very moment, making like he was the cavalry riding to the rescue. The offer was so stunning, it was hard to think. I wanted to hear King tell me why I shouldn't take the money. The money Smith was talking was serious enough that I just might be willing to buck up against that high-priced legal talent of King's. Might just be willing to tell him: "See you in court, jack."

When he finally got to Easton, King came on like gangbusters, cursing Smith and pointing fingers and making threats. Harold didn't scare. That impressed me. For me the crucial issue was—

where did all this money that Harold Smith was throwing around come from?

King told Smith: "I had you checked out with Dunn and Bradstreet and they couldn't find any legal business you owned."

I doubted King had gone to that trouble.

"Like I've told Larry," said Smith, "my backers are oil men from the Middle East who want to be anonymous."

He was responding to King, but really talking to me.

"The money is clean, Larry," Smith said. "Ask any of my fighters. You can call 'em now, right in front of me. I don't care."

I just listened.

Harold went on: "There's plenty of money with these backers and Don's pissed 'cause for the first time it's going to the fighters and not to guys like him."

King and Smith went back to arguing and cursing. If anybody had been standing under the window out there on the street and heard the kind of threats being made, he'd have been obliged to dial 911 and ask 'em to send a squad car.

Don kept saying Harold's loot was drug money. And truthfully, I couldn't think of any other explanation for all that cash in a goddamn pillowcase. That wasn't the way respectable men did business. If Harold Smith had had two more of those little peach-colored checks, I might have signed. But that pillowcase was something else. Finally, I told Harold Smith I had to pass it up this time around.

Smith didn't push it. He said, "The money's good, and it's always here for you, Larry. Think it over."

If he was desperate, I figured he would have pushed a little more. But no, he just said to think over his offer. He wished me good luck against Scott Le Doux and said he'd keep in touch.

Smith called me at home about a month later with another interesting offer. A million dollars for the right to promote any two of my fights. The million would be in addition to my purses. I never heard of a deal quite like it. Just kind of joking, I said, "Harold, I already have a million."

"Larry, I'll make it two million." He wasn't joking at all.

I'd have thought the guy was blowing smoke if I hadn't already seen the color of his money—peach and green. I passed that deal up too. Funny, all my career I was complaining that managers and promoters were ripping me off, and when a guy finally came along who wanted to pay me what I think I'm really worth, I got scared off.

But the subject of Harold Smith was not dead. When we got to Minnesota, while training for Le Doux, Giachetti said maybe it *was* time to put King in his place and give Smith a chance.

"Hey, we'd get more money, a better promotion with this guy," Giachetti said. "Don don't give us the goddamn money."

King somehow found out what Giachetti was recommending, and had us come by his room.

King was pissed. "What the fuck are you telling Larry?" he said to Giachetti.

The two of them got to arguing and cursing one another, really heating it up with threats. Finally Giachetti charged at King and threw him backward onto his bed. With his fist cocked, Richie started toward Donald when an aide of King's, Duke Durden, and I grabbed Richie and pulled him back.

"Don't you *never* put your hands on me!" King screamed, as he raised up in bed. "I'll fuck you up. I'll kill your ass."

"Try it and I'll kill *you* right now," Giachetti answered.

"I'll walk you down, motherfucker," King said.

"You ain't shit, nigger. All your talk about brothers this and brothers that . . . and you fuck *all* the brothers. Cheat 'em out of their money."

Whoo boy. The air was thick in that room. I pulled Richie out of there.

Giachetti could go off like that. I'd seen it before. We'd be crossing a street somewhere—he'd see a guy looking at him. And: "What the hell are you looking at?"

But in this case he had stood up to King, and for the right reasons.

King *was* taking advantage. But for now at least it went back to the sugar packets argument. I'd been a long time without them.

Maybe King wasn't overly generous with the sugar. But it was a whole lot more than I'd ever had.

And after I knocked out Le Doux in seven rounds, King did what other promoters tried but couldn't do. He got Muhammad Ali's signature on the dotted line. King, bullshitter that he was, claimed he'd talked Ali into fighting me. Not so. Ali simply needed the money. The same old story.

The last time Muhammad and I had traded punches, I had let him feel as if he were still the man. Remember that open-ended sparring session? I'd held back and told him I quit. This time I'd show him the real deal. It was my turn now.

CHAPTER
ELEVEN

When the Holmes-Ali match was announced, the oddsmakers made me a 3–1 favorite.

The odds would narrow by a lot, as money came in backing Ali. That was understandable. The public's affection for and support of Muhammad ran deep.

But anybody who wagered on Ali for reasons other than sentiment—who truly believed he was *still* the fighter he had been in his prime—was deluded.

Ali had not been the same since he and Smokin' Joe went at it in Manila in '75. That fight had seen the last flicker of his genius. And even then he was an athlete in decline.

In fact, one of his corner men, the doctor Ferdie Pacheco, had abandoned the Ali camp in '77 as a kind of statement. He felt that Ali risked permanent injury by continuing to fight and should retire.

In the five years since the Thrilla in Manila, Ali had gotten victories that owed more to his popularity than to his performance, against Jimmy Young (April '76) and against Norton (September '76). And after that he had only gotten older and slower, incapable of the kind of movement and volume of punching that had made him unique among heavyweights.

Never mind that he had regained the title for the third time against Leon Spinks in '78. Spinks was a boxing beginner, and the fight Ali waged against him was a nonfight, with Ali holding and playacting at aggression. He'd bullshitted his way to the victory, and everybody pretended it was the greatest thing since the Wright brothers got their plane up at Kitty Hawk.

Hell, Spinks had had eight fights when he'd beaten Ali. He was raw and inexperienced—a boxer who'd been lucky to get a draw against Scott Le Doux in an earlier fight. Yet folks wanted to view Ali as still being the man who could float like a butterfly, sting like a bee. It was the emperor's clothes. Nobody wanted to say Ali had been stripped naked of the gift he'd had.

It put me in a tricky position. A no-win situation, really. What would it prove if I beat a thirty-eight-year-old Ali? Not much. People would do an about-face on Muhammad and say, "Well, it wasn't the real Ali."

And if I lost—as impossible as that seemed to me—it would be disastrous. It would negate and nullify all that I had accomplished. I told the press that if that were to happen, I would quit the sport.

Yet what could I do? I believed Ali had no business fighting me. He was far past his prime and, I sincerely believed, would be batting practice for me. I did not relish the idea of beating him up in public view.

If, however, I tried to wriggle out of a fight with him, it would make me look lame—as if I was afraid. Afraid? Please. Since the midseventies, I believed I could whup the man, and suspected he had come to the same conclusion too. How else to account for his avoiding me at a time I was a world-ranked fighter, and instead taking on chumps like Wepner, Jean Pierre Coopman, Richard Dunn, and Evangelista.

Ali was my friend. I was fond of the man, and grateful for his help in my career. He was not a saint, even if here at the end of his career folks were beginning to think of him as one. I had seen moments of bad behavior—abusing sparring partners and taunting opponents cruelly. I had seen an Ali who could be self-absorbed and occasionally cruel to those close to him. Yet for the most part he was a good man, generous and enormous fun to be around.

He had a real flair for and vision of being more than just a fighter. He had sought, and gotten, a stage that was larger than any fighter had ever known. It wasn't simply because he was a prize specimen in the ring. It was more than that. He was a personality, a sunny and quick-witted man who engaged the larger world.

In fact, when talk first surfaced of Ali coming back to fight me, Muhammad had seen a bigger opportunity. At that time, during the presidential administration of Jimmy Carter, Iran was holding dozens of Americans captive. Remember the outrage of our citizens on seeing our blindfolded hostages being paraded before the Iranian public?

Well, Ali thought he could free the hostages by offering to stage our match—Holmes vs. Ali—in Tehran. Okay, Ayatollah. You get the fight, free of charge, live and in color. We get the hostages. That was what Ali was proposing.

"The day the hostages are released, give me two weeks to get my crew together and then two more weeks to get there," Ali told reporters.

"I'll train in Iran for four weeks before the fight. I have a lot of fans in Iran. There are a lot of God-fearing Muslims there. They've been wanting me to come to Iran for years."

For whatever reason, it didn't happen that way. Holmes-Ali was not a diplomatic tool but rather business as usual. The fight was set for Caesars Palace in Las Vegas on October 2, 1980. But because of the box-office potential, the casino decided the 4,500-seat Sports Pavilion was too small for a fight of this magnitude. Caesars went ahead and constructed an outdoor arena in

Family portrait, Sept. 23, 1982 (from left to right): Daughter Kandy, wife Diane, the infant Larry Jr., and heavyweight champion Holmes.

Holmes's championship ring. The date June 9, 1978 represents the night he won the WBC title from Ken Norton in a grueling match.

The Home of **LARRY HOLMES!**
WBC CHAMP "The Easton Assassin"

Holmes: "I was never more comfortable than when I was in Easton, Pennsylvania." The champion's hometown was proud of his accomplishments. Here a banner hangs from the St. Anthony's Youth Center, proclaiming its support.

Holmes on broadcaster
Howard Cosell:
"A front-running phoney."

Holmes, shown here with son Larry Jr., 5, peeking through the ropes, and daughter Kandy, 7, watching from below, chats with spectators following a workout at his training center in Easton.

Holmes with promoter Don King, remembered as "an equal-opportunity abuser." King once threatened to have Holmes's legs broken when Larry told him he might switch promoters.

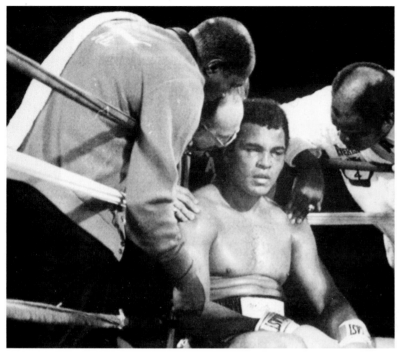

Holmes on beating his boyhood hero, Muhammad Ali, in Oct. 1980: "In between rounds, I sat on the stool and prayed I wouldn't have to hurt him." Holmes stopped Ali in 11 rounds and cried afterward.

By the mid-1980s, Holmes could boast of a business empire that included a five-story office building on 3.2 acres on Larry Holmes Drive in Easton. Here he takes in the view from the office of Larry Holmes Enterprises.

Holmes in his office with former
heavyweight champion,
Jersey Joe Walcott.

Over the years Holmes has given back to
the Easton community, through financial
support of youth programs and through
fund-raising events like his "Run with the
Champion" race, above.

More than a month before Holmes
stopped Gerry Cooney in 13 rounds in
June 1982, he posed with his support
team at the Larry Holmes Training
Center in Easton (left to right)—
brother/assistant trainer, Jake Holmes;
trainer, Eddie Futch; and
champion, Holmes.

Holmes hitting the speed bag:
"Boxing is hard damn work.
But you know what? I loved
the sweat and toil."

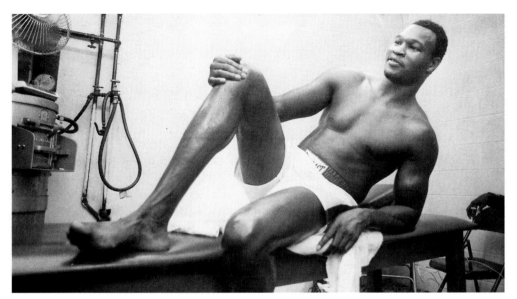

Holmes relaxing after a workout: "It was, when you came down to it, easier to feel at ease with the hard wages of a boxer when you could look at it through the rose-colored glasses of a champion."

Holmes not only mocked challenger Lucien Rodriguez while beating him handily, but he promoted the March 1983 bout in Scranton, Pennsylvania.

Tale of the Tape

LARRY HOLMES		MUHAMMAD ALI*
NOVEMBER 3, 1949		JANUARY 14, 1942
CUTHBERT, GA.		LOUISVILLE, KY.
30	AGE	58
215**	WEIGHT	225**
6'3"	HEIGHT	6'3"
81"	REACH	82"
43-1/2"	CHEST (NORMAL)	47"
45-1/2"	CHEST (EXPANDED)	49"
15-3/4"	BICEPS	16"
13"	FOREARM	14"
35"	WAIST	38-1/2"
25"	THIGH	26"
16"	CALF	17"
17-1/2"	NECK	17"
8"	WRIST	7-3/4"
13-1/2"	FIST	12-1/2"
10"	ANKLE	10"

* MUHAMMAD ALI MEASUREMENTS ARE NEW, TAKEN AS OF FIRST OF AUGUST. HE WILL BE MEASURED AGAIN ON HIS ARRIVAL IN LAS VEGAS EARLY IN SEPTEMBER.

** EXACT WEIGHTS WILL BE ANNOUNCED FOLLOWING AN OFFICIAL WEIGH-IN CONDUCTED BY THE NEVADA STATE ATHLETIC COMMISSION.

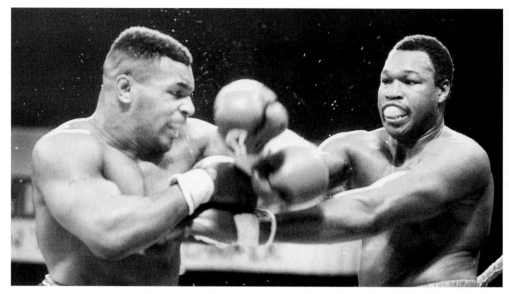

A Holmes comeback in January 1988 was foiled by then-champion, Mike Tyson, left. But a subsequent comeback proved more successful as Holmes beat Ray Mercer and fought valiantly in championship bouts against Evander Holyfield and Oliver McCall.

Larry on his way to winning the title from Ken Norton.
(Photo credit: UPI/Corbis-Bettmann)

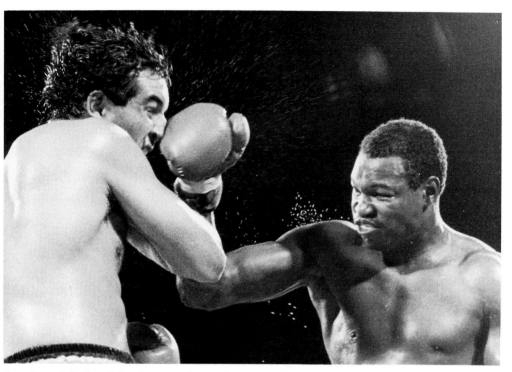

Another right hook lands squarely on the nose of Cooney.
(Photo credit: UPI/Corbis-Bettmann)

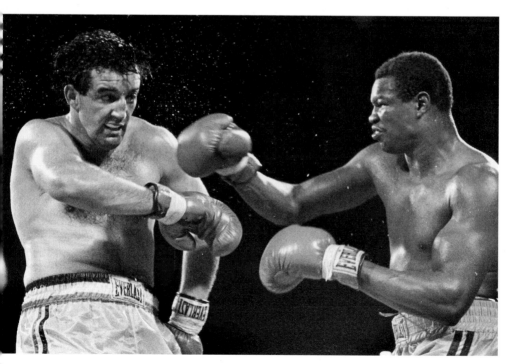

Droplets of water flying from his head, Gerry Cooney shows the effect of a right hook
by WBC heavyweight champion Larry Holmes. *(Photo credit: UPI/Corbis-Bettmann)*

Larry Holmes: "Against the odds, I succeeded." *(Photo credit: USA Network)*

its parking lot that would seat more than 24,000 paying customers.

Ali was guaranteed $8 million, and my guarantee was $5 million. That matched what Harold Smith had offered, but with King in the picture the money would settle out at half of that, before expenses and taxes.

I didn't begrudge Ali the larger purse. The poor guy had more people than a ship has barnacles clinging to him for a piece of the action. There were the ex-wives as well as an entourage of a whole lot of gofers and crap artists and a few legit professionals. In one article that I read it stated that in retirement, without most of his entourage, Ali's daily expenses were still about $10,000 a day and that there was a $20,000 antique couch sitting in his Los Angeles home that Veronica wouldn't let anybody sit on, not even Muhammad.

So no, I didn't begrudge him the money. Besides, Ali had the magic name that would fill that outdoor site at Caesars. I wasn't deluded to think the casino was building that arena only on account of Larry Holmes

Once the fight was a reality, I couldn't help think of my history with Ali, which, like my time with Earnie Shavers, was coming full circle. Only with Muhammad the time had run longer . . . and deeper.

I mean, this was Muhammad Ali I would be fighting! The man I had seen fix his tie and collar for five minutes just so it would be perfect when he talked to the kids at the Boys Club in Easton. This was the man who was doing magic tricks for African kids in a rainstorm a couple of hours after he had taken George Foreman's biggest punches and then found a way to beat him in Zaire. This was a man who gave me money to get back to Easton when my car broke down in Deer Lake.

Obviously, Muhammad had meant a lot to me. And while I did not put those memories out of mind, I was not about to be taken in by sentimentality either. Plain and simple: this would be a fight that I would do what I had to to win. This was business. This was my future.

155

In a way I hoped that in beating Muhammad, it would clear the way for people to finally take a long look at Larry Holmes. I say I "hoped" that that would happen, but I realized it might not. Muhammad had occupied the world's consciousness for two decades, and made an indelible impression.

Sure, I wanted to be accepted by the public. Who wouldn't? I wanted the acclaim of the masses, the recognition that a heavyweight champion figured to get. But like other men who had succeeded popular champions—Ezzard Charles after Joe Louis, even Gene Tunney after Jack Dempsey—it could very well be an uphill battle.

I had no control over how the world would come to regard Larry Holmes. I had to go on with my life—fight whatever opponents were put before me—and raise a family. Do the best I could on both fronts.

When the rumors intensified that Ali was coming out of retirement, I had begun enjoying the spoils of what I had accomplished so far. In '79, I'd started looking for land to build a dream house on. People would say to me, "Hey, you're heavyweight champion. Why don't you get you a place on top of a mountain, where you can be secluded?"

But that wasn't me. I didn't want to live where the goddamn bears hung out. I wanted to live with neighbors. I wanted to look out over the hedges and say to the guy next door, "Hey, what's up over there?"

I found three acres of land in Almer Township, on the border of Easton. Price: $10,000 to $15,000. At least that was the price until they found out it was for Larry Holmes. Then the price got jacked up. I didn't care. It was what I wanted, and I paid the $32,000 gladly. That was a lot of money then. It'd be cheap now.

On my travels to Vegas, several times I'd rented a house belonging to Liberace's mother. I liked the way the place had been done up. So I hired an architect and we flew out to Vegas so he could take his cues from this house. The architect brought a camera and snapped a whole lot of pictures—of the fireplace, of the pool that was shaped like a piano, and so on. And back to Easton we came.

As the Ali fight sent me into training, my thirteen-thousand-square-foot dream house was taking shape, built from scratch for $390,000. It would have five bedrooms, one of which Diane would use as a dressing room, complete with a barber chair and a sink and a TV that she could watch while making herself up. An indoor pool would be shaped like a boxing glove, and there would be an outdoor pool too. A full basement would have a steam room and sauna and a sitting area with a rec room and bar. Upstairs I'd ordered a big-screen TV and wet bar in the living room, and off the living room was a playroom for Kandy, which later would become a computer room for her and her brother Larry Junior. The house would have eight bathrooms in all.

Outside there would be a combination tennis court/basketball court. And by the outdoor pool—a cabana with two rooms and a bathroom. For the six-car garage, I already had a Cadillac Opera Coupe and a 450 SL red Mercedes, and two Lincoln Continental Mark VIs (with radio-telephones, stereos, and air conditioners).

Once training began, I switched my focus to Ali . . . and being ready for him. Part of that had to do with not letting him get to me with his jive. Lord knows, I'd seen him do it with plenty other fighters. The difference was I was used to it. I figured it'd have no effect on me, though until you're there you don't know for sure.

Well, the Ali that we found a couple months out from the fight was still pudgy but no longer gray around the temples. Uh-uh. Ali had discovered the magic bottles, and had dyed the gray away. And he had grown a mustache. Giachetti took one look and dubbed him "Dark Gable"—rhymes with Clark. Ali laughed at that, and said hereafter I would be known as "the Peanut" because, according to him, my head was shaped like a peanut.

Ali said, "I'm going to shell him and send him to Plains, Georgia."

In case you don't remember, Plains, Georgia, was where President Jimmy Carter came from, and in earlier times he'd been a peanut farmer.

I got into the spirit of things by mocking Ali in a poem, stealing a trick from his book:

On October second
this is the thing
Ali meets Holmes
in the middle of the ring.

Ali swings with a left,
he swings with a right;
It's just a matter of time before Holmes
knocks him out of sight.

People get frantic because
they've never seen a "Dark Gable"
Cross the Atlantic.

When Red Smith asked me whether Ali could psych me out, I told him: "It's the same old broken record I've been hearing as long as I can remember. That kind of talk don't win no fights. It might convince Ali and it might convince some people, but the guy he's got to convince is Larry Holmes, and the only way he can do it is to do it.

"Remember that tune 'The Song Is Ended but the Melody Lingers On'? Well, Ali's got no more melody."

Meanwhile, I was getting in shape. In Easton. I'd run about five miles each morning at a seven-minute pace along the Delaware River canal, following one of the Lincoln Continentals that led the way with a flashing red light while the other Lincoln trailed. In Easton, Lafayette College sits on a hill over the city, and I got up it by running a mile straight uphill. I pushed myself harder every day by telling myself it was finally Larry Holmes's turn in the spotlight.

Afternoons, I'd be at St. Anthony's Youth Center doing my

gym work—hitting the heavy and speed bags, shadowboxing, sparring, skipping rope, doing my sit-ups.

Before Ali started his training he weighed more than 250 pounds. At the time it was not just his weight that worried folks. Pacheco was quoted as saying Ali risked serious damage to his organs, and reporters worried in print about the same thing, some of them referring to the increased slur in his speech that I had noticed.

But in July Ali had gone to the famous Mayo Clinic in Rochester, Minnesota, for a two-day medical examination, the results of which got forwarded to the Nevada State Athletic Commission. The commission looked at the reports and cleared Ali for the fight.

That was enough for a lot of folks to buy into the Ali mystique and figure he would whup my butt. I remember being on an interstate in New Jersey when the Lincoln Continental Mark VI I was driving hit a piece of pipe that ricocheted under the car and up into the gas tank, busting a hole in it. Giachetti in the trailing car saw gas leaking and hollered for us to abandon our vehicle.

Wouldn't you know when I called for a tow truck, and identified myself, the guy on the other end starts telling me Ali is going to knock me out.

I tell him: "How can Ali knock me out? How can he? He hasn't knocked anyone out in more than four years! How can Ali knock anyone out? The fight won't go ten. Believe me? . . . Can you bet money? Yeah. Bet a thousand. I'll guarantee it for you."

In September, toward the end of my training in Easton, I had a scare. While sparring with LeRoy Diggs, I hit him with a right that sent pain shooting through my hand—the kind of pain I had felt when I broke it against Roy Williams.

We hurried over to the hospital to have the hand X-rayed. Doctors said the X rays revealed a bone bruise and soft-tissue trauma in the carpal bones of the wrist and the metacarpal bone junction just above the thumb.

Kleven began treating it three times a day, and devised a foam cast that I wore under the tape during workouts. I'd wear the cast at night too, taking it off in the morning before any reporters showed up.

Three weeks out from the fight, we headed for Vegas. Settling into suite 4520 at Caesars Palace, I taped up a huge hand-printed sign that said: *FIRST: MY WIFE. MY CHILDREN. MY FAMILY. MY HOUSE. P.S. MY POOL.* Over it I put a picture of Diane and Kandy, who was now six months old. Next to that, on a purple art board, was an architect's drawing of the home being built in Easton. All of that was to remind me what I was fighting for—to keep me focused.

By this time Ali was *looking* like Ali, fit and trim, no mustache. Yup, he'd knocked off a lot of weight, and was acting like the Ali of old, talking his talk.

Saying stuff like: "I'm not thirty-eight like other Americans. I'm not a normal American. I'm a Superman."

And: "Holmes must go. I'll eat him up. I'll hit him with jabs and right crosses. He can't dance: I'm gonna dance fifteen rounds. This old man will whup his butt. Pow! Pow! Pow! I see it all now. He's exhausted. Bam! The right hand over the tired jab. And Holmes is down! Ali goes to a neutral corner. Seven, eight, nine, ten! And for the world-record-setting never-to-be-broken fourth time, Muhammad Ali is the heavyweight champion of the world."

Of course, there were the usual insults too that Ali couldn't resist. He said, "Holmes is so ugly, his grandmother said when he started to cry, the tears would stop and roll down the back of his head."

Hadn't I heard him use the same material for Smokin' Joe Frazier?

Whatever. When both camps arrived in Vegas, all the guys that I had known from my days as Ali's sparring partner now were giving me the fish eye. Like Kilroy. He started mouthing off the first time he saw me. Told me: "You're nothing." I said, "No, you're nothing." And gave him a playful smack. For some reason Gene went ballistic. He grabbed a garbage can and came charging at me: "You black motherfucker." Caesars security had to break it up. We didn't speak for maybe six months after that until one day we shook hands and picked up as if nothing had happened.

Once we settled into Vegas, the posturing mostly stopped. With Muhammad and me it was pretty much the usual cartoon kind of jiving, with him showing up at my workout and knocking on the door of my dressing room while leading the crowd in chanting "Ali, Ali, Ali." I returned the favor a few days later.

At the final news conference to pump up the fight, Giachetti presented Ali with a drawing of a pig named "Porky," which was what we'd been calling Ali. Ali? He yelled "Peanut" at me. Big deal, right?

As the countdown to the fight began, people were taken by the fact that Ali had lost so much weight and looked fit and trim. But reports that we got said he was terrible in his workouts—that his sparring partners were whupping on him. Even so, in its prefight cover story, *Sports Illustrated* had Ali on the cover, making that I'm-gonna-get-you face of his, while on the pages inside Muhammad was quoted as saying: "They say I'm going to get hurt. When did I ever get hurt? They say I got brain damage. Liver damage. They all lied. I spent three days at the Mayo Clinic. They stuck wires in me: I looked like Frankenstein's monster. I passed every test. Look how pretty I talk. How could I have brain damage? I'll show those lying . . ."

But other guys watched a slimmed-down Ali and knew looking good was not the same as having the goods as a fighter.

A veteran corner man, Bill Prezant, saw Ali train and then told reporters: "He's just a shell. A beautiful shell, but there's nothing inside. The legs are gone."

"You can't put Humpty Dumpty together again," said Teddy Brenner, the former Madison Square Garden matchmaker.

Even after Ali weighed in at 217 ½ pounds, the lightest he had been since he was 216 ½ for Foreman, Dave Anderson, *The New York Times* columnist, would write:

But the emphasis on Ali's weight, by himself and by others, is merely another of the magic tricks he enjoys doing.

"I am a master of illusion," Ali likes to say. "I make you see something that you don't really see."

By emphasizing his weight, Ali has created the illusion that he is what he used to be. And perhaps he is. But neither he nor anyone else will know that for sure until the fight begins. Ali can dye his gray hairs black, as he has done, but he cannot dye his internal organs. Weight loss by itself is proof only that he has pared down from 254 pounds over the last seven months. But at age 38, it's not the shape of a boxer's body that counts as much as the inside of that body—his ability to take a punch, his reflexes in throwing accurate punches when an opening occurs.

Four days before the fight, I caught a bad break. While sparring with Wendell Bailey, I suffered a slight cut across the right eye that was largely concealed by my head guard. The gym was crowded with media. I didn't want word to get out. Ali would have a target to shoot at if he knew. So I called time and, back in my corner, I told Giachetti: "Richie, cover my eye with a towel, fast."

Giachetti covered up the blood and pinched the cut closed. I went back to sparring and finished the round with a flurry of punches. At that point, Giachetti took off my head guard and covered my eye, shouting, "That's all! You're in great shape, champ. You're going to kick Ali's butt. That's all."

I told the reporters who came around that Wendell had thumbed me and that I would be just fine. I was worried some of the sharper guys would pick up that I'd been cut. Richie applied pressure with the towel while we walked to the dressing room.

When I left the dressing room I had on dark glasses and a hat. Giachetti said, "If anybody asks you to take off the glasses, take your hat off first. But when you take the glasses off, tilt your head back so your eyelids go up. Then tell them to look at your pretty face." But nobody really caught on.

It was no nick but rather a cut severe enough to need medical attention. We found a doctor who could close up the injury and promised to keep word of it to himself. To encourage his silence, he was very well paid for the eight tiny stitches he used to close the cut. As was the case with the biceps injury suffered before the Norton fight, I had no intention of delaying the match because of the injury.

Sure, there was a chance the cut would reopen. But it was a chance I was willing to take. I wasn't going to have my opportunity of a lifetime canceled. What concerned me as much as Ali getting lucky with a punch and opening the cut was that the commission doctors would discover the stitches during the prefight examination and call off the fight. To pass muster, we put some of Diane's makeup over the cut. When the doctor examined me, he didn't notice anything amiss with the eye. That tells you something about those prefight physicals.

By the day of the fight, I was reduced to a slight favorite, a 13–10 choice, man to man. And there was plenty of action at the Caesars Palace sports book on the bout. The casino was jammed with a lively fight crowd. To get this match, Caesars had paid $4 million for the rights to the live gate and let's say another million dollars to construct the outdoor arena. The gate was expected to be $3.5 million, yet Caesars figured to make up the difference at the gambling tables.

The casino had sent invitations to 2,500 of Caesars' high rollers. That's how over the last twenty years Vegas and Atlantic City and even Reno have been able to land the major fights. They can put up humongous site fees that arenas like Madison Square Garden cannot hope to match. For the fights are a surefire way to increase the volume of play at the casino. In other words, it's a bigger pie on fight nights that the house odds are working on. Increase the volume of players, you increase your net profits. Those net profits motivate the casinos to go after the next major fight. For Las Vegas, Atlantic City, and Reno, it's worth it . . . and then some.

For Caesars the gate proved to be more than $6 million, minus the estimated $500,000 that the house gave away in comps. That meant the break-even point had been reached by the time Muhammad and I arrived at the small trailers that served as our dressing rooms on fight night.

After Gladys Knight and the Pips sang the national anthem, Ali left his trailer and headed to the ring at a little past eight o'clock, Vegas time, escorted by two rows of motorcycle officers. I could hear the cry of "Ali, Ali, Ali" from the sold-out crowd, ranging from the $500 ringsiders to the $50 spectators in the wooden bench bleachers.

We had anticipated all kinds of theatrics from Bundini aimed at unnerving me once I climbed into the ring. So we had planned ahead to deal with him. The strategy was to turn my brother Jake loose on Bundini. When Jake got himself psyched, he was one of the craziest muthas alive, fearful of no man and with a mouth on him that would corrode cement walls.

Well, when we got to the ring, Bundini looked like a crazed dog as he circled the ring, encouraging the crowd to chant Ali's name. Ali? He was being restrained by Youngblood and Angelo Dundee as he hollered at me, "I want you, Holmes. I want you." Meanwhile, I stepped toward the neutral corner, where the commission had laid out a resin box for the fighters to rub their shoes in, the better to grip the canvas. Well, Ali decided to block my way, his idea of one-upping me psychologically. Without a word, I shoved him aside and went to the box. No mind games for me, Ali. I am here to fight. To get the Ali monkey off my back.

Behind me I heard shouting and scuffling. It was Jake and Bundini. They were going at it, and security people, even the referee, Richard Green, were trying to separate them. Everyone was shouting and bets were being made on the fly. I heard Jake and Angelo Dundee bet $500 on the fight.

The bout started. By now, the sun, which had gotten into the eyes of the prelim fighters, had set behind the foothills of the Sierra Nevada, so it was comfortable in the canopied ring. And even though I had anticipated Ali being nowhere near the fighter I'd sparred with, I was startled by how far back he had gone. The man was slower than Heinz ketchup. The pow-pow-pow that Ali had talked about before the fight was a reality, except he was on the receiving end of it. I couldn't miss him with the jab.

As for Ali, his jab—once a stinging dart—was a push, like a bear pawing the air. It was nothing. In the second round, he landed a couple of rights, and between rounds Giachetti said, "That's all he's got—the right hand."

But even that fizzled out. Ali had no spark, no energy. He was a shell of himself.

All he had was his bravado. It was as though he thought he could talk himself into this fight. From almost my first punch, Ali began cursing me, insulting me, even as—or maybe especially as—my punches were landing with loud thuds against him.

"You dumb motherfucker . . . asshole . . . fuckhead. You ain't shit as a fighter . . . never were. . . ."

Stuff like that. On and on without letup.

The harder I hit him, the worse the language. And what was odd about it was that out of the ring, Ali rarely used foul language. When I'd known him at Deer Lake, he resisted cursing—I used to wonder whether it was part of his being a Black Muslim. Even when we'd go out on Saturday nights to Pottsville and someone would hassle him, his language never strayed to cussing.

My response to the profanity was to ignore it and just do what I had to physically. In the early rounds, I "bogarted" him—that's a fighters' expression for manhandling the other guy. I figured that his effort at losing weight might have taken something out of him. So when the two of us were at close quarters, I would lean my weight on him, turn him, toss him. In clinches, I'd try to get a hand free and bang him to the body. All of which was meant to wear him down *and* to let him know that I was no longer the docile sparring partner who would oblige him because of my relying on him to be paid.

The first couple of times he tied me up and I bogarted him, I was amazed at how weak he was. Ali used to be a real strong fighter inside because he understood how to use leverage and to lean his weight on you, make you do the work. His strength was

165

something most outsiders didn't even know about. But this Ali was different, so easy to push around he didn't even seem like the same man. It had to be his weight loss—he had lost too much too fast.

By the second round, there was a reddening under Ali's left eye. By the fourth round, blood was trickling from his left nostril. Toward the end of that fourth round, I hit Ali with a big right hook to the kidney—probably the best punch to the body I ever threw in a fight. I heard Ali moan. He started to fall. That's it, I figured. Then, all of a sudden, I saw him jerk himself upright. His damn pride wouldn't let him fall. There's not another man on earth who would have stayed on his feet after that punch. That same pride was why he took so many beatings in fights, even in the fights he won. And it was why he was one of the greatest fighters of all time. In my opinion, the greatest.

That was when, however, I realized what I was up against on this night. Ali was not going to quit. He was there to take a beating, a beating I was not eager to deliver. The dilemma for me was how to bring an end to this fight without doing permanent damage to the man. Somehow I had to convince Green, the referee, that he needed to step in and call this fight off.

I began fighting in bursts to show Ali he was defenseless against me, then stepping back so I didn't do too much damage. What's the formula of aggression that would show the referee enough is enough? It's tough to find exactly how many punches it takes to make a referee step in. A couple of times I thought he would and I stepped back to let him, but Ali tried to keep things going. It went on and on like that—it seemed forever. Damn you, Ali.

I'd go back to the corner and say to Giachetti: "What am I supposed to do with this guy?"

In between rounds, I sat on the stool and prayed I wouldn't have to hurt him.

Meanwhile, the crowd was booing Ali.

Ali was trying. He danced, he stood flat-footed. He went to the rope-a-dope. He fought from a crouch. Nothing worked.

Whatever he came up with, my answer was always the same. I was too much fighter for him, too quick, too strong.

In the ninth I hit him a vicious right uppercut that sent Ali into the ropes, where he hung from the top strand like a rag doll. When he wobbled away, I hit him with a right to the kidney that made him double over in pain.

At the end of the round, Dundee would ask him, "Do you want to do it?" meaning did he want to continue. He did.

Of round ten, Sylvester Stallone would say it was "like watching an autopsy on a man who's still alive."

After round ten, on a signal from Herbert Muhammad at ringside, Dundee told the referee, "That's all." When Bundini pleaded for one more round, Dundee screamed, "Fuck you, no!"

When I realized the fight was over, I felt relief and then a certain sadness. I stepped across the ring to Ali. I was crying when I kissed him.

I told Ali: "I respect you, man. And I love you. I hope we're always friends." He was too defeated and dejected to understand what I was saying.

Most of the people around me were celebrating—another victory, my eighth in a row as champion, the thirty-sixth without a defeat as a professional. Naturally I was happy—happy that I won, because you can never take that for granted before any fight; happier that the mess the fight became was over; happiest that Ali was behind me and that I could get on with my career. It was a real bittersweet thing, beating Ali, who had not won a single round on the scorecards of the judges.

I visited Ali later that night in his darkened suite at Caesars. Ali had not yet showered. He'd gone straight from the arena to his room. When I arrived, he was lying on his bed, still in his trunks and wearing his robe. Only his shoes were off. I imagined the emotional pain Ali was feeling, the confusion that was going on in his mind. His eyes were puffed up, almost closed. He looked very old.

"You okay, man?" I asked.

He nodded, with a sad little smile.

"I didn't want to hurt you out there," I said.

His eyes got bigger: "Why'd you do it then?"

I mumbled something, then asked him if I had really thumbed him as Dundee had tried to convince Richard Green during the bout.

Ali said, "Hell no, man." He was quiet a moment, obviously struggling with his thoughts. Finally, he looked at me and said, "The thing I can't figure out is why I fought so bad. Larry, something was wrong with me. Either I was too old or I was too light."

"Probably both, Champ."

I told him I hoped he wouldn't fight again. If he needed money, I'd be glad to lend him some. There was no reason he had to prove anything to anybody after what he did for boxing—and for me—all those years.

He didn't say anything for a while. Then he put his hands to his face, cupping them around his mouth, and real slow and quiet began to make a crowd noise. Then it became a chant—"I . . . want . . . Holmes? . . . I . . . want . . . Holmes." He wouldn't stop. The chant got louder: "*I want Holmes! I want Holmes!*" I started to get embarrassed and felt like it was a good time to leave, as he kept right on chanting, "*I want Holmes!*" I thought Ali would be okay. I never figured he'd fight again. How could he—there wasn't anything left in the man. I was wrong. He fought Trevor Berbick down in the Bahamas the following year; Ali lost the decision and took another beating. It was sad.

I had a theory about why Ali stayed too long, and took too much punishment. By my thinking, it went back to his refusal to be drafted into the armed services during the Vietnam conflict. Even though most of the nation eventually was against the war, Ali was left out there on his own, a dangling man who for a long time was viewed as a coward.

It was to overcome that stigma, I think, that led Ali to show people how tough he was when finally he was allowed to fight again. It gave us Ali standing up to Foreman on the ropes, taking the best shots Frazier could unload in Manila, surviving on sheer guts against me until his corner decided enough was enough. And in the end it gave Ali the dues to pay—the Parkinson's syndrome that left him slower in speech and movement.

In the days that followed the victory over Muhammad it gave me pause about my own career and what it would be like at the end. Naturally, I didn't dwell on it because I was at the height of my career, earning more money than I knew existed . . . and with no opponents around who I thought could beat me. But in those quiet moments at night before I fell asleep, I wondered if I'd know when to quit. Or if I would end up like Ali, staying too long. Not all champions did. Rocky Marciano, for instance.

He was 49–0 when he retired in 1956. The ultimate gladiator, as brutal in the ring as any champion before him. And yet he'd walked . . . and never looked back. Packed it in at age thirty-three after only six title defenses. I tried to imagine why he'd retired and what kept him from changing his mind, as so many champions before him did. In the Ali fight, because of my not wanting to hurt him, I sensed something that I had been noticing in small ways all along—whatever instinct I had to do damage to an opponent had limits to it. Was it that, or some other reason, that had nudged the undefeated Marciano to retirement?

And what about me? Would I know when to say adios, or would I linger a fight too many? Back in 1981, I couldn't be sure what my choice would be.

In the days that followed my victory over Ali, information would surface regarding Muhammad that would convince him that what I'd done to him in Caesars' outdoor arena was a medical miscalculation on his part and not the inevitable result of his declining skills.

Seems like Herbert Muhammad's personal physician, Dr. Charles Williams, had given him a thyroid drug called Thyrolar, prescribing one tablet a day. Whether Thyrolar had, as some claimed, dangerous side effects, I'm not expert enough to say. But apparently Ali brought on problems by taking three of the pills a day, as he often did with the vitamins that were recommended. The result was, according to the reports I read, Ali felt fatigued.

Ali's biographer, Tom Hauser, would quote Dr. Williams as acknowledging the pills "led to heat exhaustion that went into heat stroke with an intermediate period of slight stupor and maybe delirium. I may have placed him in jeopardy inadvertently."

Less than a week after the fight, Ali held a news conference at which he said: "If the pills did it to me, then I want to fight again, and right now I feel sure that the pills caused the problem."

I had no desire to fight Ali again. I knew that Ali would never be Ali again and it was lunacy to think he would. What's more, with the revelations about the pills, everything connected with the October 2 fight had become tainted. Even the aftermath.

I'm talking about the nutcases who began phoning me with death threats. I got the first call back in my room after the fight. There was a guy on the other end. He said, "I'm gonna kill you, Holmes." I figured he was one of Ali's crazy fans making a crank call. But more calls followed while I was in Vegas. And when Giachetti picked up, or Jake did, they heard the voice on the other end say, "We're gonna kill Larry Holmes." I'm lying in bed and the next thing I know I got ten security cops outside my room.

I didn't think too much about it until I got a call in Easton and that really got me mad. Calling me in the sanctity of my home is a whole lot more invasive than dialing me up at Caesars. The death threats were repeated through several calls to my home. The same guy, the same voice each time. Eventually, he stopped. But it added to the sour feeling that I was left with in the aftermath of the beating I gave Ali. I had hoped that in defeating Muhammad, it would switch the public's focus to Larry Holmes in the way that, say, Marciano's knockout of Joe Louis had brought Marciano to the spotlight.

But for whatever reason, it didn't quite happen that way. The respect that I'd hoped would result from beating Ali was slow to come.

Then again, so was the money Ali was to get for the buttwhupping he took from me. Donald King was an equal opportunity scumbag—screwed boxing legends as easily as he did the rest of us. When it came time to pay Ali his $8 million, King shorted him by a little over $1 million. Ali's lawyer, Michael Phenner, was ready to go after King in court. In fact, he sued King in June '82 in the Northern District Court of Illinois. But King had a Muslim friend of Ali's fly out to L.A. with a briefcase filled with $50,000 in cash and a release saying Ali would forgo the rest of the money—$950,000—due him. The friend caught up with Ali at the UCLA Medical Center, where Muhammad was being treated for health problems. With a notary public present, Ali took the money and signed the release. The King of trickerations had struck again.

Me? I went back to Easton and was greeted by a drum-and-bugle corps at the Allentown-Bethlehem-Easton Airport.

A motorcade whisked us to downtown Easton. It was a cheering sight to see fans along the route with banners that read "Welcome home, champ," and "Larry Holmes, we love you."

About five hundred folks in Center Square cheered when I stepped out of the white convertible.

I told them: "Thank you for the turnout. It's one helluva crowd. A fighter, or any other athlete, does not have to come from a big city to be successful. I just proved it because I'm from Easton. Thanks to my mother, because without her there wouldn't be no Larry Holmes."

An Easton department store had a four-tier, one-hundred-pound cake with a boxing ring on top baked for the occasion. After I left for home, slices were distributed to the crowd.

CHAPTER
TWELVE

With New Year 1981, Harold Smith was still shaking things up in boxing. He had big-name fighters like Hearns, Pryor, Matthew Saad Muhammad, Eddie Mustafa Muhammad, and Jeff Chandler under contract to him. Fighters were getting in line to catch those briefcases brimming with hard cash.

Then came word that Harold was promoting a big championship tripleheader February 23, 1981, at Madison Square Garden featuring Hearns versus Benitez, Saad Muhammad versus Mustafa Muhammad, and Gerry Cooney versus Ken Norton. It looked as though Smith was becoming a major player in the fight game.

That's when the other shoe dropped. Suddenly clouds hovered over Harold Smith as word spread that lawmen wanted to talk to him about all that funny money he'd been throwing at the fighters. Where was Harold Smith? In the boxing community, there were the usual conflicting stories that put him all over the damn globe. Only one thing was certain. Harold Smith had dropped out of sight.

King was gloating: "Didn't I tell you you couldn't trust the guy?"

Then came the news. The FBI wanted him for embezzling an undisclosed amount of money from the Wells Fargo Bank in California. Harold was on the lam. One of the early reports had him "armed and dangerous," but that proved to be erroneous and was quickly corrected. He was just a guy running from trouble.

For a few days, trying to find Harold Smith stayed a big story. The amount he stole and how he did it kept changing every day. It was in the millions, but how many millions exactly no one knew for sure. I remembered back to that day in Easton when I got the sweats over two of those millions.

Fighters he had paid those exorbitant sums were checking in with their attorneys to find out if the bank or the feds were going to ask for the money back. The lawyers said no, but I wondered if Wells Fargo would have a different response.

Every day a bit more of the story emerged. It turned out that Harold Smith wasn't even Harold Smith. His real name was Ross Fields. It was as Fields that he had been a member of a mile-relay team at American University that had won an IC4A indoor title in the sixties. Soon after, Harold dropped out of school and somehow persuaded the entertainer Sammy Davis Jr. to let him use his name on a discotheque he ran in Washington, D.C. It was back there that he began writing bad checks, enough of them so that by 1976 he and the woman living with him as his wife had graduated to an FBI wanted poster, charged with "interstate fradulent checks." Authorities later claimed that he had left a trail of one hundred bogus checks through thirty states. By growing a beard, putting on fifty pounds, and changing his name to Harold Smith, he took on a new life in L.A.

While it lasted, Harold did it up in high style. He lived in a fancy home in the expensive Bel Air section of Los Angeles and also owned two Marina del Rey condominiums. He leased an executive jet, and owned an $80,000 power boat, a $40,000 cus-tom El Dorado convertible, and a Seville; his wife drove a Mercedes 450-SL. A *New York Times* story stated: "He is suspected of being the undercover owner of three race horses, including John Lee 'n Harold (named for his son, his wife and himself), a 3-year-old colt who won the recent California Breeders Stakes at Santa Anita and is eligible for this year's Kentucky Derby."

Eventually, Smith was arrested in a motor home near Dodger Stadium. Little by little, the story of how he embezzled the money emerged. He had accomplices, a couple of assistant managers in Wells Fargo branches, who made the scam work. Originally, Harold used his connection with Ali—he introduced them to the champ—to get these fellows to trust him and eventually to cover a few of his checks. These guys knew how the Wells Fargo central computer worked. It turned out there was about a week's delay before checks bounced. They just set up new accounts for Harold to pay off his old accounts before the old ones came due.

It went on like that for more than a year, with his inside men— both promised a share of the profits—covering old money Smith didn't have with punched-up money Smith didn't have. Smith had hoped to catch up on his kited funds with a big score on his promotions and return the money before it was missed.

Funny thing is his heart was in the right place. Harold wanted to unify the titles in each weight class and kill the governing bodies with their corrupt ratings and political skulduggery. He wanted a panel of forthright boxing people to rank the fighters so that fighters got title shots on merit and not the usual back-room maneuvers.

It wasn't to be. Harold's house of cards came crashing down when a small check that was misdated caused the bank to check on the account. It took a while for the feds to figure out how extensive the damage was. Finally, they indicted Smith for embezzling $21.3 million from Wells Fargo.

When I received a subpoena from the federal government to go out to California and testify, I called Harold to tell him.

"Hell, man, I understand," he said. "There's nothing you can do about it. The only thing I regret is that you never let me promote any of your fights. We would have made a real good team, Larry."

Harold Smith was convicted of embezzling the money from Wells Fargo and received a sentence of ten years in prison, a $30,000 fine, and three thousand hours of community service.

Harold had reached for the stars and come tumbling down to earth. Like him, I had tried for a better life and damned if I hadn't found it.

Heavyweight champion.

By 1981, I had my dream house and a normal family life to go with it. I was making the commitment that John Henry Holmes was never able to make.

I was committed to my hometown too. When the Boys Club, located right by the Delaware Terrace projects, was threatened with closing, I organized a "Larry Holmes Run with the Champ"—a five-mile run to raise money for the club. The run became an annual event for many years . . . until the Boys Club began using the money for its payroll rather than to buy games and books for the kids, as we had agreed on. That bothered me enough to stop doing the event.

During those years, I also sponsored a "Larry Holmes Kids Day" in the town center. The whole city of Easton was invited to take part. Black kids and white kids alike got free hot dogs, hamburgers, T-shirts, live entertainments, pony rides, the chance to play various games. A day of just plain fun.

When I was younger and just starting out in the fight game, I didn't dream of million-dollar paydays and championship belts. As I've said, my ambitions were far more modest. My hope was to make enough money to own a nice little house, with enough left over to have a business of my own—like, say, a nightclub. For me, the club would be a place to go to and call my own—a place where friends could drop in and have a good time.

Well, in '79, I heard about a building at 413 Northampton Street that was up for sale. To keep the price from soaring, I had a friend buy it for me for $117,000. The building needed a lot of work, but I thought it would be a good site for a nightclub. At the time, my brother Bob was working in town as a baker. I talked him into quitting the job to run the club, which we called Round One. Actually, it was a nightclub/restaurant. See, in order to have a liquor license, you had to serve food. The restaurant part we called the Four Corners Lounge, where for $2.95 you could purchase a Muhammad Ali burger.

We renovated the building, putting another $350,000 into it and installing what became my office upstairs. On the office door it said, "Larry Holmes Enterprises." And pretty soon there actually were enterprises. Not just the nightclub but also a sportswear store two doors down from Round One and the Larry Holmes Training Center on the 200 block of Canal Street that I bought with the money I made for whupping Ali.

Round One did very well. I was happy to see people partying, having good times. The only problem was parking. There just weren't enough parking spots along Northampton to accommodate customers. Then one day a guy came to me who owned a couple of buildings across the street from Round One. He said the bank was about to foreclose on him and suggested I buy his buildings.

I knew the buildings were old, creaking structures that hadn't a whole lot to offer. But then it dawned on me. Tear the damn buildings down and I'd have an excellent parking lot. So . . . I agreed to pay off his loan and sweeten things with another ten grand for him to get started in some other business. And that was that: Round One had a parking lot.

Life seemed pretty good to me early in 1981. I was happy in Easton, raising a family and seeing a few businesses get off the ground. Not bad, I thought, for a seventh-grade dropout. Not only that. I had made eight title defenses since whupping Norton in '78 and won them all by knockout. That string of title-defense KOs broke the record of seven set by Joe Louis. That was pretty amazing too. I mean, Joe Louis—he was a legend, and one of the first sports heroes of black folks.

As I looked ahead at the start of '81, I figured to keep rolling right along. I didn't see anybody out there who could beat Larry Holmes. And as much as I could expect, the Ali monkey was off my back. For the first time in my career, it looked like smooth sailing ahead.

Then one morning in early '81, a shiny black car rolled into my driveway. On the TV security system I saw two men get out of the car. They were wearing business suits and carrying brief-cases. They looked like lawyers. I watched them move to the front door. I could tell by how they moved that the older man was in charge. He stopped at the front door and looked the place over, nodding as if he was impressed. By the time the doorbell rang, I had them pegged as feds.

"Mr. Larry Holmes?" the older guy said.

"That's right," I said, shaking hands.

"Special Agent Joseph Spinelli," he said. "Federal Bureau of Investigation."

I didn't bother looking at the IDs he and the other man flashed.

"I have a subpoena for you to testify before a federal grand jury in New York," Spinelli said. "But I'd also like to talk to you for a bit before we go back to New York."

I invited them in, maintaining a cool front but feeling uneasy about their visit. As Spinelli and the other agent settled in, I phoned Spaz and let him know what was going on. Spaz told me to bring the subpoena to his office ASAP.

I hung up, and asked Spinelli what this was all about. As Spinelli handed me the subpoena, he said: "I'm in charge of a special investigation into corruption in boxing. If you just tell the grand jury what you've seen throughout your career, you'll be doing a lot of other fighters a good turn. We are just trying to make sure some of the promoters who cheat fighters don't get away with it any more."

"Look at this house," I said. "Would you say I've been cheated?"

My distrust of cops was instinctive, based on a boyhood of uneasy encounters with them.

"Maybe not you, Larry," Spinelli said. "But you know there

177

are plenty of deserving fighters who never get to own a house like this because they get ripped off by promoters. You know the fighters and you know the promoters and you know exactly how they do it. That's why we want you to testify."

Easy enough for Spinelli—who seemed an okay, sincere guy— to say. Like a lot of others before him, he thought he could make things right in boxing. If he could, great. But I wasn't about to let him do it at my expense. The truth is Joe Spinelli wasn't the first man, and for damn sure wouldn't be the last, who thought he could change boxing. More than a decade later, a senator from Delaware named Roth would pull together a subcommittee to investigate boxing, but nothing much would result from it.

Boxing had always been a business where the rascals running things took advantage of the fighters. Shortchanged them, and sometimes worse—sometimes forced them to participate in fixed fights. There'd been mobsters like Frankie Carbo in the fifties who'd been investigated and even jailed, but the bullshit kept happening. Get rid of a Carbo, and from nowhere a Don King would surface.

Spinelli had done his homework. As we talked, he ticked off some of the abuses he was aware of. He mentioned how money was skimmed and kicked back. He knew about the tickets fighters were forced to buy and the money they had to pay the sanctioning organizations—usually one to two-and-a-fraction percent of their championship purses. He knew which managers were really just fronting for promoters, and how boxing commissioners and certain fight judges played footsie with this promoter and that one.

"We are hoping, Larry," Spinelli said, "that you would appear before the grand jury as a friendly witness, someone who really knows the story and comes forward willingly so we can make our case to the grand jury."

Where I come from, "friendly witness" sounded an awful lot like a gussied-up way to say "rat."

"Look, Mr. Spinelli," I said, "I'm just a fighter trying to turn a couple of bucks in the few years I have."

"No you're not, Larry. You're more than that. You're the heavyweight champion of the world. And that gives you a certain credibility and responsibility that goes along with it."

He wasn't wrong. The idea of cleaning up boxing was a good one. But I would proceed with caution, keeping in mind what I fought for—the greater good of my family.

As I listened to Spinelli describe his investigation, I kept waiting to hear him call out King's name. But he was careful at this point to speak in general terms and not link the FBI's probe to one particular promoter. But my hunch was that King was the target of the feds and that having me in their camp, a willing witness to Donald King's games, would be a real coup for them. I wasn't eager to do that. Testifying against Don King wasn't the smartest thing I could do for Larry Holmes.

Spaz's advice was to take the Fifth Amendment—refuse to answer all grand jury questions on the grounds that answering them might tend to incriminate me. Spaz said that while doing so we'd get a glimpse of whatever case the feds might think they had against me, if any.

At the time Spinelli and his partner turned up at my door, I was signed to defend my title against Trevor Berbick, a Jamaican who was living in Halifax, Nova Scotia. Berbick was a big, strong guy with an awkward style and a record of 18-1-1. He'd been knocked out by brothel owner Joe Conforte's fighter, Bernardo Mercado, and had fought a draw with Leroy Caldwell. His reputation had been made by knocking out John Tate the previous year. Otherwise, he had fought a lot of unknowns, including a man named Hoss Geisler, who fought under the name "Him." One sportswriter, when he heard about Him, said, "Berbick beat half of a towel set." Holmes-Berbick was set for April 11, 1981, in Vegas on Home Box Office.

On the morning of my grand jury appearance, I got my roadwork in before Spaz and I drove to the Federal Building in downtown Manhattan. On the way there, Spaz told me that his gut feeling was that the FBI investigation was targeting King and, given that Rudy Giuliani, the new U.S. attorney in Manhattan, was trying the case, the feds might have some strong evidence of wrongdoing. Spaz said that Giuliani was young and tough and was trying to make a reputation for himself. My taking the Fifth Amendment was a way, he thought, of getting his real objective—to have the feds offer me immunity.

Spaz explained to me how the Fifth Amendment worked. Other than my name, address, and profession, I couldn't answer any questions at all because by answering even one of them, I opened things up for more questions on the same subject, which I then had to answer or I could be held in contempt. Without knowing the government's case, the Fifth was my best protection.

Because I was Larry Holmes, heavyweight champ, the jurors were all smiles when I arrived. The smiles turned frosty, though, once I began asserting my constitutional right, the Fifth Amendment, in response to the questions posed by Giuliani's assistant, a young woman named Ronnie Mann. Spinelli was there too, and he didn't seem too happy with the "unfriendly" position I was taking.

Mann kept asking questions—most of them general in nature—and I kept responding by taking the Fifth. Then Mann wondered about a five-thousand-dollar check I had written to the WBC to take out a full-page ad in its program for its annual dinner. It was considered the politic thing to do—a way of assuring friendly relations with Senor Sulaiman and his organization. There was no formal requirement as champion to do so, like there was to pay a sanctioning fee for title defenses. But if you wanted the WBC to approve your opponents it was considered the smart thing to do. Who knows? Down the road, it might also figure in how WBC judges scored your fight. Stranger things had happened. So while I wasn't obligated to cough up the five grand, I did it, regarding it as a subtle form of kickback.

Now what Spinelli had done was track the check I had written. It turned out that Sulaiman himself had cashed it at Caesars Palace. That the money had ended up in Sulaiman's hands was not exactly a shock to me. But I *was* surprised he did it so openly. I began to understand for the first time why both the WBC and

WBA were based outside the United States. It put them out of reach of U.S. law enforcement agencies.

While Mann's questions revealed those facts about the five-thousand-dollar check, and surprised me some, the next few questions she fired at me really raised my brow. These questions brought up things I had said in confidence about Don King to Giachetti, and no prosecutor would have known them without being tuned in to those conversations. Had they wiretapped Giachetti . . . or me? The government's knowledge of them made both Spaz and me wonder whether Giuliani was looking to stick me in the defendant's box too.

Once recess was called, Mann, Spaz, Spinelli, and the grand jury foreperson huddled up. As a result of their conversations, it was agreed that I would be given immunity in return for answering all their questions. They took me downstairs and found a judge who swore me in and we all signed the immunity papers.

Turned out it was no wiretap. Yes, there were tapes of conversations between Giachetti and me—a whole bunch of them. But they were tapes that Giachetti, not the feds, had made. Later on, Giachetti would tell the feds that both of us had agreed to tape our conversations. Baloney. It was Giachetti doing for Giachetti, for reasons only he could tell you.

With Giachetti knowing the tape was running, he would egg me on to talk shit about Don King, which, tape or not, wasn't hard for me to do. In the bargain, though, Giachetti was covering his butt, layering in remarks meant to make him sound innocent of any wrongdoing. It was pretty transparent what he was up to, and I was convinced the grand jury and Spinelli recognized that.

Anyway, I answered all of Ronnie Mann's questions. I answered directly. I answered truthfully. I answered factually. No opinions, no interpretations, and I did not volunteer anything that could open up any new lines of inquiry. If the government knew what facts it wanted to develop, great. But I wasn't about to broaden their knowledge. If boxing was a dirty business, let them prove it. Meantime, I had to truck along with the promoter I had.

181

Teflon Don had slithered free of the scandal that followed the U.S. Boxing Championships. But I wondered if he would escape the long arm of the law this time. The government seemed to have been thorough in its preparation.

Which brought me back to Richie Giachetti.

Giachetti had sucker-punched me with those tapes, and I couldn't forgive him for that. Richie and I had had a long and often bumpy ride together. Give Richie this: he was a forceful presence, who had the knack of motivating me. He knew exactly when to go crazy, shout and scream at me, raise my emotional pitch, and get me psyched to fight. Yeah, Giachetti was a go-getter and a decent trainer. We could talk to one another, and we laughed a lot. But there were times he could be a real pain in the ass. Being around him was an emotional roller coaster.

Part of Richie's problem was that unlike, say, Angelo Dundee with Ali, Giachetti wanted to be front and center, boss of bosses. And while I didn't mind it so much when I was a heavyweight wanna-be, once I became champion I found his I'm-the-man act annoying. I was flexing my own authority. After all the years of being a boxing bobo, I was stepping up.

Over the years, Giachetti would do things, and say things, that would make me wonder about him. I never thought of him as a racist, but damn . . . there'd be times when he'd go off and leave you scratching your head. I remember once we were walking out of a restaurant in California. A car came by and Richie had words with the driver. As the car sped off, Giachetti mumbled, "Fucking niggers." I thought it was pretty weird inasmuch as everybody in that car was white.

Another time, back in '75, we were in Deer Lake, getting ready to fight Charley "Devil" Green. Saturday nights at Deer Lake, everybody went over to Pottsville for a good time. Through those weekends more than a few of us ended up fathering Pottsville children, and among them was Belinda, a daughter of mine now attending college and for whose welfare I provided as she grew up.

Anyway. This particular night we hunkered down in a bar

called the Alley. Richie had eyes for a white girl who wasn't interested. He was coming on to her and she was shooting him down while at the same time indicating she wouldn't mind going back to the room with me.

Well, back at the room (which Giachetti and I were sharing), Giachetti wouldn't take the hint and leave. Instead, he kept after this girl and even tried to force himself on her. There was no way I was going to let him do that. When I pulled him away from her, he started calling me every nigger insult I ever heard.

"Calm down, man, before you really piss me off," I told him.

But that only incited him more. He started grabbing my clothes from out of the closet and drawers and throwing them all around. He rassled me onto the bed. I was tempted to hit him, but held back because I had a fight coming up in just a few days.

I got the girl out of there—it was about 2 A.M.—and drove her home. I didn't go back to the room that night. Next morning, I phoned Spaz to tell him what had gone down. Spaz already knew about it. He said Giachetti had called him and said, "Us Italians got to stick together. Those niggers are gonna be lying." I told Spaz I was finished with Richie Giachetti.

The Devil Green fight was in Cleveland, Giachetti's hometown. No surprise, Richie came by, looking to get his job back. He was contrite as he could be and insisted that it was the booze that had made him act badly. I doubted that. If it's in you to talk that racial garbage, it's in you. And never mind how much you've had to drink. Yet even though I felt I couldn't really trust Richie Giachetti, I gave him another chance.

But once I heard him on those tapes, that was it. I fired Giachetti and hired Eddie Futch. Futch, who was sixty-nine years old at the time, went back a ways in the boxing wars.

When it later came out in the press that the tapes were what led to my firing Giachetti, he would tell reporters that while he made the tapes, he didn't cough them up until the government subpoenaed them. But that didn't explain satisfactorily why he'd taped our conversations to begin with, or the way he'd manipulated them. There was no way you could say those tapes were meant to benefit Larry Holmes.

So . . . Giachetti was out, and Futch was in. As an amateur fighter, Futch had been on the same boxing team in Detroit that had included Joe Louis. Over the years, he had trained champions like Don Jordan, Alexis Arguello, and Smokin' Joe Frazier, among others. I wasn't worried about being without Giachetti. Truth is, I put less stock in the importance of a trainer than most boxing guys do. I'm not saying all fighters know more than their trainers, but my years as a sparring partner and my belief that I was a "thinking" fighter led me to trust my own judgment more.

Almost all the trainers I knew well, and that included Angelo Dundee as well as Giachetti and Ernie Butler, always liked to take too much credit for the successes a fighter had and none of the blame for the failures. I never once heard a trainer say, "It was my fault. I gave my fighter bad advice." When I was fighting for Ernie Butler, every time I had a bad round he told me it was because I didn't do what he said. Every time I had a good one, it was because I followed his instructions to a tee. I swear there were plenty of times when I knocked out an opponent doing what I figured out for myself and damn near got knocked out following a trainer's advice. For most fight trainers it's heads I win, tails you lose.

I was called back to the grand jury while in training in Easton, and even later while in Vegas.

I wasn't happy about them breaking my focus on Berbick.

At both grand jury sessions, there were more questions that suggested the government knew the kind of trickerations that Donald King used. Questions about moneys in and moneys out—how I got paid and what stuck to my pocket.

I did my damnedest not to be distracted by these proceedings. What the hell: I had immunity and King did not. It was *his* problem. Let him worry about it. For me, Trevor Berbick was all that need concern me.

I beat Berbick decisively—the scoring was 150–135, 146–139, 146–140—but wasn't able to knock him out. Berbick was a powerful guy, with thick trapezius muscles bunched up high between his shoulders and neck. He took the punches and kept trying.

Two months later, on June 12 in Detroit, I went back into the ring to fight the first opponent I truly wanted to hurt: Leon Spinks.

CHAPTER
THIRTEEN

Remember what a strange case Spinks was?

This was the Leon Spinks who had caught Ali in his declining years as a fighter and beaten him in only his eighth fight as a professional.

And then he'd gone and acted like a buffoon of a heavyweight champion.

In the weeks and months after he'd beaten Ali, he had been sued by his landlord in Philadelphia for back rent; sued by a motel for unpaid bills; arrested and then photographed in handcuffs for driving the wrong way down a one-way street without a license; then been caught possessing drugs. He was a loose cannon, a guy who exposed himself as a dumb bastard the more you saw of him. I knew he'd end up a jive ex-champ, driving a Cadillac with about three bucks in his pocket and a brain like cornflakes.

But back when he was making millions—undeservedly so, I thought—I was fighting in Scranton and getting paid in the hallways with ten-dollar bills. That might have served as excuse enough to dislike Spinks, but in truth it had nothing to do with my grudge.

My problem with Leon Spinks arose in 1980 at a dinner in Las Vegas honoring Joe Louis. At that time, Louis, in failing health, was confined to a wheelchair. The end, it was plain, was near. I was one of many champions seated at the dais while Diane was at a table up near the front. Spinks, it turned out, was at the same table. He was loud and obnoxious, and bothering Diane.

I had one of my guys go over to him and tell him to cool it. That's when a ruckus started, with Spinks and my people pushing and shoving and shouting. I hurried over and found Spinks and Diane pulling on a small, gold souvenir boxing glove that was at the center of the table. Leon had been taking them from the various tables and throwing them around. Diane had told him not to take the one on her table, but he had ignored her and grabbed it at the same time she did.

When I got there, I told him let go or I'd knock him on his butt. He let loose with a stream of profanity, and when I pushed him his bodyguard tried to get at me. His bodyguard was a muscular guy with a Mohawk haircut and a lot of attitude. Nobody knew him back then, but in time he would surpass Spinks as a celebrity, becoming an actor going by the name of Mr. T.

I'd have whupped Mr. T and Spinks right where they stood except for the importance of the occasion, to honor Joe Louis. I didn't want to muddy that with violence, so when Spinks let go of the souvenir and both he and Mr. T relaxed their threatening postures, I backed off.

But I marked Spinks for a good buttwhupping, deciding right there I'd try to get him in the ring as soon as I could. Get him in the ring and beat him bad. Hurt him.

That was what I had in my mind when the bell rang in Joe Louis Arena for Holmes versus Spinks. I didn't have to go looking for Spinks. He was charging at me, bobbing and weaving like a disco dancer in a frenzy, trying to get inside my longer reach.

But he was also firing away, like some damn kamikaze in boxing shorts. Some of his shots hurt, but I took them because what I was laying on him was even better.

Still, he kept coming. There was a lot of fight in him. By the third round, though, he seemed to be slowing. And I wasn't. I nailed him on the jaw with a right hand. Spinks dropped slowly to the canvas, fell facedown on the lower strand, and rolled over onto the canvas, landing on his back. He was on his feet at the count of nine. The referee, Richard Steele, asked him if he was okay. Spinks nodded and came toward me.

I hit him with one right hand after another, and he took the punches. That's when I suddenly began to feel sorry for Spinks in spite of the way he had insulted Diane. I stepped back from Spinks and yelled at Steele: "Stop the goddamned fight. You want me to kill this man?" But he didn't stop it. It didn't get stopped until Leon's brother, Michael—who would fight Eddie Mustafa Muhammad the following month for the WBA light heavyweight title—came charging up the steps yelling at Steele while another guy in Leon's corner threw a white towel into the ring. Steele would tell reporters afterward that he never saw the towel—he was going to stop it then and there on his own.

Whatever. The fight was over. The rage was gone from me by then, and I was feeling pity for Leon Spinks and regret for the malice I'd had for him. My God, this was one dirty business, what with beating men senseless and working for people who had the feds looking over their shoulders all the time.

A couple weeks later, poor Leon had another run-in with the cops. He was pulled over and arrested for having a concealed weapon, a gun, in his car.

But in the immediate aftermath of my knockout of Spinks, the talk was of another man, a rising contender who had been ringside to watch the fight and had gotten a boisterous welcome from the crowd when introduced before the bout.

Gerry Cooney, an undefeated white fighter from Long Island, all of a sudden was the talk of the town.

Some of that talk had it that Cooney—six-foot-six and with a left hook that had knocked out twenty-one of his twenty-five foes—was good enough to beat Larry Holmes.

A month earlier, Cooney had scored a dramatic first-round knockout of Ken Norton. But the Norton that Cooney fought was a ghost of the Norton I had gone against. Mandingo was almost thirty-eight years old, and looking it. In his previous three fights, he had been knocked out by Shavers, fought a draw with Le Doux, and won a ten-round decision over Tex Cobb.

Still, Cooney had bombed him, leaving Norton glassy-eyed and defenseless in a sitting position on the ropes. It was a dramatic and emphatic ending, with Cooney pile-driving the left hook until the referee jumped in and stopped it less than a minute into the match. If you didn't know any better, you would have thought you were looking at the Irish Godzilla.

Pardon me if I saw less than met the gaze of the goggle-eyed average Joe who jumped on the Cooney bandwagon, proclaiming him the next heavyweight champion. I thought talk like that was wishful thinking, and was looking forward to the chance to prove it.

For a while, it didn't look as though Holmes-Cooney would happen. Not right away at least.

King had offered Cooney $5 million for the match, but word was that Cooney had signed to fight Mike Weaver, the WBA champion, in October '81. It made sense: Weaver was the easier fight and, if Cooney were to win it, he'd be in a better bargaining position in the negotiations for Holmes-Cooney.

Trouble was the Weaver-Cooney fight seemed hamstrung by the WBA's hard-line position on Weaver's next challenger. The WBA was threatening to strip Weaver of his title if he didn't fight James "Quick" Tillis in his next defense.

For me, a fight with Cooney made sense. No opponent out there stirred public passion the way Cooney did. That passion would translate to big box office . . . and bring me, I figured, at least double the $1.9 million I'd been guaranteed for fighting Spinks. More if I was lucky.

Cooney was managed by a couple of real estate guys, Mike

Jones and Dennis Rappaport. Boxing writers called them "the Whacko Twins" on account of their unconventional ways of doing things. Rappaport was big for making waves with off-the-wall promotional stunts. Before he and Jones signed Cooney, they had themselves an undefeated (20–0, 7 KOs) middleweight named Ronnie Harris, a capable boxer whose concern for self-preservation made for dull fights and precious few offers from promoters.

To combat that, Rappaport stirred up interest by giving Harris a nickname, Mazel, from the Yiddish word for good luck, and then creating a controversy by insisting Harris be allowed to wear a yarmulke, a skullcap, when he fought. Of course, the boxing commissions said hell no, prompting Rappaport to go to court in a failed effort to overturn the commissions. But he had not failed in the more important aspect of getting attention for his fighter.

His next objective was to get Harris a fight in Madison Square Garden. As he told a reporter: "After realizing how much publicity I generated by the court case with the yarmulke, I said to myself, let me try to embarrass Gulf & Western, the parent company of the Garden, and generate publicity. I called up every newspaper and TV station and told them, 'Be at the Garden tomorrow at one o'clock.' At one o'clock, Ronnie Harris and I showed up at the lobby of the Garden with a gorilla. John Condon, who was with Madison Square Garden Boxing, was so annoyed by the scene we created he threatened to have us arrested. Teddy Brenner, the Garden matchmaker, calls Mike Jones at home. 'Get this crazy man outta here—he's embarrassing Gulf & Western. I'll give Harris a fight against Sugar Ray Seales for three thousand dollars.' Mike Jones said, 'Five thousand.' Brenner said, 'I'm hanging up.' "

Harris got his fight with Sugar Ray Seales in March '77, beat him, and the next year, in August '78, got a title shot against Hugo Corro in Buenos Aires. He lost, but for a couple of so-called whackos it wasn't a bad job of managing.

They had been clever too with Cooney—building his reputation against tomato cans and big names way past their prime like Norton, Ron Lyle, and Jimmy Young. Now when I say tomato cans, I'm speaking of guys like Bill Jackson and Joe Maye. When Cooney made his pro debut against Bill Jackson in February '77, Jackson was reported to have lost eighteen straight fights. Cooney knocked him out in one round. When Cooney fought Maye in November '77, Maye had lost seventeen fights in a row over a period of slightly more than two years. Cooney knocked him out in four rounds.

I wasn't sure whether the Whacko Twins were stalling the negotiations with King to agitate Cooney's price upward, or whether they were just plumb scared of me as an opponent. Maybe it was both. Maybe they figured: let's get every last penny out of this fight, which Gentleman Gerry, as he was known, isn't likely to win.

Who knows? But when Weaver signed to fight Tillis in October 1981, it didn't leave Cooney many big-money options out there. But even with a scarcity of other multimillion-dollar bouts for Cooney, Rappaport knew he was dealing from strength. In white America, Cooney was a marquee attraction. King tried to defuse Rappaport's leverage any way he could.

As Rappaport would tell a reporter: "A sticking point in the negotiations was that King didn't want Cooney to have parity with Holmes on the purses, and I insisted there had to be parity. I guess King heard I had been a civil rights activist because when we were in Chicago working on the deal, he came up to my hotel room with Reverend [Jesse] Jackson. Reverend Jackson said to me, 'You could retard the progress of the civil rights movement thirty years, fifty years, if Cooney gets parity.'

"I told him, 'Reverend, with all due respect, this is not a black-white issue. It's a green issue. The best attractions are beyond the color of skin. Muhammad Ali and Ray Leonard are bigger than Rocky Marciano or Ingemar Johansson were. The only reason Larry Holmes is getting as much money as Cooney is because he's champion. I'm bringing the charisma . . .' As I started going over the socioeconomic history of boxing, Reverend Jackson winked at King and said, 'God bless this crazy man,' and walked out."

As far as I was concerned, charisma was just Rappaport's code word for "white guy." What Rappaport really was telling Reverend Jackson was: "I'm bringing the white guy."

And in the boxing business that was worth something. Always had been.

The summer went by. The feds' investigation of King continued. In August, a *New York Post* headline stated:

GIACHETTI FEARS FOR LIFE

Holmes' ex-trainer links "contract" to boxing probe.

The story, written by Mike Marley, quoted Giachetti as saying he feared there was a contract on his head.

> *"I am fearful for my life," Giachetti said . . .*
>
> *Giachetti, 41, who either quit or was fired in April (after spending nine years developing Holmes) believes he's caught in a squeeze play between Holmes' promoter, Don King, FBI agents, and the federal grand jury in Manhattan that has been investigating boxing for the past 12 months.*
>
> *"I think they would try to make it look like a mugging. A bombing, an outright killing, would be too obvious," Giachetti said.*

As for King, he had more than the feds to worry about. When Ali agreed to fight Trevor Berbick in the Bahamas in December 1981—it would be Ali's last fight—King went down there in advance to get his money's worth for the option he had on Berbick's next fight. I guess he figured he could flash his papers and those island boys would run to the bank vault and fill his briefcase with hard green dollars. When he told me what he was going to do, I warned him: "Those boys on the island have been known to play very rough." King just laughed at me.

Not long after, King called and, in a funny-sounding voice, started telling me what had happened down there. Seems like he'd waved his paper and they had put a gun up to his bushy head.

King may have been too big a deal to fool with in the States; down there he was just the right size. The island boys stripped him of his clothes and stuck him on a plane back to the States in his bathrobe.

"You sure were right, Larry," he told me on the phone. "Those boys down there did me from stem to stern. From stem to stern. Har, har, har."

As he spoke, I realized there was something odd about the way he was speaking. I told him, "Man, you sound a little funny."

He said, "Course I do. That's what I was trying to tell you. They knocked a few of my teeth out. Har, har, har. Anyway, we got some business to talk."

The talk was about Holmes-Cooney, and both sides were slowly narrowing their differences. Emphasis on slowly. It seemed as though Rappaport was in no hurry to finalize a deal. I think he figured it couldn't hurt to let Larry Holmes wait. I was thirty-two at the time. Rappaport probably figured I could only grow older while Coooney, who was twenty-five, would still be in his prime.

Later that year ('81), when I stepped into the ring against Renaldo "Mister" Snipes in what was to have been a tune-up bout, the deal was just about done. But the Snipes match proved again that it's dumb to ever take anything for granted in the boxing business. Snipes was so discounted as a challenger that Las Vegas sports books refused to put the bout on the boards. But in Pittsburgh's Civic Arena, Snipes damn near ambushed me and the big bucks that Cooney and I were awaiting.

Through six rounds, I had been boxing smartly against Snipes, who would come toward me bobbing like a cork on a storm-swept sea. But in the seventh round, out of nowhere he landed a right hand against my head, just above the left ear, that knocked me to the canvas. When I got up at the count of six, I was on shaky legs and lurched forward, hitting my head against a neutral-corner turnbuckle.

Snipes came after me, but as my head cleared I began fighting back. I hit him with a succession of rights—one reporter counted eleven straight punches that landed before Snipes scored with a hook just before the bell.

By the eleventh round, I was pounding Snipes, who was helpless enough to require the intervention of the referee, Rudy Ortega. Ortega stopped the fight.

No doubt the Whacko Twins and Cooney breathed a sigh of relief when the fight was over. I know I did.

Soon after Holmes-Cooney was made for March 15, 1982, at Caesars Palace in Las Vegas, at which time it was announced Cooney and I would be making $10 million apiece.

I didn't like the idea of parity. I was a champion who'd struggled like crazy to get to the top. Cooney had not. He'd been cautiously matched to avoid serious risk while creating the image of a heavy-handed knockout artist.

I told King: "Don, I'm the undefeated heavyweight champion of the world. I've been that for four years. I've got to get more than the challenger. It's always been that way in the fight business."

"I know, Larry," he said, "but this fight's not just big, it's b-i-i-ig. And half of something this big is better than anything else that's around for you or is ever likely to come along. You got to take it."

There was something strange about Don's agreeing with Cooney's people so easily. He was supposed to be my man. Still, his logic was right. The fight was a monster.

Just the same, it troubled me to have Cooney getting parity. But that was the boxing business . . . and the world it reflected. Like Ali used to say of other fair-skinned fighters, Gerry Cooney had the complexion to get the connection.

What I had—and would continue to have—in the months that led to the fight was a firsthand encounter with how deep ran the racial currents in this country. It was not a pretty picture.

CHAPTER
FOURTEEN

Years after we fought, Gerry Cooney and I got to be friends.

I found him to be a good-hearted fellow, easy to be around. Whenever one of us was involved with a charity event, the other guy would lend his support by showing up.

But back in the 1980s, it wasn't like that. To be strictly accurate, we didn't like each other.

For my part, it had everything to do with the unequal circumstances by which we'd made our way through the ranks as fighters.

By my view, Cooney had had it easy. Nobody in the business except Giachetti had wanted my success, or fought on my behalf. Cooney? Another story. He had the VIP pass, the fast track to the top, and it was based on race.

The complexion to get the connection.

If you're a fighter with the sort of pride I'd shown again and again, climbing off the canvas and beating off strong men, well . . . that gets to you.

It got to me. I was angry about this new guy, Cooney. I knew he hadn't paid his dues like I had. I recognized the inequity in our experiences.

I also knew that boxing was like that—that historically the black man had been the odd man out. In the sport's distant past—the 1920s and 1930s—the black fighter was often excluded, not given the same chance the Irish, Italian, and Jewish boys got. Only an elite few blacks were viewed by promoters as worth bothering with.

But as the immigrant classes of poor Irish, Italian, and Jews prospered and moved to the suburbs, the supply of white fighters diminished, leaving thousands of black kids waiting in line. I know because I was one of them. And because I wanted it so bad and was willing to make any sacrifice—and I guess because I had some talent too—I succeeded.

I remember what a shock it was for me when I saw the movie *The Great White Hope*. It must have been in 1973 because I was working as a sparring partner for Ali in Deer Lake, and he was getting ready for one of his fights with Norton. After some of us saw the film, we talked about it into the wee hours of the morning. We all had heard Jack Johnson was a great fighter who had his title taken away, but none of us realized how hated he was by the white establishment and how the government did everything it could to beat him down. It really bothered white people in those days that the champion of the world was a black man and especially that he had a taste for white women.

In fact, when the film of Jack Johnson's July 4, 1910, victory over James J. Jeffries, the white hope, was shown in southern movie houses, riots ensued. That would lead to the passage of a law by Congress prohibiting interstate commerce in fight films. From that point on, the people who dealt in old fight films would be the same mobsters who bootlegged whiskey.

There is something about boxing, especially with heavyweights, that brings out deep racial instincts. I remember when Norman Mailer was in Zaire to do his book on the Foreman-Ali match—*The Fight*, it was called—he talked about what that difference was.

In baseball, basketball, even football, when a black man goes up against a white man, it is skill against skill. In fighting it is man directly against man—one's toughness and courage against the other's. If one fighter is black and the other is white, race pride is almost automatically at stake. It is a race war every time it happens. These days, it is what the public—especially white people, hoping for a white champion after so many years—will always pay to see.

And so it was in 1982 when Cooney and I were matched.

As Bert Sugar, then editor of *The Ring*, would say: "The Irish still constitute the largest and most vocal ethnic group of white boxing fans, and not just in New York. They haven't had a hero since Billy Conn almost beat Joe Louis. Gerry Cooney is their new hero, and they'll pay against all logic to see him."

Much later, on the eve of the fight, when *Time* magazine put Cooney on its cover along with not Larry Holmes but Sylvester Stallone, Allen Barra would write in *The Village Voice:*

> *The Cooney campaign strategists hit upon a brilliant ploy of selling Cooney as a real-life Rocky, though in fact by fight time Cooney was much better known to the general public than the champion he was challenging. But in retrospect, the Cooney-Stallone cover made perfect sense since the financial success of the biggest prize fight ever and the most popular boxing movie of all time were due in large measure to tapping the vein of racism that feeds the white hope fantasies. . . . And if* Time's *equation of Cooney with Rocky was an admission that Cooney's media campaign for the heavyweight title was in itself a national wish fulfillment, it was also convenient to treat the white hope fantasy as a fairy tale and ignore its uglier implications.*

From the moment Cooney appeared on the scene as a likely opponent, he touched a nerve in me—the same nerve that Braverman had struck when he joked about how he had tried to ambush me by overmatching me and I'd responded with fuck you.

The same awareness of the obstacles I'd had to overcome and

the lack of respect I'd gotten on the way up made me view Cooney grudgingly. Back in December 1980, it had led to a nasty encounter when we had run into each other in a restaurant in Mexico City during a WBC convention. Cooney and I had exchanged insults, with Cooney saying: "You need me more than I need you. Don't forget that."

When we stepped toward one another, Jose Sulaiman had risen from his table to break it up. In the shoving that followed Sulaiman had ended up with a bloody nose.

Later, when I'd fought Leon Spinks and was being interviewed by Cosell afterward, Cooney was steered in our direction.

I told Cosell: "Howard, if he comes over here I'm gonna slap him."

"You got no class," Cooney said.

I lunged at him and, during the skirmish, accidentally elbowed Cosell in the mouth, slightly cutting his lower lip.

Still later, at the postfight news conference, I said of Cooney: "If he was black, he'd be nowhere. You know it, I know it. We all know it."

The parity issue did little to soften my feelings. The truth is that while it was announced that both of us were guaranteed $10 million, the facts were otherwise. The way it broke down was each of us was guaranteed $3 million and 35 percent of all net receipts once it hit a certain number. The promoters, King and Cooney's guy, Sam Glass, would divvy up the remaining 30 percent of the net receipts. The way they had it figured—and most times you can predict gross dollars with reasonable accuracy—that would give Cooney and me each $10 million.

I can tell you this. I never saw $10 million. My take was $7.5 million, which shrank to $5 million once King and Spaz got their shares.

I can't say what Cooney ended up with, but from what I later heard and read he did better than I . . . by $2 million, $3 million.

One other thing. I never signed a contract for the Cooney fight. Now, a promoter is supposed to file contracts with the Nevada State Athletic Commission for each card of his. And I figure

King must have given them a contract for me. Early on in my career, I signed a whole lot of paper for King. Whether he slapped one of those pages from the past onto a whole lot of other pages, and what those pages might have said about Holmes-Cooney, I can't tell you. But I wouldn't be the first fighter of King's who thought Donald might have played fast and loose with his contracts.

In that *Village Voice* article that caught the craziness of Cooney being on the cover with Stallone, the writer, Barra, noted that unlike the *Rocky* movies, there was no villain for Cooney to play off—no Apollo Creed or Clubber Lang—but rather "Larry Holmes, a soft-spoken . . . man outside the ring and a meticulous craftsman inside it."

Well, if I wasn't Barra's Hollywood-style villain, the rest of America saw it otherwise. It didn't take long for me to be up to my ass in racial mudslinging. Tell you the truth, though, I saw it coming. Both King and Rappaport were hell-bent to extract every last dollar out of the promotion, and they knew by pitching it to the public as a fight between a black man and a white man—the great white hope angle all over again—they would fill the arena at Caesars Palace, expanded for Holmes-Cooney to thirty-two thousand seats, and have fight fans salivating for closed-circuit seats and pay-per-view screens. Me, I thought Cooney and I could avoid the racial cesspool by playing against it. But when in private I told Cooney that, he smiled and looked away, not bothering to say anything. I knew then that the worst was yet to come.

From the outset of my training, bad things began to happen. In the driveway of my home, there was a metal statue of a jockey—you know the kind: a figure in riding clothes and cap holding a lantern. This particular one was a white jockey. Well, one morning when I went out, I discovered that somebody had painted his face black.

That was the start of the unending racial assault on my family and me. Vandals blew my home mailbox apart with cherry bombs and painted the words "nigger nigger nigger" on the wall of the entrance to my house. Bullets smashed the window of my restaurant on Northampton Street. When we ran outside, we saw the letters "KKK" painted on the wall of the parking lot across the street. At my office, the phone would ring and, when I answered, the caller would say: "Cooney's gonna kick your black ass." Or, "You can't fight, nigger."

I began screening the calls. They still got to me. My receptionist would say that Don King was calling. I'd pick up the phone and it would be a white guy saying: "You ain't shit. Cooney's gonna kick your ass."

I'd tell him: "Fuck you. You better kill me now 'cause I for sure am going to beat your boy."

They got to calling me at home too. And when I'd answer them back, challenging them to meet me on the street, it upset Diane, who was pregnant with what I hoped would be our first son. For sure I wouldn't let *her* answer the phone and have to hear that garbage.

I'd had this kind of call before—"So and so's gonna whup you"—but never with the racial curses that were coming now. "Nigger bastard." "Black faggot."

There were threats too. "We're gonna burn down your house tonight." And: "Don't start up your car tomorrow, nigger."

Of course, I knew that the people doing this were nutcases. But the frequency of their provocations got to me . . . and made me angry. Damn angry. I said things then that maybe I shouldn't have. Said Cooney wasn't the great white hope but a great white dope. Other times I called him a great white hoax. My anger at what I was having to put up with made me strike back. I was determined not to be intimidated by the collective desire of white America to see me get beat . . . by an America desperate for its first white heavyweight champion since Ingemar Johansson KO'd Floyd Patterson in 1959.

In doing so, I was soon tagged by certain writers as a racist. That hurt. I knew it wasn't so. I'd grown up among Italians and Irish and Lebanese. We all hung around and played together. It wasn't perfect—there were racial sparks from time to time—but it didn't preoccupy us.

What's more, I'd always tried to look beyond the color of a man's skin. I'll give you an example. When I bought the Holiday Inn, a 131-room hotel just across the river in Phillipsburg, the whole white staff—except for four people—quit. They just didn't want to work for a black boss. That hurt. But when I replaced the staff, I didn't hire all black people. I hired qualified people who would give me an honest day's work. That got black people criticizing me for not taking care of my own. That's how it goes. In Easton today, there are still white folks who resent me because I'm the boss and I'm black. And there are black people who have it in for me because I don't hire exclusively black. That's my definition of racial lunacy.

Everything connected with the Cooney fight was race, race, race. I took to carrying a gun because the gunshots and cherry bombs meant there were some real crackpots out there. But the big problem was that I began to get leery of white people just because they were white. That's what I mean about the atmosphere getting poisoned. I began to think, "What do they think about me?" I began to imagine I could read their minds, and naturally what I read was prejudice. If I came across a white man who said, "I hope you beat Cooney, Larry," I thought he was just being sarcastic and making fun of me.

Meanwhile, King and Rappaport were nudging the media toward the racial angle. The press were like spiteful schoolboys, trying to incite Cooney and me. "Hey, Larry, did you hear what Gerry said?" Or: "Gerry, Larry called you a . . ."

Rappaport regularly brought up the racial issue to denounce it, with this slogan: "He's not the white man, he's the right man."

I phoned King and told him about the gunshots and the threatening calls in Easton and that I thought he could cool things down by backing off the black-white approach to the fight. He wasn't all that bothered by what I was experiencing. It was, according to Donald, what happened when a white and black fought. But I knew he was full of crap. When I'd fought Le Doux in Minnesota, his home turf, the racial vibes were minimal.

Cooney himself wasn't saying anything directly racist, so I thought he might be the guy who could help me defuse the situation. I tried to get through to him on the phone, but there was no way. Dennis Rappaport had Cooney so protected he never returned my calls.

I finally got my chance to talk to Cooney when Howard Cosell interviewed us before the fight. It was a little late in the game, but the racial thing figured to get even more explosive as we came down to the last few weeks in Vegas. The studio people weren't quite ready to tape and we were each sitting alongside Howard. I leaned across Howard and said, "Man, no one knows what's gonna happen out there. Either I kick your ass or you kick mine. We'll each try to do the best we can to win. Either way, Gerry, we're the ones who are putting it on the line. Those guys who are talking all this shit, they don't risk anything. They're gonna collect our money no matter what happens. We're the ones who got to get beat up. So the one thing we ought to do is be friends."

He just dropped his head and never looked at me, like a mercenary who had been taught not to have feelings or concern. I was disappointed by him. But over the years I thought about the pressures he must have been under, feeling as though all of white America was depending on him to beat me. Gerry was sincere— maybe too sincere—in feeling he had an obligation to those people. It weighed on him and probably colored how he thought of me.

But if the pressures of being a white hope weighed on Gerry, I had my own burden. Everywhere I turned, people were in my face, letting me know they wanted me to lose. On the flight to Vegas, we stopped in Chicago, where folks said, "Good luck, Holmes. You're gonna need it."

In Vegas, it was worse. Caesars Palace was like downtown Dublin. There were green signs everywhere proclaiming we were in "Cooney Country." Green signs and shamrocks, like the four-leaf clovers Gentleman Gerry wore on his trunks and robe. As a champion who had fought at Caesars often, I felt slighted. I felt I deserved better.

But it was, as they say in *The Godfather*, not personal. Just business. Cooney was from Huntington, Long Island, and the casino was jammed with his supporters. That meant they were spending at the hotel, and Caesars wasn't about to do anything to upset paying customers.

Executives from Caesars told me they would be glad to accommodate my fans and hang up signs for Larry Holmes. But Easton was a largely blue-collar city and at that time was experiencing a business slump. So my fans were back in the Delaware Valley, leaving me to move among the aggressively hostile Cooney crowd. More than once their rude remarks triggered near-confrontations with the guys in my camp.

The first day Cooney trained at Caesars members of my camp went over to watch. When they were discovered and asked to leave, they did so but only after harsh words between both camps were exchanged. Cliff Perlman, Caesars' chairman of the board, called in both sides separately and asked them to behave. But I felt the casino was putting too much blame on my guys.

Let's face it, you keep getting that sort of reception wherever you go, it makes you leery . . . and maybe a touch paranoid. But enough strange things had happened to me in the months leading up to the fight that there were times I couldn't be sure whether I was being paranoid or being abused.

For instance, when I settled into Caesars, I became suspicious about the food. The first meal I had in my suite was a steak that had a peculiar fishy taste. The next few meals, the vegetables had an acidy taste.

Meanwhile, hotel construction was waking me up at four, five, in the morning—jackhammers blasting away. I wondered whether Cooney's room suffered the same noise pollution. My guess was that it didn't. When there wasn't the banging from the construction, my phone would be ringing at odd hours with the kind of crank callers who'd been bugging me in Easton. Paranoia or reality, I didn't care. I made a move.

There was a fella at the Dunes—a chef who was a fan of mine. He got me a suite at the Dunes, which sat catty-corner from Caesars on Las Vegas Boulevard. The suite had a kitchen, and my friend the chef would have the food brought up. Then he and his staff would prepare the meal right in my suite.

I never checked out of Caesars, just didn't eat or sleep there. I would awaken at 6 A.M. at the Dunes, cross the street to meet the guys for my morning roadwork. On one of those mornings, as I was standing on the corner of Las Vegas Boulevard and Flamingo, a car waiting for the light began honking its horn. I figured it was another of the Cooney nuts who wanted to do nigger this, nigger that. But no, it was a black guy, who stepped out of the car, walked over to me with a big grin, and said, "Larry Holmes! Me and my wife drove all the way here to bet on you. You got to beat this boy, y'hear! Look in this bag."

The paper bag his wife showed me was full of money they were going to bet. Well, after being treated like Public Enemy No.1, boy did it feel good to hear this. That couple really lifted my spirits. At the time it felt like they were the only strangers in Las Vegas who wanted me to win.

As the fight drew near, the hordes began descending on Vegas. *The New York Times* reported that Caesars had invited only those guests who had a $50,000 line of credit. Unlike Atlantic City, where the casinos are required to reveal their weekly income, Las Vegas casinos don't have to report what they make. But the rule of thumb was that only the big fights rival New Year's Eve in Las Vegas for a night's casino gross. And the word I got was that Caesars had *cleared* a record $10 million for the week of my fight with Ali. Holmes-Cooney was expected to do even better.

Caesars had paid $6 million for the live-site rights and, with tickets priced at $600 tops, the casino anticipated a record gate of $7 million or more. *Time* magazine said that 2.5 million paying customers were expected to watch the fight at closed-circuit theaters.

If a guy from Mars had landed on the Strip, the main drag of Las Vegas, in June 1982, and been asked to judge from the outward evidence which fighter was the champion, you can bet he would have said Cooney. I mean, the week of the fight, *Sports Illustrated* had a lush color painting of Cooney in his shamrock green trunks on its cover . . . and guess where Larry Holmes was? On an inside flap.

Sure it bothered me. I won't pretend it didn't. The magazine covers. The TV commercials that dropped in Cooney's lap. The celebrities like Sinatra and Stallone who hovered around him. I had been a champion for four years, fighting regularly and winning . . . and not bringing any disgrace on the game with misbehavior outside the ring. Yet once Cooney appeared, it was as if I was a supporting player—the other guy, so called. Cooney was presented in the media as a gentle giant—the photos of him always had him smiling or kissing babies. Me, the pictures showed a scowling, angry man.

> *And so* [wrote Allen Barra] *after more than a year of the cleverest campaign strategy since Carter's presidential bid, the Cooney campaign had not only managed to exploit racism but to reverse the tables and put Holmes on the defensive as a "racist"—the same Larry Holmes who grew up with and still lives near white friends in Easton, Pennsylvania, who has four brothers married to white women, whose personal secretary is white, whose close friend and corner man Luis Rodriguez is Hispanic, and whose special trainer, Daeshik Seo, is Korean.*

Experts, it seems, have always lowballed Larry Holmes.

And that didn't change when it came time to fight Cooney. There seemed to be a feeling out there that I was slipping—that at thirty-two I was beginning to show my age.

Still, I was surprised at how many of them thought Cooney could whup me.

Al Braverman was at the head of the parade, predicting that Cooney would flatten me "like a latke [potato pancake] within five." *That* sure as hell didn't surprise me.

Norman Mailer said, "Cooney will win because he's got one

205

of the best left hooks I've ever seen in a heavyweight and because he's young and strong. Holmes is a fine boxer and a hard hitter but he's looking just a little old."

Carmen Basilio, the former world champion welterweight and middleweight, said, "Cooney's got youth, height, speed, and punching power. The fight won't go more than six rounds."

On and on it went. Even Ali got into the act, saying: "Cooney will hit Larry so hard he'll jolt his kinfolk back in Africa."

Was Muhammad jiving—doing the promoters a favor by being outrageous? Or was he just bugged that his former sparring partner had given him a good whupping?

Whatever. Talk was talk. And now it was time to fight. I had no doubt that I would beat Gerry Cooney. There was just no way he was going to outtough me. He grew up in the suburbs. He graduated from high school. His father, a construction worker, made good steady money. And because he was white and big and could fight a little, he didn't have to box in Scranton for sixty-three dollars. He didn't have to fight thousands of rounds as someone else's sparring partner. He didn't have to face the moment of truth and take on a fighter as tough as Roy Williams until he was already a top contender. Gerry Cooney didn't have to pay his dues the way I did, the way most black fighters do. He didn't have the hunger in his belly that I did.

It gets hot in Vegas in June—that dry desert heat. And on the day of the fight, temperatures soared to over one hundred degrees. By evening, the air temperature during the preliminary bouts reached ninety-nine degrees.

It was 7:55, Vegas time, when Cooney left his trailer and made his way to the ring in a green robe, with the hood pulled over his head. In my trailer, I could hear the chant of "Cooo-ney, Cooo-ney." My guys were getting me revved: "You're the man! ...You're the champ! ... Let's kick his ass!"

Then it was time for me to head to the ring. As I made my way there, I could hear cheers mixed with boos. A few of those thirty-two thousand fans leaned toward the aisle and shouted: "Cooney's gonna kill you!" Others shouted encouragement. I looked to the ring and could see Cooney on his knee in his corner, praying . . . while Rappaport raised a huge mock-up of a wristwatch with the notation ". . . tick, tick, tick." The idea was, I guess, that time was running out on me.

On the way to the ring, I couldn't help notice that green and white flags flew all along the perimeter of the arena and that the ushers were wearing green shirts. That told me that Caesars Palace was looking to a shamrock future—that a Gerry Cooney was worth a whole lot more to the casino than Larry Holmes.

Cooney as the challenger had been the first fighter in the ring. That was boxing tradition. But when they announced the fighters and introduced me first, that broke tradition—a champion was *never* introduced first—and reinforced the overwhelming bias toward Cooney I'd had to deal with practically from the day the fight was signed. Even the president of the United States, Ronald Reagan, was in on it. Earlier in the day, he'd had Secret Service guys install a phone hookup in Cooney's dressing room so that he could congratulate him if he won. I guess Reagan didn't feel the same urgency to say hello to me, because he hadn't bothered to wire my trailer.

All of this put me in a foul mood, and as I stood in my corner, glaring at Cooney, I was truly mad. But it was a smoldering anger. I wasn't going to let it get out of control and make me do something stupid. Cooney turned his eyes away every time he saw me glaring at him.

Before the fight, I had told the press: "I ain't going to fight Gerry Cooney. I'm going to box him. You have to make a guy drunk before you mug him." That was just a way of saying I would not be swept up in the emotion that had built for this fight. I would fight *my* kind of fight.

That meant circling to my left away from Cooney's hook, and applying my jab to his face. Break up his rhythm and, when he pivoted to throw the hook, step to the side, out of harm's way. I was cautious, I was careful in that opening round. And I was watching Cooney, registering his rhythms, his patterns, figuring the distance at which I could make him a target.

The first round was what they call a "feeling-out" round—a round in which we were both getting a sense of how the other fellow moved without committing to full-tilt aggression. I thought Cooney was slow and would be easy to hit with the jab.

By the second round, I was snapping off jabs that landed with impact—three, four in a row right in his puss. I figured: What the hell, try something off the jab. I delivered the jab and then brought the right hand over it—the oldest combination in boxing. And damn: the right landed flush on Cooney's jaw. Cooney lurched halfway around the ring before falling to his knees in my corner. It was the first time as a professional fighter Cooney had been knocked down. Cooney got to his feet at the count of five with a sheepish smile and took the mandatory eight count from the referee, Mills Lane.

Do I go after him and try to put him away? Or do I stick to my plan and make sure I've got him out on his feet before I try to finish him? I put myself in his position, which wasn't hard because I knew about being knocked down. Given it was the first time he'd hit the deck, there was no telling how he would handle it. It was early, he still was strong. What if he tagged me coming in? Even though I'm a gambler sometimes, I wasn't going to risk it all this early.

Cooney rallied over the next few rounds, getting that left hook of his in there. Give him this: he could punch. The left hurt when it landed but I usually could see it coming. My objective was to get him to punch himself out. Cooney was used to quick knock-outs and, big as he was, he didn't figure to possess lots of stamina. In his twenty-five fights, he'd never gone more than eight rounds. If he had to fight a distance fight, I figured on his wearing down.

While Cooney got his shots in from rounds three to five, I was setting myself to take them, and keeping the fight where I wanted to . . . in the center of the ring. By the fifth round, I was scoring regularly with the jab and the overhand right. Unless he got lucky, I had no doubt at all that I was going to beat the man.

Through those middle rounds, I was working Cooney over, hitting him and hurting him. In the sixth round, I staggered him with a right hand to the head and this time went after him. At one point the ropes prevented Cooney from spinning out of the ring. By the seventh round, blood was trickling from Cooney's left eyelid and from the bridge of his nose. I was up on my toes, punching and dancing away like I did with Ali in the old sparring days. It made me feel young and gave me pleasure to show I was still a very good athlete.

In my corner between every round, Futch was mumbling stuff for me to do. I couldn't hear him, and since things were going pretty well, it didn't matter. Ray Arcel, an old-timer who was assisting Futch, was there mostly to handle cuts. I must have told him a hundred times in training that I couldn't stand smelling salts, but he was a big believer in them. They used them in the old days, but they were illegal now in Nevada. I told him to keep them out of my face. Then, for no reason at all, after the seventh round he sticks one right under my nose. I went crazy and warned them to keep Arcel away from me.

By the tenth round Cooney was tired. He was hurt. He was bleeding. He had been knocked down. But he held together and really showed me something in that tenth round. It wasn't just boxing anymore. It was fighting. We just whaled on each other. I took his best body shots. He took my combinations and kept coming forward, throwing punches. The crowd was roaring. During the action Cooney hit me low for the umpteenth time and Lane, who had warned him earlier, deducted a point from his score. When it happened again, Lane took another point. Then we went back to letting the punches fly. When the bell rang, we stopped and tapped each other with our gloves. Respect in a simple gesture.

There were still five rounds to go. I was prepared for them. Cooney wasn't. Finally, he looked drunk enough to be mugged, although he stayed real game and took a terrible beating. By this time Rappaport was trying to rally him by shouting: "America needs you!" Rappaport had spent the night spouting that cornball nonsense, telling Cooney: "Win it for your dead father." And: "Win it for the kid with leukemia."

209

Before the fight, some of the so-called experts didn't think Gerry Cooney had a big heart. They were wrong; there were lots of chances for him to quit and he refused. He did hit me low again a couple more times—maybe his arms were tired—and lost another point.

By the thirteenth round, Cooney was moving in slow motion, blood smearing his face. He was, I knew, ready to be had. I hit him with one shot after another, measuring him for the right hand. Cooney staggered but wouldn't go down. Part of me was thinking: "Man, why am I doing this to another man?" I'd never thought like that before I won the title. Moment by moment, Cooney was grinding down, slogging about the ring. I threw a left uppercut and a right, and Cooney went reeling backward, grabbing the top rope as he slid toward the canvas. By taking hold of the rope, he was able to keep his bottom from touching but not able to prevent his other glove from scraping the canvas— a knockdown.

At that moment, Cooney's trainer, Victor Valle, climbed through the ring ropes. Lane turned to wave him away—the corner cannot stop a fight in Nevada—but Valle ignored the referee and went over to his beaten fighter, forcing Lane to stop the bout at 2:52 of the thirteenth round.

Cooney told Valle, "I'm okay," as Valle led him across the ring.
"That's enough, son," Valle told him. "That's enough."
Tick tick tick: the clock had run out on Gerry Cooney.

But I knew I'd been in a fight. My ribs were aching, and would continue to for a full week. My feet were blistered and bleeding because the canvas had been so hot. But I wasn't going to let any of that stop me from having my say at the postfight press conference. Maybe it would have been wiser to be more gracious in victory. But as I figured it out years later, what my detractors said fueled me as a fighter . . . and that fuel couldn't be turned off just because the bout was over. That anger sat in me like a hot coal, and probably cost me a whole lot in public relations.

On this night, there was added fuel—the judges' version of the bout. It turned out that while I was beating Cooney up, the judges were doing Looney Tunes scoring. Through the first twelve rounds, Jerry Roth had it scored 115–109 in my favor. But the other two judges, Duane Ford and Dave Moretti, had me up by only 113–111. That meant that if you didn't factor in the three points that Mills Lane had deducted for Cooney's low blows, Ford and Moretti would have had Cooney ahead after twelve rounds. That was surreal, given what I had done to him. In that Sunday's *New York Times*, the headline asked: COULD HOLMES HAVE LOST A DECISION?

The *Times*'s man at ringside, Michael Katz, wrote that Larry Holmes "was never more convincing than he was Friday night [against Cooney]. Except to the judges."

I told the media in my usual charming manner that I hoped this fight put to rest the issue of whether I could really fight. They gave me the best young—and I emphasized *young*—contender around, and I gave him a boxing lesson. Why did I have to go on, year after year as champ, proving myself all the time?

"I have killed all the critics," I said. "Rocky—Sylvester Stallone—*Time* magazine, *Sports Illustrated*. I'm very sorry to not be what you expect. I'm not Muhammad Ali. I'm not Joe Louis. And I'm not Leon Spinks either. But I wasn't born to be these people. I was born to be myself, Larry Holmes."

I could tell from the questions posed in the press conference what the slant in a lot of the stories was going to be:

Gerry Cooney [I figured they would say] was not the fighter his record and the experts led us all to believe he would be. That as opposed to: Larry Holmes, still the undefeated heavyweight champion of the world, fought a smart, tough fight tonight against a good contender.

There it was again, the Larry Holmes Curse. I might be champion of the world for a lot of years, but I could never get the respect that goes with it. I guess you can't have everything, and I certainly did have more money and fame than I ever imagined possible. Still, not having that respect always ate at me. And there was no way to let people know how I felt without coming off bitter and ungrateful. I know the best way of handling it is to say nothing and let history sort out the kind of fighter I was. But that wasn't my style back then.

In fact, after the news conference, I wandered through the casino at Caesars in my boxing trunks and robe, telling people: "You lost your money betting on Gerry Cooney. Now who's the man?" Early on in my stay at Caesars, there'd been a Cooney supporter who'd made a point of betting against me when I shot craps. I saw him now and laughed at the guy.

Meanwhile, Cooney had to go to the local hospital for about a dozen stitches over his left eye. We met up at 4 A.M.—7 A.M. back east—for a live interview with Howard Cosell for *Good Morning America*. When I got there, I had to force Cooney to shake my hand. He looked peculiar, not just beat up but defeated inside. I told him he fought a good, game fight. "Everyone gets beat," I told him, "and sometimes losing makes you an even better fighter. Hell, you're only twenty-five years old." He didn't seem to believe me, but it was true. Gerry Cooney, I thought back then, had the stuff to become a helluva fighter. Lots of heart. And a punch that I could testify was a hurting thing.

A few days later, I was back in Easton watching the news on TV. They showed Cooney returning home and saying, "I'm sorry I let you all down."

At the time, I remember telling Diane: "Why's he feel sorry for the guy who bought a ticket? He didn't let anybody down. He did his best."

In the years that followed, I'd get into arguments with people who would try to tell me Gerry Cooney was a bum. I really felt otherwise. That he never did get to be champion puzzled me. I believed in him. I even bet and lost five grand on him when he fought and lost to Michael Spinks. And I lost another five grand when George Foreman knocked him out.

Ask me what happened with Cooney, and I'm still at a loss. Something on the mental side, I suspect. Maybe, as some experts said, Cooney never really wanted to be a boxer. In the beginning, he was pushed to it by his disciplinarian father. Against me, he was doing it for white America. Maybe the reasons Cooney walked into that ring were never compelling to him. I don't know. Gerry would have to figure that one out. All I can tell you is if you don't have the fire in your belly, it ain't gonna happen for you.

And thank the Lord, I still had the fire.

Diane gave birth to Larry Holmes Jr. a few months after the Cooney fight. I finally had the son I could be a father to. It helped me put the bitter memory of the racism surrounding the Cooney fight behind me. But it also made me wonder what kind of life my children would have in a world that wasn't changing very much for the better. I knew that being the son and daughter of a famous father and even having money wasn't going to protect them from some painful racial incidents in their lives. I was fearful about their future.

CHAPTER
FIFTEEN

Say this about Gerry Cooney, at least he got the public worked up.

For a guy like me, it was important to have challengers who could rouse interest. A champion without worthy contenders was like a doughnut without the hole. It was hard to recognize him for what he was.

That was my situation after the Cooney bout.

But business was business. You did what you had to. You fought what was out there.

By November of '82, more than five months after beating Cooney, it meant taking on Randall "Tex" Cobb down in Houston. One-point-six million bucks to meet Cobb on ABC-TV.

Cobb was a unique character, a beer-drinking, fun-loving fella who'd played a little offensive line at Abilene Christian and been a kickboxer before taking up the manly art. The writers loved him because Tex was good "copy," saying outrageous things in a homespun funny way. For instance, Cobb claimed never to have been knocked off his feet except for the time he was floored by a 130-pound bar patron: "But I don't think that counts because someone was swinging him by the heels at the time."

As a fighter, he was awkward, and crude. He couldn't even box a trifecta. He was a human block of cement no one had ever knocked down before. In twenty-two fights, he had lost only twice, to Ken Norton and Michael Dokes.

Although Cobb was a white guy, the fight would be without the racially charged atmosphere of the Cooney bout. That was because it was widely conceded Cobb hadn't much of a chance. What Cobb had was the ability to absorb punches. What I had was way too much quickness and skill. It was like fighting a heavy bag. I threw punches, Cobb took them, trying gamely but without any real success to lay something on me.

Very quickly, Cobb's face got swollen and bloody. But Tex just kept walking forward, straight into my punches. The referee is supposed to stop a fight when a fighter is helpless, but Cobb wasn't helpless. He was just mismatched, terribly mismatched.

By the eighth round, as the swelling around his left eye became more pronounced, the referee, Steve Crosson, asked Cobb if he could see okay. "Sure," said Cobb. "I can see you. You're white."

After the fourteenth round, Cobb staggered around the ring, trying to find his corner. He went to a neutral corner, realized his mistake, and after another false start finally figured where he had to go.

Enough of this, I thought. I'm not gonna hit him in the final round if I don't have to. For the first minute and a half, I did my best to stay away from Cobb. But the guy had no reverse gear. He just kept moving toward me, like Robby the Robot, throwing punches, forcing me to fight back.

I knew I had the fight won and had no desire to pound Tex any more, even when the crowd started booing at my reluctance. Screw 'em. I knew that the fifteenth round was too often that one round too many that caused another ring fatality. Tex Cobb was a good man with a lot of courage. I just didn't want to hit him any more.

The sight of all this had Cosell babbling: "A mismatch like this is pre-cisely what's wrong with this so-called sport of boxing. . . . This is pitiful. . . . This is disgusting."

After the fight—a lopsided fifteen-round decision for me—Co-sell said he would never announce another fight again. He acted as though he had just discovered boxing was a brutal sport.

After Cosell said sayonara to boxing, Cobb would quip about his role in Howard's defection: "If I cured cancer or eliminated heart disease, I don't think I could give a greater gift to mankind."

Me, I thought Cosell used the mismatch as his way out of covering sports. He always thought he really was bigger than sports and should be sitting at the anchor desk on ABC's *World News*. Boxing, and especially Ali, had made him, but he didn't talk about how rotten boxing was then. Or when he was a shill for ABC's U.S. Boxing Championship. Or when Ali was fighting the same sort of mismatches—against Floyd Patterson, for instance.

Cosell always struck me as a very strange man. One time, Howard, Don King, and I were sitting at the bar in Caesars, and I felt this hand rubbing on my knee and then up my thigh. *What the hell is this?* It was goddamned Howard. I looked at Cosell and growled: "What you doing, man? Get your hand off me!"

Howard turned it into a joke, slurring his words and saying, "But I love you, Larry. I wanna make love to you." King started laughing his big dumb laugh—"Har, har, har . . ." It bothered me a lot because even if it was a joke, his touching me there wasn't funny.

A year later, we were at Caesars again, right after the Cooney fight, and this time Diane was sitting with us. Damned if I didn't feel Cosell's hand rubbing me in the same place. I got angry again. Don laughed in the same way. And Cosell turned to Diane and slurred, "What do you see in this guy? I could treat you so much better than he does. Why don't you come away with me?" Supposedly he was kidding again.

I told Howard it wasn't funny. But he wouldn't quit. So Diane and I got up and moved to another table. Don just kept laughing. For the life of me I couldn't figure what Cosell was up to. One thing I knew for sure: when I got drunk, I didn't touch other men's thighs and then make jokes about it.

Back to Cobb. When the fight ended, Tex embraced me and said, "Hey, next time let's fight in a telephone booth."

I shook my head and grinned: "I tell you what. I'll just give you my home phone number and you call me about the fight."

In later years, Cobb would become an actor, appearing in films like *Raising Arizona* as a crazy-ass bounty hunter, in *The Golden Child* as a henchman of Satan, and in *Police Academy 4* as a guy who beats up an old lady. I saw him on TV shows like *Miami Vice* and *Moonlighting*, playing tough guys, and then he'd turn around and charm the audience with his wit on *Late Night with David Letterman*. Like when the subject of his beating at my hands would be brought up, Tex would say, "Larry Holmes didn't beat me. He just won the first fifteen rounds." What a character.

At the victory party after the fight, King approached me and said, "Larry, I lost seven hundred thousand dollars on this fight. I'm going to have to cut your purse another two hundred thousand."

"Like hell you are," I told him.

See, my purse originally was to have been $2.1 million. But when the bout was switched from a Friday to a Monday, the decline in TV revenues was the pretext King used—and maybe it was a justified one—to reduce my purse to $1.6 million.

But I remembered King telling me about a $300,000 hit he'd taken—allegedly taken—earlier in the year when Salvador Sanchez fought Azumah Nelson. He'd laughed about it in recounting it. So now I told him: "Well, you just take your seven-hundred-thousand-dollar loss and laugh now. You aren't going to cut me another dime."

When the press got wind of what occurred and asked King about it the next day, he pooh-poohed it, claiming he had been drunk at the party—there was nothing to it. Don King always had a story.

Back when he was the man on top, Ali told me what has to happen before any fighter can possibly beat the system. He said, "It hardly ever happens, but if fighting needs you more than you need it, you better get yours real fast because you won't be in that situation for long. And be ready to pay the price, because they're gonna get even." I never forgot his words.

I believed the time had come to take a shot at independence. Spaz and I had talked about it for a long time and decided to move on it in 1983. We had set up a production and promotion company called Sports/Cor. The plan was for me to promote my own title defenses as soon as I figured a way to lose Don King.

I knew I was breaking new ground—dangerous ground. It was one thing for a fighter to try to hold out for more money against a promoter; it was another thing to challenge the basic structure of boxing, where the promoter is the master and the fighter is his slave. Somewhere down the line there was probably going to be a price to pay, but the same angry spite that drove me in the ring was driving me now. Also, I was after justice for a lot of other fighters besides myself. I wanted to try to change the boxing business.

With the feds still hounding him, and an indictment supposedly imminent, the time seemed right to loosen King's death grip on my future. In early '83, I told King I'd be defending my title against the European heavyweight champion, Lucien Rodriguez, and promoting the bout. King went "Har . . . har . . . har" and then began talking about the paper he had on me that bound me to fight Tim Witherspoon next. I told him he could take his paper and shove it. Come hell or high water, I would fight Rodriguez for Sports/Cor.

"Don King," I said, "the only way I'll ever fight for you again is if you let me fight for me. And I'll sue your ass if you don't."

He knew I wasn't playing this time.

Take a guess who I heard from next. King's WBC bobo, Jose

Sulaiman. He said his organization would not sanction Holmes-Rodriguez. Some surprise.

Next I heard from Sig Rogich, a WBC vice president, who later would become a spin doctor for President George Bush and still later for Mike Tyson after Tyson bit a chunk off of Evander Holyfield's ear. Rogich threatened to strip me of my title if I fought Rodriguez.

"I'm the people's champion," I told him, "and have been for more than five years. The people will recognize me if the WBC won't."

King must have sensed I wasn't fooling, and backed off. He said he'd sign a release so that I could promote the Rodriguez fight if I agreed to face Witherspoon after that. Once I did agree to that, the WBC rolled over again and quit their threats.

Now that I was in business as a fighter-promoter, I discovered a curious fact. At CBS-TV, I was a nonentity.

The lawyer I was referred to at the network told me: "We have a corporation policy, Larry. We don't talk to fighters."

Really. Well, okay. If CBS wanted to play that . . .

I asked Dick Lovell, an old friend who worked for me, handling my press and public relations, to talk to CBS. The network offered half a million dollars for the fight.

ABC was still smarting from the bad ink and Cosell's harangue on the Tex Cobb match. And though Jim Spence at ABC had no problem talking with me, he had a problem doing business on an opponent as so-so as Rodriguez. ABC said "pass."

At NBC, Ferdie Pacheco was the guy who was advising the network what fights to buy and how much to pay. Pacheco, who also did commentary for its matches, knew me from my days as a sparring partner of Ali's, back when he worked Muhammad's corner. Yet it wasn't like some kind of nostalgic reunion when the two of us sat down and negotiated. Truth is, Pacheco was another of the many guys who had treated me like a second-class passenger on the Good Ship Ali. Pacheco was, like King, like

Cosell, like Braverman, your run-of-the-mill front-runner, treating you well only if he thought you were important. I guess I'd become important. Pacheco advised NBC to take the fight for $600,000. Not a lot of money for a title fight, but enough to guarantee we'd make a little profit.

I made a decision to stage the fight in Scranton, the site of so many of my early low-paying fights. Up to World War II, Scranton had been a coal-mining hotbed. But after the war, as oil replaced coal, the mines shut down and the population shrank drastically, from 155,000 to 86,000. But Scranton was my launching pad, and having won the title allowed me to feel warmly about those hard beginnings now. Back then—another story. But as heavyweight champion, I could look back on Scranton as the bottom rung on the ladder I'd climbed to the top. There was a certain kind of symmetry to going back there that I liked.

Pacheco knew when he advised NBC to buy the fight that the network had an event—a heavyweight title defense—more than a killer-diller match. Rodriguez had lost to some obscure opponents, like Ngozika Ekwelum and Lorenzo Zanon. Evangelista had KO'd him three times. Michael Dokes had beat him by decision. Nobody was expecting Rodriguez to be the last action hero.

On the other hand, we were hoping he'd put up a fight—show some passion. But Rodriguez ran like a bandit. He was there to survive. Guys like that make for lousy fights. It *was* a lousy fight. An easy win for me—I won every round on the judges' scorecards—but a lousy fight. For a first promotion, that was a disappointment.

Witherspoon was next, less than two months later. I remember at the press conference for the fight trying to tell him how to avoid King's trickerations so he would get out of the fight game with some money.

"Shut up—I'm gonna knock your ass out," he told me, practically in midsentence . . . like he didn't need to hear it.

Maybe he thought I was high-hatting him, rather than just warning him, fighter to fighter, as Earnie Shavers had once warned me. I don't know. All I can tell you is when I was coming up, I listened to what Ali and other guys had to say about the business end of boxing, and locked it in my mind on the chance that someday I might need that information.

Witherspoon? He would be screwed royally by King. For instance, after he beat Tony Tubbs in January 1986 for the WBA title, King matched Witherspoon against Frank Bruno of England, telling him he would be paid $550,000. For a new champion, that sounded like a decent enough payday. But that was before Witherspoon found out that King was allocated more than a million dollars by HBO for the July '86 match—as much as $1.7 million some reports said—most of which was supposed to go to Witherspoon. And it was before he learned that Bruno, the challenger—paid from a separate allocation by *his* promoters— would end up with more than the champion. And when it came time to be paid, it was even worse. Where Bruno, the loser, ended up with $900,000, Witherspoon, the winner and champion, got a check for $90,094, thanks to a $275,000 cut taken by his so-called manager, King's adopted son, Carl, and thanks to King's fancy bookkeeping, which hung all kinds of expenses on him.

Witherspoon was so depressed by that, and subsequent trickerations of the family King, that he was mentally out of it at the time of his next fight, against Bonecrusher Smith. Smith knocked him out in one round that December ('86). Witherspoon's career floundered after that and, though he recouped more than a million dollars in a suit against King years later, he could have done a lot better if his career had run its course. Witherspoon was, I thought, a talented fighter.

I can tell you this. He gave me hell when we fought. The bout took place in a newly built outdoor stadium at the Dunes on a sweltering Vegas night. At the time Witherspoon was a relative unknown, undefeated in fifteen fights, with his biggest victories over Alfonzo Ratliff and Renaldo Snipes. He'd come to boxing after a brief career as a tight end at Lincoln University in Missouri and a stint as a waiter in the doctors' dining room at Philadelphia Hospital, where his mother worked as an electrocardiograph technician. The insulting way the doctors treated him led him to a local boxing gym, where he could take out his frustration on the heavy bag. That in turn led to a brief (six fights) amateur career and on May 20, 1983—some three and a half years after turning pro—to a shot at the heavyweight title.

Witherspoon worked out of a wide-legged stance, with his right hand in front of the left side of his face, a style similar to that of Ken Norton. Like Norton, he punched well to the body. Unlike the night I fought Norton, I hadn't the snap on my punches I did when I won the title. The heat was sapping my strength, and, I realized afterward, so was Father Time. Although I escaped with a split decision that night, I learned that my body was taking longer and longer to recover after a fight. Seven weeks—the time between the Rodriguez and Witherspoon fights—had not been long enough for a thirty-three-year-old Larry Holmes. I began thinking of the possibility of retirement.

But that changed abruptly when a pair of promoters, Murad Muhammad and Bob Andreoli, offered me $5 million for a two-fight deal—Scott Frank and Marvis Frazier. That was, I thought, practically like white-collar crime. Easy money. Found money. I couldn't imagine either Frank, a white kid from New Jersey, or Frazier, the son of Smokin' Joe, lasting more than a few rounds with me.

The hitch here was convincing King to butt out so I could sock away these easy paydays without his getting a taste. What's more, I had promised King that I would fight another heavyweight of his, Greg Page. Both Page and King were concerned that at my age, who knows—maybe the worst would happen and either Frank or Frazier would knock me off.

I was able to convince Page that the wait was worth it . . . and don't worry, neither Frank or Frazier would lay a glove on me. Besides, I told him, he wasn't going to make better money fighting any other heavyweight. Page went along with it.

But King. . . . well, he was his usual greedhead self, reluctant to cut a fighter of his—even one who, like me, had made him millions of dollars—a little slack. That really angered me. And when I get angry, I either laugh or cry. I couldn't hold the tears back when King and I began arguing and cursing one another. Finally, I looked him in the eye and told him that if he tried to stop these fights I would retire—and that he would have a cut of a fight that would never happen. He looked at me and saw I meant what I said . . . and backed off.

Scott Frank was a wild swinger who had no style whatsoever. I stopped him in five rounds in September '83 in Atlantic City.

A week before the Frazier fight, the WBC held its annual convention in Vegas, where Holmes-Frazier was to take place. Earlier, Sig Rogich, the WBC's VP, told me his championship committee would strip me of my title if I fought Frazier instead of taking my mandatory bout against Page. Rogich had once been the chairman of the Nevada boxing commission and was used to ramrodding his decisions through. Seemed to me he was still bugged about not being able to stop me from fighting the Frenchman, Rodriguez. And who knows? Maybe he was acting on the urging of Donald King. King and the WBC—hell, they were tighter than canned sardines.

Anyway, I had hardly set my bags down in Vegas when here comes the little senor, Sulaiman, to give me a lecture on ingratitude. All that the WBC had done for me . . . why wasn't I grateful?

I told him: "Jose, what about all I did for the WBC? What about my staying in it and being its champion all these years? And what about all the damn kickbacks I paid?"

He said, real deadpan—as only Jose could—"Kickbacks? What's a kickback?"

It was an Oscar-winning performance.

At the convention, the WBC boys were still threatening to strip me of my title if I went ahead and fought Frazier. I had brought a young Vegas attorney, Mark Risman, with me to speak on my behalf. The WBC boys treated him like dirt. Next day, I showed up with Oscar Goodman, one of the most important lawyers in

Vegas, a man who defended some of the biggest moneymen out there. The tone was completely different. It was, "Yes, Mr. Goodman. Of course, Mr. Goodman."

Toward the end of the convention, Rogich was still making noise about the mandatory defense against Page, eventually proposing that the matter be put to arbitration. Maybe I didn't go to school that much, but I'm not stupid. I wasn't going to let them do that. There was no arbitrating Larry Holmes's independence. On the last day of the convention, I stepped to the microphone and told them how disappointed I was with the organization, how after all my years of loyalty they weren't giving me any consideration. I guess they thought I was going to appeal to their sense of fairness. But I wasn't. I called their bluff. I said, "You don't have to strip me of my title. I don't want to be your champion anymore. I resign."

Well, that shook them big. You could hear gasps in the room, and some of the WBC members shouting no, no, I wasn't allowed to resign. Not allowed? Hell, didn't they hear? I just did it. Rogich said his committee "would take it under advisement." Fine, you do that, Sig, but I'm out of here.

Marvis Frazier had been a hotshot amateur fighter, but was, I thought, miscast as a heavyweight in the pro ranks. He was taller and leaner than Smokin' Joe—six-foot-one, two hundred pounds—and probably would have been better suited to be a cruiserweight. There were a lot of folks who thought the decision to have him fight as a heavyweight, and the aggressive style that he fought with, were influenced by his father—that Joe wanted a carbon copy of the fighter he had been. A second-generation Son of Smokin'.

Both Joe and Marvis would deny that, but anybody who had seen Marvis as an amateur, trained by George Benton, would recognize the differences in the way he fought then and later, when his father had taken over training him. Benton himself would tell reporters that he had styled Marvis to be a defensive-oriented fighter—a boxer type. "Then somewhere down the line he became more a brawler-type fighter," Benton said.

Marvis himself would say, "The only thing Pop added was my standing my ground a little firmer. Rather than my being defensive, a little more offense was added."

As for Joe, he told people: "Size don't mean nothin'. It's like a bee. A bee ain't built big but it still puts knots in your butt."

By the time Marvis fought me he was twenty-three years old and undefeated in ten fights, with decision victories over James Broad and Joe Bugner. I had known him from back when he was a peewee, hanging around Frazier's Gym on North Broad Street in Philadelphia. Known him and liked him. Marvis was a good kid, a Bible-reading youngster who was respectful of his elders and not the least spoiled being the son of a celebrity. Even though he had talked a lot of trash in the weeks leading up to the fight—stuff about me being washed up and ready to be taken—I figured it was Smokin' Joe that was putting him up to it. That was more Frazier senior's way than Marvis's.

In fact, Joe wasn't shy about putting the knock on me either. He told the press: "Larry makes too many mistakes. He used to work with me sparring, and I set him down every day. Guess he got tired of that because, as I remember, he took his money and went home."

All of that got my juices going. The Witherspoon fight had generated a lot of talk about me being in decline as a fighter. I wanted to set the record straight.

On the night of the fight, in November '83, our dressing rooms were separated by a thin wall and I could hear the Frazier guys going: "Woof. Woof. Holmes is going to fall. What time is it? It's KO time." Then they'd howl like dogs and laugh.

I had the last laugh. Midway through the first round, I nailed Marvis with a right hand high on the head and he fell face-forward to the canvas. It kind of scared me the way he dropped. I didn't want to hurt him too much. But he beat the count and I began hitting him while he was against the ropes. I hit him with three right hands, stopping after each one to motion the referee, Mills Lane, to stop the fight. Lane ignored me. So I fired six

225

more rights and a left hook to the body, and finally Lane stopped the fight at 2:57 of the first round.

I walked to Frazier's corner and told Marvis and Joe: "I don't want to fight no more. I don't like having to do this."

The fear that had been growing in me, the fear of how dangerous fighting was, got stronger than ever after the Frazier fight. Maybe I was becoming too civilized, too happy with Diane and Kandy and Larry junior, to stay heavyweight champion of the world for much longer.

Let me tell you the twisted tale of my big-money South African adventure.

It starts with Gerrie Coetzee, a fighter from Transvaal, South Africa, winning the WBA title from Michael Dokes in September 1983 on a tenth-round knockout.

Two months later, I beat Marvis Frazier.

Now for Coetzee's people, a fight with Larry Holmes seemed a natural.

For the government of South Africa, it seemed an opportune way to legitimize its country at a time when most nations were shunning it for its apartheid policies.

How do you overcome the negative image of apartheid? Well, if you're South Africa, one way is to do as Mobutu did in Zaire—you import a major fight on the mistaken assumption that you can paper over your worst sins with a celebrity-driven event—make it seem as if the country is normal.

Which is how it came to pass that the Shapiro brothers—two businessmen who were active in Atlantic City—came to my door with an offer of $30 million to fight Coetzee in Pretoria.

The Shapiros said that the stadium would be integrated for the match and that they would meet any other condition I wanted.

Thirty million dollars. Don't just skim over those words. Look at them again. Think about them for a minute. I thought about them for months and months. Sometimes I still think about them.

Now when the Shapiro brothers made their offer, I recognized it for what it was, a bribe—as sweet a bribe as a black man had seen this side of Cape Town. I also understood that the money came from the South African government and the Shapiros were their go-between. I'd be a liar if I didn't say the money was tempting.

When they heard I had been approached, Harry Belafonte and Arthur Ashe, the chairmen of Artists and Athletes Against Apartheid, contacted me. I got calls and letters from them warning me what I would be getting myself into if I ever agreed to fight in South Africa.

The United Nations had the Special Committee Against Apartheid, which published a list of people who went over there to perform. That's so you couldn't just sneak over, do your thing, fill your pockets, and slip back without anyone knowing what you did. It was a sort of list of shame. A copy was sent to my office by the U.N. delegate from Ghana. Black African countries were strongest in pushing the antiapartheid boycott. I'm sure Belafonte was behind my getting the list.

The list was kind of amazing. Frank Sinatra not only performed in Sun City, a big hotel and casino near Pretoria, in 1981 and got $1.8 million, he went back and did it again for more in '83. There were even major black performers whose names would surprise you. No way they were for apartheid. Still, they took that South African money in 1982 when they should have known better.

Me, I said pass to the $30 million, feeling I could not be any part of racism that was killing black people.

But it didn't end the effort to make a Holmes-Coetzee fight, which would take all kinds of twists and turns before it played out.

See, what happened was a Texan named Kenny Bounds of JPD Sports materialized soon after, looking to match me against Coetzee. Bounds, who owned a cable system in Texas, wanted a two-fight package. John Tate first, *then* Coetzee.

"How much?" I asked.

"Fifteen-point-three [million]."

I tried to be cool. "Where would I have to fight these guys? South Africa?"

"Hell no. Las Vegas."

That sounded damn good to me . . . and still did when the Tate fight fell out and Bounds was willing to pay $13 million for just the Coetzee fight. We shook hands on $13 million. Bounds gave me a $3.5 million check as a nonrefundable advance; I signed his agreement. Holmes-Coetzee was set for June 8, 1984, at Caesars Palace.

But Bounds was new to the game and he had miscalculated on what the fight was worth. Four, five weeks before the fight, he realized he might be looking at a potential loss of $10 million.

Well, on May 15, Caesars Palace pulled the plug, canceling the fight while saying JPD Sports had failed to post a guarantee bond. The June 8 date was blown and, as it turned out, that would be as close as I would ever get to fighting Gerrie Coetzee, who would lose his title to Greg Page that December (1984) in Sun City.

Don King saw an opportunity to fill the void when the Coetzee fight fell out and offered as an opponent James "Bonecrusher" Smith, a big, awkward heavyweight, who'd knocked out Frank Bruno in his last fight. The bout was set for November 9, 1984, in Las Vegas for the International Boxing Federation heavyweight title.

The IBF, based in Newark, New Jersey as opposed to the south-of-the-border locations of the WBC and WBA, was the newest governing body in boxing, and when I'd blown off the WBC, I'd approached the IBF about being its heavyweight champion. Quicker than you could say Sulaiman, the IBF agreed.

Smith was a college graduate who had been working as a prison guard down in North Carolina, a job so depressing that he had turned to boxing as a possible Plan B. He had been knocked out in his very first fight by James Broad back in November 1981, but he hadn't been beaten in the three years since. Fourteen straight victories, thirteen by knockouts.

Well, I snapped the string, stopping Smith in twelve rounds. But I hadn't fought in a year, since knocking out Marvis Frazier, and it showed. My timing was off, my thumb was again a problem (hurt but not broken), and Smith—a very strong man—cut me on the brow of my left eye and hurt me with body shots.

As I had done before, I reached down and gutted it out for my forty-sixth victory in a row.

I had been thinking of retiring—I had just turned thirty-five and sure as hell was feeling it after the Smith fight. But . . . the victory over Smith—hard as it was—had been my forty-sixth victory in a row since turning pro. And now the press began to write that I had a chance to break the undefeated record of Rocky Marciano, who had won forty-nine straight fights before he announced his retirement in 1956.

That was enough of an inducement to get me to go on—and it came at a time when the government indicted King and Connie Harper, the vice president of Don King Productions (DKP), on twenty-three counts of tax fraud and conspiracy. The indictment was announced in December '84 by the U.S. attorney, Rudolph Giuliani.

King was accused of skimming money from DKP and not paying the taxes on it. Giuliani told newsmen: "The scheme involved obtaining cash from casino cages on several occasions—on one occasion as high as seventy thousand—and not reporting it as income."

Back when I talked to Spinelli and then testified before the grand jury, the focus seemed to be on what King did to his fighters and whether he had any organized-crime connections.

The indictments' emphasis on tax evasion meant the government hadn't been able to nail King on the other charges.

To fight his legal battle, King settled on Vincent Fuller of the Washington, D.C., law firm of Williams & Connally, the same Fuller who would represent—or misrepresent, according to most observers—Mike Tyson when Tyson was charged with rape in 1991.

I stopped David Bey in ten rounds in March '85 in Las Vegas, in a bout that King promoted, and then decisioned Carl Williams in May in Reno in a Sports/Cor promotion.

That made me undefeated in forty-eight straight bouts. But what the Bey and Williams bouts shared with the Bonecrusher Smith fight was this: I was working like hell to hold it together against these younger guys. I was no longer Larry Holmes, the Easton Assassin, but I was still a pretty good thirty-five-year-old heavyweight champion. And I was also the only promoter I knew who had to bust his gut, and even bleed, to stay in business.

I now had made twenty successful defenses of the heavyweight title. Only Joe Louis held the title longer and won more title defenses than I did. Yet rather than praise me for long and meritorious service to the sport, most of the writers were saying Larry Holmes was losing it. It seemed like when the press looked at me, the cup was always half-empty rather than half-full.

I thought—and hoped—that might change if I could tie Marciano's record.

One to go.

CHAPTER
SIXTEEN

Michael Spinks was Leon's brother and the light heavyweight champion of the world, undefeated in twenty-seven bouts. In '85, after Spinks defended his title against David Sears and Jim Mac-Donald, his promoter, Butch Lewis, announced that Spinks was stepping up to the heavyweight class to challenge me.

There had never been a light heavyweight champion to make a success of that transition. One of the best of them, Bob Foster, who packed a real wallop as a light heavyweight, was cannon fodder when he went up against Smokin' Joe Frazier. Frazier knocked him out in two rounds.

Before him, Archie Moore, the wily ole Mongoose, hadn't done it either, getting knocked out by Rocky Marciano and later by Floyd Patterson.

And going further back, Billy Conn had come damn close against Joe Louis but ultimately had been stopped by the Brown Bomber late in the fight.

For Spinks, moving up in class made sense. He had been light heavyweight champion since 1981 and had cleaned up the division, beating some pretty good fighters—Eddie Mustafa Muhammad, Dwight Braxton, Yaqui Lopez, and Marvin Johnson—as a contender and as champion. But the money in the light heavyweight division was nowhere what it was in the heavyweight class. For fighting me in September '85, Spinks would be getting $1.1 million—or eleven times what he had made in his last title defense, against MacDonald. My purse was $3.5 million, which would bring my career earnings to more than $65 million.

Spinks, who had fought at 175 pounds as a light heavyweight, went on a conditioning program designed to bulk him up, give him the muscle to cope with heavyweights. Under a fitness coach, Mackie Shillstone, he ate lots of carbohydrates, lifted weights, and ran sprints. But I knew that even if Spinks managed to get to, say, 200 pounds, he wouldn't pack the wallop of the natural heavyweights I'd been fighting.

I was thankful for that. I was getting tired of getting hit shots by those big boys. After fighting Carl Williams, I had been so puffy around the face and hurt all over that I had skipped the postfight news conference so that I could go back to my room at the MGM and sit in a hot bath.

My only concern about Spinks was his awkwardness. The guy threw punches at weird angles and fought with unconventional rhythms. As a reporter had written:

As a champion, Spinks turned out to be one of those athletes who appear to get results almost in spite of themselves. There were a few like him, competitors who might not have the picture-perfect moves their peers did, yet managed to excel anyway. Billy Kilmer, the quarterback, threw passes that did not spiral and were jokingly referred to as "wounded ducks." Yet he could do what quarterbacks are supposed to: make a team win. As the baseball executive Branch Rickey once said of Eddie Stanky, the second basemen: "He can't run. He can't throw. He can't hit. All he can do is beat you."

Spinks was stiff-gaited, and his herky-jerky movements were accentuated by the knee wraps he sometimes wore. . . . Lurching and twisting and sometimes actually running from a punch, Spinks made a mild case for winning ugly.

But the fact was that Spinks had done that against light heavyweights. I was sure I'd be able to impose my will on him when we met.

When the fight was made, Eddie Futch claimed a conflict of interest. He had trained both Spinks and me, and didn't want to choose between us. In need of a trainer, I decided the time was right to bring back Richie Giachetti. Mean and sneaky as Richie could be, I knew he was the motivator I needed. And when Richie knew I was watching his ass, he'd stay in line and really do a job. Besides all of that, there was something in me that couldn't help liking Richie.

The oddsmakers had me a 5–1 favorite when the fight was announced. Because the bout appeared to be one-sided, the emphasis in the media coverage shifted to my going after Rocky Marciano's record. And that meant once again I was back in the racial swamplands. The fact that two black men were fighting for the title was secondary to my challenge of Marciano's record.

At my hotel in Phillipsburg, and at my gym in Easton, Marciano's picture was up on the walls, one of an elite group of fighters whose photos I'd framed. To me, Marciano was a great fighter. But to white folks, Italians in particular, he was more than that: he was an icon.

To sharpen that promotional angle, Marciano's family, his brother Peter, who owned a sporting goods store in Hanover, Massachusetts, and Rocky's two children, thirty-two-year-old Mary Ann and sixteen-year-old Rocky junior, had been flown to Vegas, where the fight was to take place in a makeshift stadium behind the Riviera Hotel & Casino. In the weeks leading up to the bout, they were interviewed more than Spinks and me.

Peter was quoted as saying to Spinks: "You know that Rocky is going to be pulling for you." To which Spinks replied: "I need all the help I can get."

Peter told the press that he was hoping I didn't break his brother's record—that he was praying and lighting candles that I wouldn't win. That aggravated me because records are made to be broken. I mean, Hank Aaron broke Babe Ruth's record and Pete Rose broke Ty Cobb's record . . . and so on. And I didn't think people should pray and wish people bad luck for breaking records.

With all this attention to Marciano, I was set up as the Darth Vader to Marciano's white knight. I didn't like it at all. As a champion I had not avoided any challenge, taking on the best contenders and beating them all. What's more, I had done nothing to disgrace the title, living a clean life, without incident. But here I was again made out to be the bad guy. If Jack Johnson had held the record, no way would it have been the most important thing in a fight between me and Michael Spinks. I knew there wasn't much I could do about it except to use what they were saying about me to spite them. But that kind of garbage just takes the heart out of you after a while.

They had a Larry Holmes–Rocky Marciano computer fight on the radio a few days before the fight. The computer said Rocky would have knocked me out in the tenth round. The writers asked me what I thought about the computer fight and I said, joking, "What do you expect from a white computer?" That got me branded a racist all over again.

I mean, how the hell is a computer going to say something about me and Marciano? If you put in all the variables—the size difference, the weight difference, the speed difference, the boxing difference—I say the computer's got to be wrong. I thought to myself: I can't fight time. I mean, how can you go back and say what I would have done with Marciano? Or how could you come forward and say what Marciano would have done with me?

But I had a bigger problem than some figment of a computer's imagination. In training, I found that whenever I threw a right hand, pain would shoot through my shoulder. Keith Kleven diagnosed it as a pinched nerve, and tried to treat it with heat, massage, and pain pills.

When we got to Vegas and the pain persisted, Kleven had a doctor he knew examine me. This doctor looked me over and thought I needed a nerve specialist to check me out. The specialist concentrated on my back and legs rather than the shoulder area, where the pain was. He looked at old X rays of my neck and back, and asked if I ever felt a tingling sensation in my fingers and toes and lower back. His diagnosis? A slipped disc in the fifth vertebra.

"If I were your doctor, I'd have you on the operating table within the hour—that's how serious I think it is," the specialist said.

Come again?

If it sounded kind of extreme to me, well, this guy was about to take it further.

He said if I went ahead and fought Spinks it'd be like playing Russian roulette. I might be paralyzed for life any time I threw a punch with the right hand. According to him, the disc might rupture my spinal cord.

Paralyzed for life.

What the hell. One minute we're talking about a pain in my arm and the next thing I'm hearing is the words "paralyzed for life." Well, we brought in other doctors. They said I could fight with the pinched nerve, no problem. They said the chance that I'd get paralyzed were practically nil.

But come fight night—after Pia Zadora lip-synched the national anthem (her husband owned the Riviera)—I found that not only was I flat and listless, I was reluctant to pull the trigger on the right hand. At 221 pounds, I had the weight on Spinks, who came in at 199 ¾ pounds. But I guess I couldn't forget what the specialist had said. Richie kept screaming: "The right hand, Big Jack! Off the jab, the right hand!" As the fight wore on, he was pleading: "Please throw the right hand."

But I didn't let the right go. Mostly it was jab jab and sometimes hook off the jab. Give Spinks this: he was hard to hit. And his punches came from places I never saw before. But I hurt him a few times, enough I thought to take important rounds late in the fight. Yet after fourteen rounds, two of the judges, Harold

Lederman and Dave Moretti, had it dead even. The third, Larry Wallace, had Spinks ahead comfortably.

So it came down to the fifteenth and final round. I managed to get off one of those rare right hands, and it landed big, shaking Spinks. Spinks ran for most of the round. But when the decision came, the man said, "Winner and neeeewww champion."

And like that, the magic-carpet ride was over. I was no longer champion, I was no longer undefeated. Never mind that Dave Anderson of *The New York Times* scored it 9–6 in rounds for me. Or that Pat Putnam of *Sports Illustrated* had it 143–141 in points for me. Or that even Peter Marciano said that he thought it close enough for me to keep my title. Never mind that lots of the ringside reporters saw me as the winner. The guys that counted—Lederman, Moretti, and Wallace—all had it for Spinks.

If I'd been emotionally flat during the fight, I felt the anger rising in me now. The best thing I could have done was go back to my room and let the anger burn off before going public with my thoughts. But I didn't and, to my regret, I said things in the aftermath that got my hide blistered—things that people still remember and still judge me harshly for. Yup, I should have stolen away into the night. But then, I guess that wouldn't be me. I'm an impulsive man, a man who says what's on his mind and doesn't sugarcoat it.

So there I was at the televised press conference and what was on my mind was not the judges and maybe the people who control them but rather Marciano's record. And in my anger I said, "I'm thirty-five fighting young men and he was twenty-five fighting old men. To be technical, Rocky Marciano couldn't carry my jockstrap."

Giachetti nudged me and whispered, "You're out of hand. You got to be humble."

But I rattled on, saying things to Peter Marciano and Rocky's kids that were uncalled for and simply wrong. Somewhere in there I must have realized I'd gone too far because in my fashion I tried to apologize. I said, "Rocky was one of the greatest fighters of all time. For anyone to accomplish forty-nine victories, even if they were all bums, is some kind of record. If I didn't think he was a great fighter, his pictures wouldn't be on the walls of my motel near Easton."

But of course it was too little too late. As they say, "The insult is halfway around the world before the apology gets its boots on."

Since then, I have apologized repeatedly for my behavior that night. I've explained what caused me to say it and what I meant by it until it's been rehashed to the point where I just want the damn thing to go away. No one's been hurt more by my angry remarks than I have. No matter what I say now, the fact is I was wrong. I shouldn't have said it. I can't make things any clearer than that.

Rocky Marciano was a great champion—you don't set the record he did without being a great fighter. Period. But that wasn't what had upset me. The experts said Marciano was better than I was. Fine, that's their opinion. But why did I have to agree with them? I truly believed I could beat Muhammad Ali in 1975. Why didn't I have the right to believe I could have beaten Marciano too? The "jockstrap" remark was dumb, but all I meant was I would have whupped the man—the man, not the legend the world turned him into.

There had been a few years there in the early eighties when I was like no one else in boxing—promoting my fights or dictating the terms I'd fight under; deciding who I'd fight for and when; and, most important, keeping most of the money I'd earned. I guess I became like the successful reformer who gets a little too arrogant, a little too sure of himself. It must have been satisfying to bring me down that night in Vegas.

There was more coming.

The next day, I drove from the Allentown airport along Route 22. As I approached the Easton turnoff, I passed the billboard that for seven and a half years had stood there—the one that said: "Easton Is the Home of Larry Holmes, World's Heavyweight Champion." It didn't say that anymore. It hadn't take them long to change over that billboard.

That November ('85), King skated on the tax evasion case.

The Teflon Don was acquitted by the jury while his codefendant, Connie Harper, was found guilty.

The jury decided that Harper, as vice president of Don King Productions, was technically responsible for filing the taxes for the corporation.

Once again, King had lateraled blame to his associates, as he had done in the U.S. Boxing Championships.

I knew that Connie—a short, plump woman—had a thing for Don, and it later would be written that she had been one of King's mistresses. But taking the fall for him was sure as hell going beyond the call of duty.

She was sentenced to a prison term of a year and a day, and ended up serving four months. When she came out, she got a job with the Cleveland Board of Elections.

At his press conference King said, "Justice like this could happen only in America."

Was there boxing life after losing?

That was the question I faced in the months that followed the Spinks fight.

On various occasions during my championship reign I had talked about retiring. At times there had even been headlines saying I was getting out of boxing. But I'd change my mind and be back at it before long, sometimes within a day or two of raising the notion of retirement.

Well, on the night that Spinks had gotten the decision, once again I told reporters who came up to my hotel room long after I'd bumbled through the press conference that I was packing it in.

But it turned out I didn't mean it any more this time than I did before. Truth is I wanted revenge—I wanted to get back at Spinks and prove I was the better man.

The rematch was set for April 19, 1986, in Las Vegas, with Spinks to get $2 million and me to get $1.125 million.

This time I closed my workouts to the public and the press, determined not to let anything, or anybody, break my focus. The press blackout was out of character for me—I'd always been available to the reporters and often sat drinking beers with them in the evenings.

But I knew that as the challenger, I no longer could claim the little edge that champions have with the judges in close fights. In boxing, there is a kind of tradition that a challenger has to assert his superiority to win a title. In a fight where that superiority is not clear-cut, the unspoken rule is that the champion gets the nod. But by the time I fought Spinks I had made enough enemies among the governing bodies and commissions to set up the ambush in the desert I found awaiting me at the conclusion of Holmes-Spinks.

In the long months that followed, I wondered why it was that through a career in which I'd fought as regularly as church bingo, and beaten every legitimate contender, I could never seem to get my just dues. Around the time I fought Spinks a *Boston Globe* sportswriter, Leigh Montville, had taken a shot at it, writing:

He forever is judged by what he is not, rather than what he is. He is not Muhammad Ali, glib and lively and pretty and controversial. He is not Joe Louis, stolid king of a thriving sport, a symbol of success in a troubled time. He is not Rocky, neither the real or movie variety, the belligerent bulldozer of a man, surviving the worst mayhem to win in the end.

Larry Holmes is the heavyweight champion who lives next door. He might have all the qualities all the polls say people want from their heroes—a family man, a suburban man, a man who stays away from drugs and under control—but he still lives next dooor. There is little romance to be found next door.

"This is a bidness," Larry Holmes always says. "I'm in this to make money. I'm a bidnessman."

The trouble is that the bidness is show bidness. The singer is not supposed to say he sings only for his supper. He says he sings for his art, his craft, whatever. He may, indeed, sing for the money, but he does not say this. Larry Holmes says this all the time.

Where are the threats of annihilation? Where are the poems for a victory? Where is the Marvelous Marvin Hagler baseball cap with the word "WAR" across the front?

It was a point of view, and maybe even true. Who could say? From how I looked at it, I was just being honest, just being Larry Holmes.

The bidness now was to beat Spinks, and do it without that vigorish that used to belong to me as champion. And given the backlash that followed my remarks about Marciano, I was not exactly riding a wave of popularity. I had to be sure that I was a whole lot better than Spinks this time.

To do that, I felt I had to tunnel into my training and work harder than I had for my recent fights. I wanted to be all the fighter I could be at the age of thirty-seven. By the time I was ready to leave for Vegas, I felt ready as Freddie. I'd run the hills of Easton, sparred hard, and was mentally all there.

I even had Spaz compose a letter to Bob Lee, the head of the IBF, saying that I hoped we could rely on the independence and fairness of the judges. We specified those judges who were not acceptable to us, hoping that that would insure a fair shake on the scoring of the fight. What it got was a holier-than-thou response from Lee, denying that I had been jobbed back in September and claiming I would be treated just as fairly this time too.

Just as fairly. That was what I was afraid of. About a week before the bout, I ended my interview blackout by agreeing to talk to a local TV interviewer after one of my workouts. He asked me what I learned from the first fight.

"I learned I have to knock this guy out," I told him. "I learned these judges get drunk when they judge fights. I learned these guys get paid off. . . ."

Sure it was an outrageous statement. I meant it to be. I was

240

trying to put the judges on their guard. If they were planning to ambush me again, I wanted to alert the public. By doing so, I figured the judges might be less reluctant to mess me over.

Four days out from the fight, the press turned up at my workout for the first time. By contract, I was obliged to let them see a training session so they could tell their readers what kind of shape I was in. I wasn't required to speak to them. I intended to go about my business and scram.

The session was at the Hilton Hotel & Casino, where Spinks and I were to fight. The press was asked to stay behind a restraining rope a few feet from the ring, but as I shadowboxed, there was Dick Young stepping in front of the rope, standing there with an attitude, obviously intent on creating a ruckus. I kind of dug what he was trying to do, it was so outrageous. Young was white-haired and sixty-eight years of age . . . but still plenty ballsy.

And as a columnist he was very much still Dick Young. Young had been working me over in print ever since the Marciano comments. He had been painting me a racist. That was just like him. He was like a dog who wouldn't let go of the bone. When Ali refused to get drafted, same thing. When Young didn't like you, he made it personal.

As I was shadowboxing, I could hear Young arguing with my brothers, calling me names. I was listening, but I can't honestly say he distracted me. It was just showbiz, and I didn't take it seriously. I finished shadowboxing and was toweling off when I heard Young say, "He ain't shit anyway." At that point, he was told: "You get your ass back of that rope." When things began heating up and I thought it might come to blows, I stepped in and said, "Listen, Dick, you're interrupting my workout, man. You be cool or I'm gonna have to have you removed."

Young argued that he was part of the working press, raising his voice so that the other news guys pushed close to see what the hell the problem was. I began hitting the heavy bag. As I did, I heard him call me an asshole. That was enough. I told him to get behind the damn rope. When he refused to and kept bad-mouthing me, I told Hilton security: "Pick the man up nice and gentle, and carry him out of here."

Well, the news guys had their story—Larry Holmes the bad guy, the bully. That's how it read the next day. "The angry unraveling of a proud and embittered Larry Holmes continued yesterday when . . ." Blah blah blah. I was quoted as saying while hitting the heavy bag: "These damn writers are always writing what they want. . . . They look at you with their lying eyes. . . . I'm fighting for the right to see my kids recognized as decent human beings."

I had given up trying to explain things since all the explanations go through the media. When they get done with your explanation, you're usually in worse shape than when you started. But it sells papers. The truth's got nothing much to do with anything. Who would have written a story that said Young turned on me after I didn't hire his girlfriend? Who would have taken on someone as powerful as Dick Young? The thing about the whole incident that disappointed me the most was that when Young was carried out kicking and cursing, the other reporters left too. They made it a freedom of the press issue. It was no such thing. Not if you knew the whole story.

I was full of fury, awaiting the opening bell for the rematch with Spinks. Awaiting it for the first time since 1978 as the challenger.

When the bell rang, I went after Spinks, looking to beat him up. But Spinks recognized how intense I was and decided, I guess, that discretion was the better part of valor.

Spinks ran, making a calculated decision, it seemed, to give away a few early rounds letting me chase his butt.

That was okay with me. I won the first two rounds and was settling into the aggressor role in the third when I felt a searing pain shoot through my elbow up to my shoulder. The thumb again . . . the right thumb was broken. I was beside myself with anger and despair. Of all the times to go on me.

Against Roy Williams, I had adjusted by hitting with my outside knuckles. But for Spinks, I said the hell with it. I would ignore the pain and hit him my best licks. I wanted this fight, and the pain would be the cost of doing business. That was all there was to it.

But Lord, it hurt when I laid that right hand on him. Still, I hit Spinks with the right and hurt him in the fifth round, and hurt him again in the ninth.

In the fourteenth round, I came over the top with the best punch I could throw with my right hand, a clean shot high on his head. Spinks stopped cold. His legs went weak. His eyes went out of focus and he stared out into the crowd. He wobbled backward. I thought he was going to fall. He didn't.

I should have been on him like a snug overcoat. But that instinct for finishing an opponent that had been second nature earlier in my career had grown dull. If you think about what to do, you're lost as a finisher. Spinks got away and was beginning to recover when I closed on him. He tied me up.

Still, when the bell ended the fifteen-round fight, I felt I had a commanding lead—that the decision was a no-brainer . . . even in the politically charged atmosphere surrounding my career. But when they announced the first judge's scoring—144–141 for Spinks—I was stunned. The crowd booed. I said to Giachetti, "Shit, I got a big mouth."

They like to announce decisions in a way that squeezes the most drama out of them. The next judge had the fight in my favor the exact opposite way, 144–141 or nine rounds to six. I wasn't going to get my hopes up; deep down I knew what was coming. The last judge had it 144–142 for ". . . the winner and *stillll* champion . . ."

Beat again. Beat by boxing bullshit.

As the crowd raised a din, booing and jeering, I stepped across the ring and shook hands with Spinks.

The postfight press conference was packed. The reporters were, I knew, trying to provoke another of those Holmes last-angry-man quotable quotes, asking if I thought my remarks about the judges being drunk and accepting payoffs had come back to haunt me. I told them that the boxing establishment had no use

243

for Larry Holmes anymore and that this second bad decision was the result. The two judges who had scored it for Spinks, well, they had "lying eyes."

Then I gave them what they wanted. I told them, "The judges, referees, and promoters can kiss me where the sun don't shine. And because we're on HBO . . . that's my big black behind."

When I said that, I heard a gasp in the room. So I knew I didn't disappoint the writers, most of whom would say in print they thought I had won the fight.

After that, I rode the limo to the emergency room of Valley Hospital, still in my robe and trunks. Diane and Dick Lovell and my brother Jake were with me. None of us talked. I looked down at my useless thumb and all of a sudden I was crying.

It wasn't the pain of the fractured thumb that brought tears. It was being screwed again after having fought my heart out. I had overcome the useless thumb, the pain, the old-for-boxing body and beaten the guy. Beaten him fair and square . . . only to be ambushed again by boxing bullshit.

I couldn't stop the tears. There in the silent dark of the limo, with the lights of Vegas blinking around us, I was bawling like a little kid who was being punished when he didn't do anything wrong. Even when I was a kid, I didn't cry . . . I fought back. But how do you fight against judges with lying eyes?

CHAPTER
SEVENTEEN

I once wrote a poem that goes:

> *Boxing's politics is what we're talking about—*
> *the only thing worse than being knocked out*
> *Promoter gets the money, fighter gets the pain*
> *That's how it goes in the boxing game.*

I was hurt, and bothered, by the politics that had deprived me of my victory in Vegas, but once in Easton I got back into the swing of things. People figured I'd go into hiding. Or maybe get a gun and blow my brains out. But the Monday morning after the fight I was thinking about how to invest the 1 million bucks they'd paid me.

In the years since I'd gone into the restaurant-club business, I had tried to expand my holdings. I'd met resistance on the local level, motivated, I thought, by the intolerance among some for a black man's making good in business. As Kenneth A. Briggs of *The New York Times* would observe:

Holmes is seen by some as an unschooled, arrogant, uncouth upstart who tried to push his way into the city's troubled economic picture by throwing his money around . . . Holmes' supporters attribute most of the opposition to envy or resistance to letting a black competitor into social and business clubs of the city.

A few years earlier, I had wanted to develop a piece of land on Third and Ferry Streets in Easton. I'd spoken to Sal Panto, the mayor of Easton, who was a boyhood friend of mine. The two of us had once sold baked goods and fried dough for the St. Anthony's Youth Center. I told Sal, "I'll give you a check for a million and you're going to tell me if I can get the land and build on it." It was redevelopment land. A couple months later, when I hadn't heard back, I called and Sal told me somebody else had been approved for redeveloping it. I felt it was a black-white issue and, in protest, I got my million-dollar check back and moved my business operation across the bridge and into the hotel I'd bought in Phillipsburg.

I thought Sal was part of the plot to undercut me, but found out that in fact he had been trying to help. So later I went back to him and we began talking about a plot of land on what once had been Riverside Drive and had been renamed Larry Holmes Drive. There were a few false starts, but eventually plans were approved for a five-story building on a 3.2-acre plot at 101 Larry Holmes Drive, looking across the Delaware River.

That was a first step. The big hitch at that point was I couldn't get financing. I was looking for a loan of $4 million. So I decided to use my own money and start building, figuring everything would fall in place once the building was up.

For the time being, I decided I was retired from boxing.

Not that people didn't try to persuade me to climb back into the ring. A promoter from Miami offered me $4 million to fight a white South African, Johnny Du Plooy, in Johannesburg. I was tempted to take the money just to spite my boxing enemies. But deep down I knew I couldn't actually do that.

An odd thing happened shortly after the Du Plooy offer became known. One day, the Reverend Al Sharpton showed up unannounced in my office. I'd never met Sharpton before, but that didn't stop him from launching right into a spiel about why I shouldn't go to South Africa. Talking to me as if he was a favorite uncle, dispensing helpful advice.

He did the whole rap on South Africa, especially how the boycott was working and how if it was broken now the whole movement would be set back for years. He didn't tell me anything I didn't already know, but, man, could he talk. He was a black Howard Cosell.

The question in my mind the whole time was: Why is this guy here and who sent him?

The more I said no to the South Africans, the more they wanted me. The offers grew, but I didn't bite. Some decisions just make themselves. This one did. Bitter as it was, my soul wasn't for sale.

After I turned the South Africans down, David Bey took the fight with Du Plooy. He went over there and got knocked out.

Life went on. I was overseeing the groundbreaking for my building, and getting to spend time with my family.

I promoted the occasional fight for my brother, Mark, a middleweight who'd won thirty-two straight before being stopped by John Collins for the vacant USBA title.

There was also a seven-man band, called Marmalade, that I sang with, doing gigs all over the country, maybe thirty a year.

In June '87, Smokin' Joe Frazier and I got invited to perform in Atlantic City during the week leading up to the Michael Spinks–Cooney fight.

I had one song that went like this:

I trained real hard to do the job,
Then beat the man and I got robbed.
Yeah, won that fight.

Everybody knows I beat Spinks,
That's okay.
Politics stinks.

Yeah, I'll admit it: those two losses still bugged me.

But late at night, when I thought about my life, I realized I had plenty to be happy about, starting at home—a wife and two kids I loved. When I'd married Diane in '79, it had been kind of spontaneous. I'd called her from the gym two days before Christmas and said, "Honey, guess what? We're gonna get married."

She laughed and said, "When?"

"This afternoon. It's all arranged."

Actually, I hadn't arranged any of it. But like that, I began phoning around. I got Reverend Jacobs to perform the ceremony at the Second Baptist Church in Easton, then notified our families. Spaz got the rings (which didn't really fit) and ordered the food and drink for the reception.

I changed from my satin warm-up suit into my blue dress suit at the church. Diane showed up in a lovely white dress. Most of the guys, though, were still wearing their training duds. We were a strange-looking crew at that church, but Reverend Jacobs never let on. He said this was a "true-spirit marriage." Ten minutes later, I kissed the bride and we went back to the house to celebrate.

Spaz had ordered a couple hundred dollars' worth of cold cuts, potato chips, potato salad, cole slaw, beer, and soda. We drank out of paper cups and ate off paper plates, played Aretha Franklin on the stereo and danced.

There was no honeymoon. I went back into training the very next morning. It took a few years of quiet nudging by Diane to get it through my skull that she hadn't had the most romantic wedding there'd ever been, and that lots of her relatives and closest friends didn't happen to be around that day. She wanted us to renew our vows. So . . . now at her church in Bethlehem, with Diane in a beautiful wedding gown this time and me in a tuxedo—before a standing-room-only congregation—we did it right. We renewed our vows in a first-class ceremony, with singers and an organ player.

Not only did we renew our vows to one another, I renewed my commitment to be a dependable father. Like our marriage, like my championship, commitment was something I knew I had to work at continually . . . and never take for granted.

By the middle of 1987, more than a year after I had lost the rematch to Spinks, the public assumed I was out of boxing for good.

Me, I wasn't so sure. While I worked out from time to time, and even joined the Easton YMCA to do laps—nineteen to the mile—on the overhanging oval track, it wasn't to get in fighting trim that I put in the miles. Uh-uh. It was just what a guy like me did to fight that middle-age spread. I'd gotten as heavy as 250 pounds while out of the fight game.

Still, I hadn't written off the possibility of boxing again. Practically every day, somebody was on the phone, trying to coax me back into the ring.

One of them was Jim Jacobs, the comanager of Mike Tyson, who had won the WBC version of the heavyweight title in November 1986, knocking out Trevor Berbick to become the youngest-ever heavyweight champion. Jacobs and the other comanager, Bill Cayton, had the largest collection of boxing films in the world and, as The Big Fights Inc., the two of them had made big bucks exploiting the commercial rights to those films. In the mid-1970s, for instance, the company made a $4 million deal granting ABC-TV exclusive rights to use The Big Fights' film library on the air. A renewal of the deal in the early 1980s was worth $6 million more.

And while those fight films—some of them dating back to the turn of the century—were a commercial venture, Jacobs had a historian's interest in the sport as well. Because of that, he wanted Tyson to fight me: he liked the symbolism of the new heavyweight star kicking the old legend's butt, as, say, Marciano had done to Joe Louis.

As for Tyson, he had been released from a juvenile detention facility to the care of veteran boxing man Cus D'Amato, who began developing him as a fighter back when Tyson was thirteen. At the time, according to Tyson, "Cus would always speak about me fighting Holmes someday. When I did my roadwork, I'd fantasize about fighting Holmes. He was the champion of the world and I was a fan of his. I always wanted Holmes to win, except when he fought Ali. I liked the way Holmes fought. He had guts. He'd get knocked down and get right back up. And he'd take some good punches, like against Cooney. He took some good shots to the body. When I was doing roadwork, I used to think of us fighting and me winning. I'd always think about outpointing him. I used to beat him good, but I never thought of a knockout. Not then."

Jacobs and I had talked about a Holmes-Tyson fight as far back as '86, before Tyson became champion. But for one reason or another no deal was made. Other promoters, like Bob Arum and Murad Muhammad, tried to horn in, making offers far better than the $1.5 million Jacobs had proposed. But Jacobs said he didn't want to do business with those guys and only he could deliver Tyson.

Maybe so, I told him, but you got no lock on Larry Holmes.

"It still takes two to tango," I said. "So it looks like we don't have a fight."

I could afford to play hard-to-get because I had money; if I didn't, I would have had to take Jacobs's original $1.5 million, or even less. Most fighters would have been very happy with money like that, but by not needing the money, I was in a position to max any deal that might be made. God bless my municipal bonds.

Every few weeks Arum would call with a sweeter deal he was

sure he could jam through. Jim Jacobs killed it every time. Jacobs didn't like Arum—in fact, he loathed him. When Cayton and he had their first champion, Wilfredo Benitez, Arum had tried to steal the fighter away from them. Jacobs didn't forgive or forget.

Don King was trying to make Holmes-Tyson too. But every time he called, we hit a stone wall arguing over money he still owed me from as far back as the Ali and Cooney fights. I'd end up calling him names and hanging up in his lying face.

By late '87, the public was clamoring for a Tyson–Michael Spinks fight, following Spinks's dramatic knockout of Gerry Cooney. But Jacobs and Cayton were taking the position they didn't need Spinks—there were plenty of other opponents out there. In fact, though, there was a shortage of worthy challengers. As a guy looking back on that period would write: "The heavyweight division in 1987 was a lot like that trick circus coupe from which a multitude of clowns emerge. The question was how long the public, and the press, would put up with watching Tyson go against the bozos."

That put me in a good bargaining position. For Larry Holmes had a name that would still put fannies in seats. Never mind that I was thirty-eight and had become a grandfather that August when my nineteen-year-old daughter, Misty, gave birth to six-pound seven-ounce Jeffrey Allen Dorsey Jr. In a heavyweight division short on live bodies, I was a name that would work on any casino marquee.

Late that year, King drove down to my house in Easton.

King has a way of stroking your ego to grease the way for getting what he wants in the negotiations that follow. So . . . when King walked into my house and was lavish in his praise of all I had—the beautiful house with a swimming pool, children who had the love of two caring parents, real estate, businesses, investments—I knew better than to take him seriously. Still, he rattled on and on.

"Don't you ever look at everything you have," he said, real

mellow, "and say to yourself, 'Man, I can't believe my life has turned out this way.' You know, Lar, I'll see myself on television or I'll see my name in lights and I'll think, 'Shit, that can't be me. That can't be the same Don King. It's *got* to be somebody else . . .' You know, Lar, when you think about all the hard times when it didn't look like we'd make it, you got to admit, finally it's all been worth it."

"Don," I told him, "everything I got in this world I earned the hardest way possible. And the truth is I'd have even more if you had treated me fairer all along."

Well, that set him off with a long-winded defense of all he had done for me—the gospel according to Don King. There were the usual lies and half-truths that he wove into his typical filibuster, giving all praise to Don King. That set us back a good hour.

As he was switching gears, I opened an envelope from the day's mail, showed him a $50,000 interest check, and told him: "See this, Don. I don't need the money."

That was just to let him know he'd better be real with the deal he was bringing me.

In fact, it was good enough: $3.1 million to fight Tyson in January in Atlantic City, with hotshot Donald Trump's Trump Plaza the host hotel.

In '87, Trump had become a player in the boxing game, stealing the spotlight from Las Vegas, first with Spinks-Cooney in June and then with Tyson–Tyrell Biggs in October. Both of those bouts went into the Convention Center, adjoining Trump Plaza, one of the two casinos he owned at the time. (Trump Castle was the other.)

The Convention Center, which could seat up to sixteen thousand spectators for boxing, opened in 1929. But in the city's recent makeover as a gambling resort, it was not until Trump's arrival in boxing that the arena was regularly used for big-time fights.

Trump had an edge over other casino operators. His Trump Plaza had the benefit of a walkway he built that ran from his casino to the arena. With that walkway, he had what no other casino man had: an arena that was, in effect, an extension of his casino.

See, in Atlantic City, other casinos lacked large on-site locations for boxing, or the sort of direct access to one that Trump had. Because of that, the staging of major fights never made business sense to his rivals quite the way it did to Trump. Casino operators do not like to move potential gamblers too far from their gaming tables.

I agreed to the $3.1 million, but insisted it had to be in the bank before I stepped into that ring. King agreed. Then I told him I wanted one other thing too—just on principle. The film and video rights to the fight.

With Jacobs and Cayton in the fight-film business, that was a tricky point for King. He claimed no fighter had ever gotten film and video rights before.

"Good," I said. "I'll be the first."

My thinking was that old movie actors never got residuals for their old movies, and old fighters never shared in the revenues made when their bouts were shown on TV. It sure would have helped Joe Louis and some of the other old-timers who ended up broke if they could have owned the rights to their films.

"Out of the question," said King about the film rights.

"Then you'll have the press conference announcing the fight without me."

When it dawned on King and Jacobs that I was serious, they yielded, finally, on that point.

The press conference announcing the fight was held at the Grand Hyatt in New York. As he often does on such occasions, King monopolized the microphone, using the occasion to stroke Trump, a man he must have seen as a future collaborator on big fights to come. In other words, a moneybags he could stick his grubby paws into. King was effusive—as only he could be—in his praise of Trump, making him out as Jesus in a business suit, the savior of our free world. He said he wished Trump would run

253

for president of the United States. If Trump was obviously embarrassed by Donald King's bullshit, it didn't stop the mouth that roared. On and on he went about Trump.

The presidential angle—that was something King and I had talked about up in my suite before we came down. I asked him, "Who would you vote for between Donald Trump and Jesse Jackson?"

King said, "Jesse's got no chance. Donald Trump's a winner. And I always got to be with the winners."

Those words were as characteristic of King as his fingerprints. Loyalty could go screw.

When Tyson and I met before the press conference, I offered to shake hands. He refused, saying: "Go fuck yourself."

I told him: "Hey, it's a game. You win, you win. You lose, you lose."

He just stared at me.

I didn't get angry. I got disappointed. "Shit," I thought, "we got to play these stupid mind games. A grown man like me."

When a reporter wondered why Tyson had declined to shake hands, he said, " 'Cause I didn't feel like it."

Most heavyweight champs think they're the baaadest cats around. Ali did, so did Frazier and Foreman, so did I. But that didn't mean the opponent wasn't worthy of respect, particularly if he had proven himself.

But Tyson—championship belt or not—had a lot of street punk in him. The fight game and all the rewards it had brought him hadn't changed that, it was clear to me. He had already had an "incident" in Los Angeles—a so-called stolen kiss with a female parking-lot attendant. He'd smacked her male supervisor when he protested, breaking his nose. The whole thing was settled for more than a hundred thousand dollars. That one had made the papers. But I heard talk of another sexual incident that Jacobs and Cayton had covered up before the press got wind of it.

Whatever. The impression I got from meeting Tyson was that this was a kid whose bad attitude was going to land him in a jam.

A big jam. I told reporters that some day down the road Mike Tyson was bound to end up in jail. When I went back to Easton, I removed his framed photo from off the wall of my gym, where I had framed photos of past and current champions hanging.

And then I went into training. I had two months to get ready.

Two months out from the fight, here I was, back at it again in the Larry Holmes Training Center in Easton. I was standing before the speed bag, talking—riffing, really—as my hands beat a steady rhythm on the small bag.

"I ain't going to do nothing to hurt me," I said, almost evangelically. "I love me. Thank you, Jesus. Lord, have mercy. Thank you for giving me the power to be strong."

Rat-a-tat, rat-a-tat went the speed bag. I took a deep breath and continued: "This old man is gonna shock the world! They're going to say, 'And the neewwww chaaaaamm-pi-ooooooon . . . !' "

After a forty-five minute workout, I headed for my private dressing room, where I did sit-ups, weighed myself (232 pounds), and began to let my mind wander on the Holmes-Tyson bout I saw in my mind's eye: "He'll be throwing forty-five to fifty punches a round—forty-eight blocked, two will graze me but look like they landed. And I'll be jabbing. Thirty, thirty-five punches a round landing. All of a sudden a right hand out of nowhere. Bam bam! Uh-oh. I changed up."

The way I am, I need to think it to do it. See it to believe it. I saw it. The question was would my body cooperate?

The answer, I'm afraid, was not what I'd hoped for.

And you know what? I sensed it even before I left my dressing room the night of the fight, January 22, 1988.

When the commission inspector said, "Time to leave, Mr. Holmes," there was a rush of panic in my chest. I'd been in this situation fifty times before, so why was I so scared now?

I heard my music out in the arena—a song called "Ain't No Stopping Me Now." That helped. But only a bit. What the hell was going on?

255

I remembered how unpredictable Ali used to be back at his hotel before a fight. Sometimes he would want to be alone or just be with a couple of people, not to talk or anything, just to stare off into space. Other times, he would want everyone there and be doing magic tricks, making short pieces of rope into long ones. I remember before the Wepner fight he took money from everyone, from Pacheco and Dundee and Kilroy, me and Jody Ballard, Don, everyone, and cut it into small pieces with scissors, and we all expected it to come out whole again. It never did, and Ali laughed till it hurt and said, "I do tricks, man. I ain't no damned magician."

As we headed for the ring now, people were shouting, "Go get him, Larry," "You can do it, champ"—stuff like that. There were more people rooting for me than I remembered for a very long time, maybe more than ever before.

When the spotlight hit me in the aisle, there was a big cheer that should have made me feel good. Should have but didn't. Didn't because I was suddenly wondering what in the hell I was doing there. A voice in my head was saying, "You ain't ready, Larry."

As I neared the ring, I had this weird thought: "Why not be the first fighter to refuse to go into the ring? All those people watching on HBO, I'll amaze all of them. I'll tell the announcer, 'I swear I'll fight Tyson next month, right after I have a tune-up. Just not tonight.'"

Richie was pulling me forward. I felt like a robot following him. The next thing I knew I was going up the steps and into the ring. No turning back now. "This is it, Big Jack," I told myself. "You gotta fight this guy."

I fought him, fought him the way I did everybody else—jabbing and moving. When he got past the jab, I drew him into a clinch. Through three rounds, I was still alive and well, growing confident enough to get up on my toes and move like I did in the old days. My plan was to get Tyson into the late rounds, where I figured I could outgut him and outthink him.

But the best-laid schemes went kerblooey with one Tyson

punch in the fourth round. He timed a right hand over my jab and landed it high on my head. I lost my balance, spun around the ring, and fell. When I fell, I pinned my leg under me and felt a twinge of pain in my knee.

When Earnie Shavers hit me, I saw stars. With Tyson there were no stars; I knew where I was all the time, I just couldn't get my damned balance back. I got upright at the count of four, shaking my head to clear it. After the referee, Joe Cortez, gave me the mandatory count of eight, Tyson was on me again. He dropped me with another right to the head. I got up at the count of two, lurched into the ropes, and then turned to face Tyson again.

I figured he might be wide-open in his eagerness to end the fight, so I made up my mind to put everything into an uppercut and see if I could change my luck. But damn, my arm got entangled on the rope and the punch died there along with my chances. Tyson hit me on the chin. I sprawled backward onto the canvas, backside first and then my head hitting the canvas. Cortez stopped the fight.

It must have looked as if I was in big trouble, lying there, because Giachetti and the other corner men came rushing through the ropes, obviously fearful. But I was as okay as a guy can be who just got his butt kicked.

Soon after, Tyson came to my corner to shake my hand. He told me: "You're a great champion."

I told him: "You're a great champion, but you still ain't shit."

He replied, "You ain't shit either."

And we left it at that.

There was one more battle to fight afterward—trying to get all my money. Remember when I said that I'd insisted on my money being in the bank before the fight? Well, King had largely complied, putting $2.8 million of the $3.1 million in my account. The other $300,000? Well, there was a story there.

One night during training camp, with the fight a couple weeks away, a bunch of us were sitting around the dinner table at my restaurant, swapping stories. One of my sparring partners, Bernard Benton, was telling how he'd won the WBC cruiserweight title from Alfonzo Ratliff while being promoted by Don King. When he lost it in his very first title defense, against Carlos De Leon, he had become that famous needle in the haystack for King.

"Don't talk to me about that man," said Benton. "Not while I'm eating."

Wouldn't you know at that very moment, who should appear in the entrance of the restaurant but Don King his damn self. Everyone froze until I said, "C'mon in, Don. We were just talking about you."

King came to talk business. I knew that because he started with: "Larry, I got to change my life. My good friend Harold Washington, the mayor of Chicago, died of a heart attack the other day. We were sitting across a table talking just last week, and he looked great. It can happen just like that. Larry, I'm getting up around the same age. It's the pressure that gets you. Man, I got to get out of this business."

Well, when Don King talks about the meaning of life, grab your wallet.

King said he couldn't give me the whole $3.1 million before the fight, which were the terms we had agreed to. Seems like he felt he was entitled to a little taste for procuring me the bout. He made it sound as if he had argued strenuously on my behalf with half the civilized world so that I would be paid properly. Anybody who'd been around as long as I had knew the $3.1 million was what HBO had budgeted for me and what Jacobs and Cayton had agreed to. But King made it seem as if he had gone on some Indiana Jones quest to get me that money. It was the usual horseshit, but pretty entertaining. Set King loose on the trail of money and he can talk up a storm. And on this night, to reinforce his argument for a cut of my money, he was acting like the bottom had fallen out on his life, claiming to have been hit hard in the stock market crash. "Black Tuesday put me down," he said. "Black Thursday almost put me out."

Well, after going back and forth on it, we agreed he'd put $2.8 million in my bank before the fight and $300,000 afterward. I knew it wasn't going to be easy getting the $300,000, but the $2.8 million up front satisfied me for the time being.

After the fight, though, when King held on to the $300,000 as his "consultant's fee," I did what so many others in boxing have done. I sued him for my money. Don King has more lawsuits against him than a crooked aluminum-siding company. In the end, rather than waste time and money in a court, I settled with him, as, I'm sure, he figured I would. I got $100,000 back, he got the rest.

Some things never change.

The $2.9 million enabled me to finish financing the five-story glass-and-redbrick office building at 101 Larry Holmes Drive.

When the building went up—all forty-eight thousand square feet of it—I owned it free and clear. No debt.

The L&D Holmes Plaza (for Larry and Diane) took in prime tenants like the Lehigh Valley Bank, the Federal Court for the Eastern District of Pennsylvania (including three jail cells), Manpower Temporary Services, and Comac (a telephone service).

I set up an office on the fifth floor. From there I looked out onto the spot where the Delaware and Lehigh Rivers come together. A red cabin marked the end of the towpath along the Lehigh. I must have run that path in training and turned back at that cabin five thousand times in my life.

The property at 101 Larry Holmes Drive—and the rest of my portfolio—kept me busy over the next few years. It tickled me that in my old age I'd become a fat-cat capitalist. Me. A seventh-grade dropout. Very satisfying.

I sold the Commodore Inn (formerly the Holiday Inn), which I had bought for $1.5 million, and made a profit of $1 million.

I bought a house in Easton as a rental property, and continued to collect on apartments I rented.

Years before, I had bought thirty acres of land in Easton for

$75,000. I sold twelve acres for about $967,000 because the highway—I-78—went through there.

I made an additional $30,000 to $40,000 a month on interest from municipal bonds I held.

And from the L&D Holmes Plaza, the first of two buildings on Larry Holmes Drive that I financed—they became Easton's version of the Twin Towers—I began collecting serious rent money.

Somewhere in there I got the fishing bug. My buddy, Charlie Conover, was a primo fisherman, and he showed me the ropes. It was a nice balance—the complexities of business against the sky-blue easy afternoons on the water.

It started with Charlie, Dick Lovell, and me fooling around in a seventeen-foot boat on the river running alongside Larry Holmes Drive. Then we got a little more serious. I bought a $200,000 thirty-one-foot sports cruiser from Sea Ray—one of those fancy luxury boats—and named it *The Easton Assassin*. I kept the boat in a New Jersey marina off the Hudson River and would go out three, four times a week, doing a lot of bottom fishing in Long Island Sound or going for bluefish off Sandy Hook. Four-thirty, five in the afternoon, at that time of day they'd be jumping out of the water. Yeah, you could catch bluefish, sea bass, whiting, ling, fluke, and flounder. You could do a whole lot of fishing out there.

When the cold weather came, we would fly down to Jacksonville, Florida, where we'd go shrimping on a second $200,000 thirty-one-foot sports cruiser of mine, also called *The Easton Assassin*. Pretty soon I'd bought two homes in Jacksonville, and when we were down there, we lived in the $400,000 waterfront home on North Laurel Green Way. The other one became a rental property. When the kids were out of school, or on vacation, we'd be there for long stretches of time.

Fishing, a little poker, the occasional boxing exhibition—they were a nice complement to the assorted business matters I had to keep track of. It was a happy time, watching my kids grow up, fussing with my grandchildren, Jeffrey and Jessica, and enjoying life in a way I couldn't when I was boxing.

I kept my hand in boxing, continuing to promote fights for my brother Mark. I never made any money promoting him—my objective was to maneuver him to a title shot and let him make as much money as he could.

But Mark had an outlook very different from mine as a fighter. I was willing to sacrifice and do whatever it took to succeed. Mark gave in easily to temptation. He liked women, and had a lot of them. He liked the late hours, and ran through them as if his body would never know the consequences.

Mark's kind of lifestyle undercut the discipline it took to train. It was a shortcut mentality that, once his boxing days were over, still ruled him. He'd once said to me: "I can make more money selling drugs in one damn day than for boxing all these years." Well, he rolled the dice on that proposition and lost. The Easton police busted him, and he ended up doing five years hard time for distributing drugs.

So did my brother Jake, who should have known better. Jake was my assistant trainer. He was great at motivating me, particularly during the years Giachetti was gone. Jake had started with me when I fought for the title, against Norton. At the time he was working as a laborer with the American Can Company in Easton. One day he up and quit, telling me: "I'm gonna work with you."

I told him, "If I don't beat Norton, I don't know how I'm gonna pay you."

"You're gonna beat Norton," he said.

Jake's gamble paid off. I gave him a weekly salary and a bonus after every fight—a bonus that might range from $1,000 to $20,000.

But as my star ascended, Jake got to believing he was born for the fast lane. The drugs got him too—cocaine was his addiction. Jake got busted about the same time Mark did, and served four and a half years for using and distributing drugs.

Their fall was a disappointment to me. I'd tried to spread the wealth, helping out my brothers and sisters, only to see it corrupt the better instincts in some of them and provoke the same kind of petty bickering I had witnessed in the members of the Ali camp.

But you do the best you can and move on.

CHAPTER
EIGHTEEN

It was in early 1990, while I was out fishing with Charlie Conover, that I said to him: "These guys I see can't fight worth a damn."

I was talking about the heavyweight division.

By 1990, Tyson had lost his title, getting blown out by Buster Douglas in Tokyo.

Douglas, grown fat as the Pillsbury Doughboy, got his big butt knocked out by Evander Holyfield in his very first title defense.

The young talent that was coming up—guys like Ray Mercer, Tommy Morrison, Riddick Bowe, and Lennox Lewis—didn't impress me. And meantime, after a ten-year absence from boxing, a new and reconstituted George Foreman was out there in the hinterlands, knocking out a bunch of nobodies and getting well paid for it, even as he joked about the quality of these opponents.

"You know," he said, "there are some who claim I don't fight a guy unless he's on a respirator. That's a lie. He has to be at least eight days off the respirator."

By 1990, George, like me, was in his forties. When he knocked out Gerry Cooney that year—his first *real* opponent—it was as inspiring as any sermon big George might have delivered in that little church of his down there in Houston, Texas.

By the end of the year, I had begun training for a comeback.

There was a lot of speculation about why I was returning to the ring. Some said it was to gain the acclaim and the respect that I had deserved but hadn't gotten when I was champion. Probably there was some truth to that.

Others said that it was, as it had been before, for the money—that comfortable as I was, financially, I didn't mind having more of the dough-re-mi. As Richard Hoffer would write in *Sports Illustrated*:

> *When Holmes says he needs the money—and he has told people that—he means it in the way that a Rockefeller might mean it. That is, after all, how you remain wealthy: You have a need for money. Holmes, ever since he discovered that boxing was a kind of ready teller, has needed money.*

There was something to that, too, I suppose. But it ran deeper than just hoarding money. See, my deepest fear, after I started making some money, has always been that I'd be thrown back into poverty again. Poverty to me was more than just a bad dream: it was something absolutely real that could happen again at any time.

For as long as I can remember, I've been afraid of being broke. I've always been a hard worker, so I knew I would always be able to provide for myself and my people one way or another if I had to, but the irrational fear of not having anything overcomes me from time to time.

When I was a little kid, my brothers and sisters would take things of mine that were valuable to me. So I learned not to leave anything lying around, and I also learned not to let anyone know what I had or to trust people until they'd been tested, and maybe not even trust them then. I was like a squirrel, forever hiding things and storing them away. I lived with a constant fear in my chest that I wouldn't be able to hold on to whatever I earned: that's why for me there has never been any such thing as "enough."

My fear of being broke never left me. In fact, when I began to make some decent money fighting main events, it intensified. I put most of the money right in the bank. But I never lost my habit of hiding cash—in the closet, under the rug, in the basement, anywhere. If I was fearful of losing everything when I was a poor kid, I got even more fearful as I got older and made more money.

There are still times when I'll feel that old panic and take a few thousand dollars out of the bank and squirrel it away in a hiding place. When you're marked as a kid, I guess you can just go so far undoing the damage.

The panic of going broke motivated me in every big-money fight I had. I always had to have something specific and concrete that I was fighting for, something my purse money was going to allow me to buy and that I would have long after the fight was over. I was like the casino gambler who goes out and buys something right away with his winnings so he doesn't risk giving it back at the tables.

That said, let me just add this: if the money factored in, as did the chance to prove worthy of applause and recognition, there was one other crucial reason. A simple reason. At age forty-one, I could do it, I could fight. Old as my body was in years, the fire in me still flickered as it had when I was starting out. Like any of the old boys in team sports—the George Blandas and Nolan Ryans and Robert Parishes, who played into middle age—I took pleasure in standing up to time and thumbing my nose at it. Like the shoe commercial says: Just do it.

I was eager to just do it. Big George's second time around was instructive. Rather than jump into a big fight right off, he had taken his time, fighting a series of patsies while allowing his skill level to return under conditions that suited him. Conditions that were not overly demanding yet gave him exposure and, because of his name, money that was disproportionate to the challenge these opponents offered.

That was how I proceeded when I came back in 1991. The slowly-but-surely route, fighting opponents that were a level below world-class but would test me enough to sharpen my skills.

Tim "Doc" Anderson was the first, in April 1991 in Hollywood, Florida. I knocked him out in one round.

Before the end of the year, I was a regular attraction on the USA Network, fighting and beating guys like Eddie Gonzales (W 10, Tampa, Florida), Michael Greer (KO 4, Honolulu), Art Card (W 10, Orlando), and Jamie Howe (TKO 1, Jacksonville, Florida).

When I had started, promoters like Bob Arum had called my comeback a joke. Then he saw the ratings I was getting on the USA Network and realized that even at age forty-one Larry Holmes was still a draw. Arum signed me to fight the winner of the Ray Mercer–Tommy Morrison fight.

By that time, Harold Smith was acting as my adviser. Smith had served more than five years and, on being released from the federal prison facility at Boron, California, in October 1988, had jumped back into boxing. He had worked briefly as an adviser to Roy Jones Jr., at the start of Jones's pro career, and had arranged a nice gig for me in Jakarta, Indonesia. For $75,000 I boxed an exhibition and then sang with my band, Marmalade.

When I came back to boxing in '91, Harold called about setting up a fight with Michael Greer in Honolulu for $40,000.

"Forty thousand?" I said. "I can't fight for that little."

"Think of it as a vacation," he said. "Help me get back."

I thought it over and said what the hell. I'd always liked Harold. Besides, it's better to hide in the shade of a toothpick than to burn in the noonday sun.

When Mercer beat Morrison, Harold helped in the negotiations for Holmes-Mercer.

He said, "Let me talk to Bob Arum for you. They think you're difficult to deal with."

I asked him how much I'd have to pay him. Harold said I didn't have to pay anything—he'd get his share from Arum. Not so, it turned out. The money ended up coming from me.

I got $1.1 million to fight Mercer, who the experts said would whup me easy. Mercer, a gold medalist at the '88 Olympics, was big and strong, and was undefeated in eighteen bouts. He had knocked out Morrison, giving him a fierce beating. He was a 4–1 favorite.

I trained for the fight in Jacksonville, in a gym I'd built at my waterfront home there. One day I walked into the gym and I said aloud, "Why the hell's it so dark in here?"

My brothers Lee and Floyd and my new trainer, Don Turner, said it wasn't dark.

"The hell it isn't," I answered.

Well, they looked kind of funny at one another and shrugged.

After the workout, I stopped in at one of those eyeglass stores on the side of the highway—you know, where they check you on the spot.

The guy looked at my eyes and said, "I think you got a real problem."

He wanted me to see a specialist.

"No way," I told him. "I got to fight."

"I don't know if you should," he said. "I think you have a detached retina in your right eye."

I got mad and left. I told my guys not to disclose the problem to anyone. As before in my career, I wasn't going to let a physical problem keep me from fighting.

I adjusted, though. I stopped sparring.

When I got to Atlantic City—the fight was at the Convention Center—I was a little concerned about the prefight exam. But the truth is a doctor can't detect a detached retina unless he looks behind the eye. So I passed. Bad eye or not, the fight was a go.

When I went into the ring against Mercer, I used my good eye to focus on him.

In the first round, Mercer jarred me with a jab. I didn't realize how hurt I was until I tried to move. But I didn't let on to Mercer.

In fact, I waved him in. Like: Come on, son. Let's see what you got. I conned him into not following up his advantage.

That was as hard as it got all night.

Early on, Mercer was walking forward with the assurance of a hit man, throwing clubbing punches. But his punches mostly bounced off my gloves or went into thin air. In time, I began frustrating him, taking the swagger right out of him.

I did it with gamesmanship—"the creaking art of self-defense," as one writer called it. I showed him a little of this and a little of that. For several rounds, I used a variation of rope-a-dope, planting my back against the ropes to spare my legs while muffling Mercer's punches and whacking the occasional combination off Mercer's head.

I bluffed, I conned, I talked to Mercer. Once, in Mercer's corner, I even turned to the television camera there and spoke to the home audience before wheeling and hitting Mercer.

I did what I had to do. And soon enough I had Mercer lunging amateurishly to land punches. He simply couldn't figure a way through my defenses.

Sometimes I used my longer reach by placing my glove on top of Mercer's head and simply holding him off. I used guile more than firepower. It wasn't photogenic. It was just an old one-eyed fighter with survival tactics who was able to break down a tough but unsophisticated pug and do it with a real economy of motion.

A computer punch count had Mercer throwing 657 punches, compared with 491, for me. But I landed 336 of my 491, or 68.4 percent, while Mercer managed to connect on 247 of 657 for 37.6 percent.

It didn't take long for the Convention Center crowd to realize that Grandpa Holmes was doing the improbable and giving the young guy all he could handle. They began to chant, "Lar-ry, Lar-ry, Lar-ry."

It was a great feeling to hear the crowd in support of me. It was even better when the decision was announced.

The judges had me winning big—117–112, 117–111, and 115–113.

HOLMES MANAGES TO PULL A TRIUMPH OUT OF HIS HAT was the headline in the next day's papers.

After the fight, I entered St. Luke's Hospital in Bethlehem, Pennsylvania, to have my detached retina repaired. I registered as "Charles Jones" so nobody would know I was there. I didn't want to jeopardize the big-money bout that beating Mercer put me in position for.

It took a couple months for the eye to heal. During that time I was told to take it easy—don't run, don't ride in a bumpy car, just let the eye heal. When I spoke to the eye doctor about continuing to fight, he was not eager to see me go on.

"But," he said, "if you're that determined . . . It's just that there are risks of permanent damage to the eye."

"There are risks in everything," I said, "and I want to do it."

When I had signed with Arum to fight Mercer, I had agreed to a two-fight deal . . . in the event—unlikely as it must have seemed to Arum—that I beat Mercer. My objective was to fight either Foreman or Holyfield, and now that I'd whipped Mercer it was pretty much my choice.

I really wanted Foreman. I just thought he couldn't beat me. Couldn't beat me when he was young, couldn't beat me now. Him on TV with that big phony smile. He didn't fool me. What kind of man calls all his children George or Georgette? Can't he take the time to remember their names? I really wanted to kick his fat ass.

But given that Holyfield was the champion, it was a no-brainer.

Holyfield-Homes was made for June '92 at Caesars Palace in Las Vegas. Smith helped negotiate a $6.5 million deal for me—Holyfield was to get $16 million—and I gave Harold $180,000 for his part in the process.

The Mercer fight had been February 7, 1992. By April, I was recovered from the eye surgery and back to running. The original date for the Holyfield bout was June 8. I asked Arum to see if he could push the date back a little. I told him I had a scratch on my cornea—I could use the extra time. He came back with June 19 as the new date.

The doctors had inserted a kind of rubber band to give the surgically repaired eye extra support. Trouble was that it threw the focus for that eye slightly out of whack. So when I returned to training in Jacksonville, I began using a contact lens to correct the focus problem. A couple of times during training, the contact lens would curl up in the eye and I'd have to take it out.

Diane knew about the contact lens and she was against my fighting Holyfield like that. But I felt I couldn't turn down that kind of money. I told her: "A man's gotta do what a man's gotta do."

The contact lens crimped my training. I was cautious in sparring, and limited the chance of a problem developing by sparring far fewer rounds than usual. Still, I figured I could beat Holyfield.

Holyfield had won the title from Buster Douglas. He had defended it against another old man, Foreman, and a journeyman, Bert Cooper, who had knocked him down and damn near knocked him out before Holyfield rallied to win. Cooper had been a replacement for Tyson, who had pulled out of a November 1991 date with a rib injury, then disappeared from our radar screens as a convicted rapist—inmate number 922335 at the Indiana Youth Center.

Because of the limited training, I parceled out my aggression the night I fought Holyfield. I fought him with the contact lens, which got dislodged in the third round. For much of the fight I stood against the ropes and from that energy-saving position invited Holyfield's lead, hoping to sucker-punch him with a right-hand counter.

As *The New York Times* reported:

For a middle-aged fighter it was a bright enough idea, and not without effect. Holyfield was there to be hit. Holmes landed his share of snapping rights and uppercuts, good punches that did not discourage Holyfield.

Holmes fought with a cunning that was admirable. . . .

He was like a junkball pitcher, using his art to keep Holyfield constantly off balance and unable to dig his heels in and turn the match into the brawl he wanted.

Still, for all my tricks, it was not quite enough. Holyfield got the decision. And when a newsman asked me afterward what I would have done differently against Holyfield, I told him: "I would have fought him in 1980."

I had hoped to be the slightly paunchy underdog who took apart a body-beautiful champion. I chased the dream, but this time it eluded me.

But it didn't kill the desire to keep on boxing. Five years and 14 fights later, I was still at it. Who would have figured? I was forty-eight in 1997, and didn't expect to be lacing them up much longer. In fact, I'd be surprised if, after 72 fights—and with a record of 66–6, with 42 knockouts—you'll ever see me in there again. Oh, I might make an exception for George Foreman. I've always thought I could beat that Texas fatboy. But otherwise . . .

While I haven't held the heavyweight title for more than a decade, during that time I've been treated with respect by the paying customers who have come to watch me, be it in Galveston, Texas, or Prior Lake, Minnesota, or Las Vegas, Nevada. Damned if after all these years, seems like I've become a bit of a sentimental favorite.

That's nice. Everybody likes to be liked, and to get the recognition. I'm no different that way. I appreciate the attention, the warm regards of the public. Maybe the critics have been a little less tolerant of my hanging around for so long. That's okay, too. I've gotten used to those "expert opinions," and don't take them quite as seriously as I once did.

To have been forty-plus and held my own with fighters quite a bit younger, well . . . that's something you have to experience to get the pleasure of. You don't last that long unless you know your business. And I've known mine. The art of self-defense. To have a punch come at you at one hundred miles an hour and make it miss—believe me, it's a hell of a feeling.

271

What does it say about the heavyweights around today that I've been able to hold my own with them?

Well, I could pretend to be impressed by them. But for better or worse—like me or loathe me—I'm going to give it to you straight. Tyson, Holyfield—you wouldn't have heard of them if they had fought back in the seventies. Smokin' Joe Frazier would have bombed Tyson out. So would have Bonavena, Lyle, Shavers, Norton, and Quarry. Those were big, strong-punching suckers. Even Mac Foster and Ernie Terrell would have beat him. Ali would have ambushed him as Tyson charged forward. Foreman? After he hit Tyson, Little Mikey would have been ready for Social Security.

There are people who tell me I'm dead wrong about this. But I'm a student of boxing and can tell you that while Tyson is a good fighter for today, he's not one of the great fighters of all time. Not even close. He can't take a punch. Every time Tyson gets knocked down, he doesn't get up. That's when you prove yourself as a great fighter.

Holyfield has a lot of courage, but as a heavyweight he'd have been a sparring partner back when Ali, Foreman, Frazier, Shavers, and Holmes were working. He simply gets hit too much. And while he can get away with it in today's heavyweight scene, he'd have been dead meat back in my time. Out of his league. Ali would have slapped him silly with the jab. It would have been a cakewalk. Foreman, who went the distance with him as an old man, would have creamed him back then.

At least Holyfield has a warrior's heart. It's more than I can say for Lennox Lewis. He's a joke—a big, athletic guy who's strictly a front-runner. Put him in against a fighter who stands up to him—like, say, Ray Mercer did—and Lewis is exposed as a man who doesn't like a real fight. Lennox Lewis is just a heavy-weight wanna-be.

Hell, he stopped by to see me in Easton once and, when I asked him why he wouldn't fight me, he said: "I can't give you a fight. You got too good a jab. Teach me the jab."

"I don't wanna teach you," I told him. "I wanna fight you."

"Nah," he said. "I don't wanna mess with that jab."

If the roles had been reversed . . . if I were the young kid and he were the old champ challenging me, I'd have told him: "Bring me the money and I'll kick your ass."

One guy who had some talent was Riddick Bowe. He punched good and had the moves. But Bowe lacked the staying power. Soon as he won the title, he ate himself into a fat man, and fight by fight seemed to lose his passion for the game. By the time Andrew Golota got in there with him, Bowe was a shell of himself. It takes a whole lot to keep it together, to have the longevity that fighters from my era—Ali, Frazier, Foreman, myself—had.

Too many fighters these days—and the heavyweights typify them—aren't in it for the long run. They get a little taste of money—face it, with pay-per-view the money's super—and they lose their focus. And I'm telling you that that's not likely to change. Because there are too many distractions out there. Fighters don't keep their minds on boxing. They're more concerned with being celebrities. They're focused on the women they can have, the cars, the big houses. Hell, I've been living in the same $395,000 home for damn near twenty years. What do you need a $10 million place for? With a staff of thirty people to keep it clean.

Fighters nowadays lose sight of the discipline it takes to stay champion. They start looking for, and taking, shortcuts. Like steroids. I don't know it for an absolute fact, but with certain heavyweights out there today I suspect steroid use. You look at their chest and back and arms and you see all these white pimples, and it makes you wonder.

I know that there was a time recently when I broke out on my back and neck with white pimples, and wondered what was responsible for them. Then I heard a report on TV that a certain so-called vitamin that I was taking had steroids in it. As soon as I stopped taking the vitamin, the pimples disappeared.

Where you see dedication today is among fighters in the lighter weight classes. Many of the Latino boxers seem to have the eye of the tiger. A kid like Oscar De La Hoya, even while making purses of $6 million to $10 million, still appears intent on fighting all the worthy challengers. That's good for the sport. Too often champions avoid the top challengers to prolong their reign.

The truth is most champions today exist in relative anonymity compared to the guys from my era. When I was ringside in Atlantic City for the De La Hoya–Wilfredo Rivera match in December '97, people were coming up to me all night for autographs. At one point, Lennox Lewis stopped by and I told the man I was signing for: "Hey, it's Lennox Lewis." He said, "Who's that?" I said, "This is your heavyweight champion." Well, that was when he decided, what the hell, he'd have Lennox Lewis's autograph too.

Imagine that. The heavyweight champion and a who's-that reaction.

Part of it has to do with all these chickenshit governing bodies—the alphabet-soup groups, as they're known. While their abundant titles provide opportunities for fighters to make better purses, too few of those fighters get recognition from a public grown increasingly confused having so many men—many of them mediocre—claiming to be world champions.

More damaging to today's fighter is the absence of network television. Pay-per-view has made rich men out of the elite fighters, with purses up to $30 million. But there are talented champions like Roy Jones Jr. who have gotten rich on pay-cable deals with the HBOs and Showtimes, as well as from pay-per-view, and still don't have the recognition that fighters from my era did. The reason is the virtual disappearance of network TV from boxing.

In the seventies and the eighties, folks got to see Larry Holmes on network TV all the time, and it made me so recognizable that when I came back in the nineties as a middle-aged fighter I still commanded big money. Same for guys like Hector Camacho and Roberto Duran, who became widely known years and years ago through free TV and are still banking big paydays because of that.

Network exposure created boxing personalities. Boom Boom Mancini shooting for the title his old man never won. Camacho strutting before the camera in sequined robes. The glare of Duran. Hit Man Hearns, Arguello, Pryor, Sugar Ray Leonard.

No more. Now the free TV is on the USA Network and ESPN, cable networks that just don't have the money for the monster fights. It's not the same as when NBC, ABC, and CBS were big players in the boxing business. As a result, a Lennox Lewis is an anonymity and wherever I go people point and smile and say, "Hey, Larry. Hey, Larry Holmes."

Things change. Now we have circus attractions like Butterbean—a fat slob impersonating a fighter—and we have women boxers. Look, I know it's not politically correct to say this, but I'm against women boxing. I've got no problem with women as referees or judges. But women are too precious to get banged up. I see women as a minority, just like black folks, and recognize that they're discriminated against. I'm sympathetic to them. But it just rubs me the wrong way to have them box. Fact is, I don't like to see women driving big tractors or fighting with guns in a war. I like to see women doing things that aren't hazardous to their health.

I watch Christy Martin. She was very attractive the last time I saw her. But she's not going to stay that way if she keeps getting cut or busted in the mouth. Sorry. It ain't for me. Christy Martin is a good fighter, but please . . .

So the fight game goes on, a little gaudier, and more honky-tonk.

At bottom, though, it's the same hard bargain for your fighter. Promotional options bind him to sleazeballs like King, who are wired to exploit the poor bastard who steps into the ring. And the governing bodies become the accomplices of the promoters, encouraged, I suspect, by fat payoffs. How else to account for the chicanery, the endless trickerations that mark their rankings and their decisions?

Some folks say a federal commission to oversee boxing would

cure the sport's ills. I doubt it. It would be just another layer of politician, another shark too easily corrupted. Boxing is boxing, a dangerous roulette. Step right up and take your shot.

I took mine, and made out as well as could be expected. Better than I figured on. Where my place in heavyweight history will be is not for me to say. My fights are all on film, and in the future people will be able to watch them and draw their own conclusions.

I know this much: I've been awfully fortunate. Look back at some of the fighters from my era and you can see that time did not treat them kindly. Ali has Parkinson's syndrome. Jerry Quarry suffers from *pugilistica dementia*, the medical term for being punch-drunk, and requires twenty-four-hour attention. Ken Norton got messed up in a car crash. Le Doux lost his wife to cancer. Berbick, like Tyson, went to jail on a rape charge. Tim "Doc" Anderson is doing time for murdering his promoter, Rick "Elvis" Parker. Oliver McCall, a boxer I fought in '95, had drug problems and suffered a nervous breakdown during a fight against Lennox Lewis in '97. Bonavena was shot and killed. Buster Mathis died of a heart condition. I saw Earnie Shavers at one point reduced to working as a chauffeur for King, and running errands for him. Jeff Merritt, who came into boxing after serving time for first-degree robbery, was seen not long ago in a Vegas hotel lobby, begging for money.

Yet here I am all these years later with good health, money in my pocket, and a family life as apple pie as those sitcoms I used to watch on the black-and-white TV in the fifties. You know, like *Father Knows Best* and *Ozzie and Harriet* and *Leave It to Beaver*.

My older daughters, Misty, Lisa, and Belinda, are doing just fine. Misty's an ordained minister, Lisa works for Kodak, and Belinda is in college. And nearly twenty years after that impromptu wedding to Diane, I'm still married, and happily so, to her. We've got a daughter who's a cheerleader, a son who plays hockey, both of them good students with a love of learning. In fact, their preoccupation with books made me start taking remedial reading lessons myself. It's been as big a struggle as walking down the aisle to face Mike Tyson, but I've made progress and refuse to be defeated.

I once saw Cher on a TV interview admit she had had trouble reading too. It took courage for her to say that publicly. Barbara Walters asked how it had made her feel. Cher replied that she knew she was smart but secretly she experienced doubts because where others could read, she could not. I knew the feeling.

My mother worked the cotton fields when she was a girl, so she got even less schooling than I did and she can't read. My father couldn't read or write either. Not being able to do what my own children could do was a great embarrassment to me. One of the reasons I pronounce some words wrong is that I've never seen them in print: I've only heard them spoken and sometimes that just isn't good enough. Because of my children, I have been able to break a pattern that's kept too many members of my family down for too long. Now I want the world to know that Larry Holmes can read.

When a man fights, you see his deepest self if you know what to look for. It's there in every move of his, but especially when he gets his opponent in trouble. You see it even more when he's in trouble himself.

I had a degree of fear in the ring, and it cut two ways—making me cautious, or bringing out pure rage.

My approach to an opponent was rooted in caution. I was not there to take punishment unless I absolutely had to in order to win. My greatest satisfaction was slipping punches or smothering them. I was the fighter who leaned back from the waist, retreating carefully, the other guy coming at me. No one fought better backing up than I did. And then, suddenly, *bam!* I'd be smashing the jab, setting up variations off it. Frustrating my opponent, outthinking him. Tying him up, spinning him, and backing away again. For me that was the art of boxing. Hitting and not getting hit. The press likes ring wars because they're dramatic and exciting to write about. But writers aren't fighters; they never take a single punch.

One of the things I'm proudest of is how few ring wars I had over such a long career. People admire Ali for his courage—I do too—but these days, looking back, I prefer my caution. But I couldn't be a cautious champion all the time and hold the title as long as I did. There came a time when the movement, the reflexes that made the art possible began to leave, and I had to hit and be hit to win. That was a dangerous time, a period when as an older fighter my body couldn't shake off the punishment as quickly as it used to, leaving me more vulnerable to damage.

When I did get into a brutal fight, that's when the part of my personality that was pure rage came out. It was the part that always scared me a little because I never completely accepted the fact that I had it in me. Early in my career, when I sensed the animal rage in me, I was like a spectator to it and sort of let it do whatever it wanted. And, I have to admit, it made me feel good sometimes to let all my rage out. Stopping me was the referee's job. Sometimes I wished they did their job better. But as the years went by, the unnecessary violence began bothering me because I knew I could hurt other fighters if I got too much out of control.

My rage had a positive side too, a survival side. When I got hurt or knocked down, I just wanted to fight for the pure feeling of getting even. It was simple retaliation: *This guy's hurting me. He's taking what is mine!* To stop him, my rage burst loose, pure animal revenge: something in me wanted to hurt back the way it was hurt. Some of the best times I had fighting were after I was hurt but still in control of what I was trying to do *and* full of rage at the same time. That was exciting because I had it both ways—rage and skill at the same time: the best way to fight.

One good side effect of my rage in the ring was that after it burned itself out, I felt—I don't know how to say it exactly—cleaner, I guess. Less complicated, less screwed up, more at peace with myself.

But my rage as a fighter was pretty much all gone after the Cooney fight. And I wouldn't even have had it then if it wasn't for all the sick racial stuff that provoked me.

My being cautious has also kept me in Easton—driving in the slow lane, I like to say—and it helped me choose a very good woman to settle down with. It was my sense of caution, or lack of trust, however you look at it, that led me to take control of my own career. My caution, based as I said on fear, is the main reason I have the financial security I always sought. It's the reason I'll never be broke again and will be able to pass wealth on to my children so they won't grow up with the same fears of being left with nothing.

Against all odds, I succeeded.

The Fights

1973

Fight # & Date	Opponent & Fight Location	Result & Round	Weight
1. 3/21	Rodeil Dupree ~ Scranton, PA	W ~ 4	202
2. 5/02	Art Savage ~ Scranton, PA	TKO ~ 3	202
3. 6/10	Curtis Whitner ~ Scranton, PA	KO ~ 1	201
4. 8/22	Don Branch ~ Scranton, PA	W ~ 6	201
5. 9/10	Bob Buzic ~ New York, NY	W ~ 6	196
6. 11/14	Jerry Judge ~ Scranton, PA	W ~ 6	204
7. 11/28	Kevin Isaac ~ Cleveland, OH	TKO ~ 3	203

1974

Fight # & Date	Opponent & Fight Location	Result & Round	Weight
8. 4/24	Howard Darlington ~ Scranton, PA	TKO ~ 4	206
9. 5/29	Bob Mashburn ~ Scranton, PA	TKO ~ 7	199
10. 12/11	Joe Hathaway ~ Scranton, PA	TKO ~ 1	208

1975

Fight # & Date	Opponent & Fight Location	Result & Round	Weight
11. 3/24	Charley Green ~ Cleveland, OH	KO ~ 2	205
12. 4/10	Oliver Wright ~ Honolulu, HI	TKO ~ 3	203
13. 4/26	Robert Yarborough ~ Toronto, CA	KO ~ 3	
14. 5/16	Ernie Smith ~ Las Vegas, NV	KO ~ 3	
15. 12/11	Obie English ~ Scranton, PA	TKO ~ 7	209
16. 8/26	Charlie James ~ Honolulu, HI	W ~ 10	207
17. 10/1	Rodney Bobick ~ Manila, PI	TKO ~ 6	203
18. 12/9	Leon Shaw ~ Washington, DC	KO ~ 1	209
19. 12/20	Billy Joiner ~ San Juan, PR	TKO ~ 3	210

1976

Fight # & Date	Opponent & Fight Location	Result & Round	Weight
20. 1/29	Joe Choiston ~ Easton, PA	TKO ~ 8	208
21. 4/5	Fred Ashew ~ Landover, MD	TKO ~ 2	207
22. 4/30	Roy Williams ~ Landover, MD	W ~ 10	205

1977

Fight # & Date	Opponent & Fight Location	Result & Round	Weight
23. 1/16	Tom Prater ~ Pensacola, FL	W ~ 8	208
24. 3/17	Horace Robinson ~ San Juan, PR	TKO ~ 5	213
25. 9/14	Sanford Houpe ~ Las Vegas, NV	TKO ~ 7	211
26. 11/5	Ibar Arrington ~ Las Vegas, NV	TKO ~ 10	203

1978

Fight # & Date	Opponent & Fight Location	Result & Round	Weight
27. 3/25	Earnie Shavers ~ Las Vegas, NV	W ~ 12	210

| 28. 6/9 | Ken Norton ~ | W ~ 15 WBC | 209 |
| 29. 11/10 | Alfredo Evangelista ~ Las Vegas, NV | KO ~ 7 WBC | 214 |

1979

Fight # & Date	Opponent & Fight Location	Result & Round	Weight
30. 3/23	Ossie Ocasio ~ Las Vegas, NV	TKO ~ 7 WBC	214
31. 6/23	Mike Weaver ~ New York, NY	TKO ~ 12 WBC	215
32. 9/28	Earnie Shavers ~ Las Vegas, NV	TKO ~ 11 WBC	210

1980

Fight # & Date	Opponent & Fight Location	Result & Round	Weight
33. 2/3	Lorenzo Zanon ~ Las Vegas, NV	KO ~ 6 WBC	213
34. 3/31	Leroy Jones ~ Las Vegas, NV	TKO ~ 8 WBC	211
35. 7/7	Scott LeDoux ~ Bloomington, MN	TKO ~ 7 WBC	214
36. 10/2	Muhammad Ali ~ Las Vegas, NV	TKO ~ 11 WBC	211

1981

Fight # & Date	Opponent & Fight Location	Result & Round	Weight
37. 4/11	Trevor Berbick ~ Las Vegas, NV	W ~ 15 WBC	215
38. 6/12	Leon Spinks ~ Detroit, MI	TKO ~ 3 WBC	212
39. 11/6	Ronald Snipes ~ Pittsburgh, PA	TKO ~ 11 WBC	213

1982

Fight # & Date	Opponent & Fight Location	Result & Round	Weight
40. 6/11	Gerry Cooney ~ Las Vegas, NV	TKO ~ 13 WBC	212
41. 11/26	Randall Cobb ~ Houston, TX	W ~ 15 WBC	217

1983

Fight # & Date	Opponent & Fight Location	Result & Round	Weight
42. 3/27	Lucien Rodriguez ~ Scranton, PA	W ~ 12 WBC	221
43. 5/20	Tim Witherspoon ~ Las Vegas, NV	W ~ 12 WBC	213
44. 9/10	Scott Frank ~ Atlantic City, NJ	TKO ~ 5 WBC	223
45. 11/25	Marvis Frazier ~ Las Vegas, NV	TKO ~ 1 WBC	219

1984

Fight # & Date	Opponent & Fight Location	Result & Round	Weight
46. 11/9	James Smith ~ Las Vegas, NV	TKO ~ 12 WBC	221

1985

Fight # & Date	Opponent & Fight Location	Result & Round	Weight
47. 3/15	David Bey ~ Las Vegas, NV	KO ~ 10 IBF	223
48. 5/20	Carl Williams ~ Reno, NV	W ~ 15 IBF	213
49. 9/21	Michael Spinks ~ Las Vegas, NV	L ~ 15 IBF	221

1986

Fight # & Date	Opponent & Fight Location	Result & Round	Weight
50. 4/19	Michael Spinks ~ Las Vegas, NV	L ~ 15 IBF	223

1988

Fight # & Date	Opponent & Fight Location	Result & Round	Weight
51. 1/22	Mike Tyson ~ Atlantic City, NJ	TKBY ~ 4 BABCBF	225

1991

Fight # & Date	Opponent & Fight Location	Result & Round	Weight
52. 4/7	Tim Anderson ~ Hollywood, FL	TKO ~ 1	236
53. 8/13	Eddie Gonzales ~ Tampa, FL	W ~ 10	238
54. 8/24	Michael Greer ~ Honolulu, HI	KO ~ 4	238
55. 9/17	Art Card ~ Orlando, FL	W ~ 10	236
56. 11/12	Jamie Howe ~ Jacksonville, FL	TKO ~ 1	236

1992

Fight # & Date	Opponent & Fight Location	Result & Round	Weight
57. 2/7	Ray Mercer ~ Atlantic City, NJ	W ~ 12	233
58. 6/9	Evander Holyfield ~ Las Vegas, NV	L ~ 12 BABCBF	233

1993

Fight # & Date	Opponent & Fight Location	Result & Round	Weight
59. 1/5	Everett Martin ~ Biloxi, MS	W ~ 10	238
60. 3/9	Rocky Pepeli ~ Bay St. Louis, MS	TKO ~ 5	242
61. 4/13	Ken Lakusta ~ Bay St. Louis, MS	TKO ~ 7	242
62. 5/18	Paul Poirier ~ Bay St. Louis, MS	TKO ~ 6	232
63. 9/28	Jose Ribaita ~ Bay St. Louis, MS	W ~ 10	243

1994

Fight # & Date	Opponent & Fight Location	Result & Round	Weight
64. 3/8	Garing Lane ~ Ledyard, CT	W ~ 10	241
65. 8/9	Jesse Ferguson ~ Prior Lake, MN	W ~ 10	239

1995

Fight # & Date	Opponent & Fight Location	Result & Round	Weight
66. 4/8	Oliver McCall ~ Las Vegas, NV	L ~ 10 WBC	236
67. 9/19	Ed Donaldson ~ Bay St. Louis, MS	W ~ 10	243

1996

Fight # & Date	Opponent & Fight Location	Result & Round	Weight
68. 1/9	Curt Shepherd ~ Galveston, TX	KO ~ 4	246
69. 4/16	Quinn Navarre ~ Bay St. Louis, MS	W ~ 10	243
70. 6/16	Anthony Willis ~ Bay St. Louis, MS	KO ~ 8	240

1997

Fight # & Date	Opponent & Fight Location	Result & Round	Weight
71. 1/24	Brian Nielson	L ~ 12	246
72. 7/29	Maurice Harris ~ New York, NY	W ~ 10	248

GV
1132
H65

BUNKER HILL COMMUNITY COLLEGE

Larry Holmes : against the odds.

DATE DUE

NOV 29 '99	
OCT 0 2 2001	
OCT 2 9 2009	